Techniques of Treasury Debt Management

Techniques of Treasury Debt Management

by TILFORD C. GAINES

A Joint Publication of
The Graduate School of Business,
Columbia University, and
The Free Press of Glencoe

For information, address: The Free Press of Glencoe,
A Division of The Macmillan Company,
The Crowell-Collier Publishing Company,
60 Fifth Avenue, New York 11

Designed by Andrew Roberts

Library of Congress Catalog Card Number: 62–11849

Preface

Robert V. Roosa

THE UNDER SECRETARY OF THE TREASURY
FOR MONETARY AFFAIRS

This book combines the results of Dr. Gaines' experience as a student, teacher, and practitioner in the arts of debt management and central banking. And in the final editing, it bears some marks of his new career as a commercial banker, concerned principally with trading and investing in government securities. In a field penetrated only by a hardy few, and described in print by only the rare individual who is so busy that he also has time to write, Dr. Gaines has made a unique contribution. Apart from a few monographs prepared for Congressional Committees or the Commission on Money and Credit, this is the first major treatise on debt management since Henry Murphy's *The National Debt in War and Transition* which was published in 1950 and Charles C. Abbott's book, *The Federal Debt, Structure and Impact,* which was published in 1953.

v

The book is divided into two parts. The first presents a detailed historical survey of debt management in the United States from the Civil War through 1957. This historical survey, in the tradition of Davis R. Dewey's *Financial History of the United States,* is a first-rate work of scholarship and should be rewarding reading for any student of debt management problems. Not everyone will agree with Dr. Gaines' interpretation of this history. He may have appraised too generously the debt management record of the distant past and has perhaps been unduly critical of the performance during the postwar years through 1957. Nevertheless, the facts are all presented with a thoroughness that enables each reader to make up his own mind.

The second part of the book deals with current problems of debt management and sets forth suggested policies for dealing with them. Some readers will find an element of internal conflict in Dr. Gaines' prescriptions. One of his principal theses is to advocate a "stereotyping" of more of our debt operations; that is to say, placing them on a regularly scheduled basis. Yet he also argues for more daring and imagination in handling debt management problems—an injunction which some would like to mean greater flexibility in using debt management as an instrument of economic policy. But even in his provocative shifts between urging adherence to fixed forms and recommending variation with cyclical or structural changes in the economy or with balance of payments developments, Dr. Gaines spins off suggestion after suggestion that today's reader will recognize as already a part of the debt management tool-kit. For this book in its typescript form was a desk-side source of historical background and stimulating contemplation for the debt managers of two administrations in Washington before it was made ready for actual publication.

It is a well-reasoned and well-written book which I commend to any student of finance.

Acknowledgments

A complete list of the individuals and institutions that played some part in the preparation of this study would leave scarcely any credit or blame for the author. To all those whose names are not mentioned here, your help was sincerely appreciated.

The study would not have been possible without the generous assistance of the Federal Reserve Bank of New York, the author's employer at the time the book was written. Under a program developed by the bank to encourage advanced study and research on monetary and financial matters, the author was granted a six-month leave in 1958 (at full salary) to pursue his research. My thanks to Alfred Hayes, President of the New York Fed, and to the directors of the bank for their generous contribution to scholarship.

The study might then have slipped quietly into the obscurity of the library stacks—the fate of most doctoral dissertations—if it had not been rescued at least temporarily by a new program, adopted in 1961 by the Graduate School of Business at Columbia

University, for publishing distinguished dissertations. I wish to thank Associate Dean Clarence Walton and the editorial staff at The Free Press for their help in making this study the first in what will be a series of dissertations to be published under the new Columbia program.

It would be completely impossible to mention all of the teachers and colleagues whose encouragement, knowledge, and assistance contributed directly or indirectly to the finished product. But an effort is called for. The Columbia Business School faculty, particularly Professors Benjamin Haggott Beckhart and Roger Murray, supplied wise counseling and guidance. Robert Rouse and Robert Roosa at the Federal Reserve Bank of New York contributed their knowledge of Treasury finance and the Government securities market. J. Dewey Daane and Robert Mayo of the Treasury Department read and criticized the original manuscript. Robert Lindsay, Jack Guttentag, and many more of my colleagues at the New York Reserve Bank assisted in countless ways. Tom Plank of the First National Bank of Chicago read and corrected the galley proofs. And Mrs. Lee Martocci, Mrs. Sophie Babski, and Miss Mary Lavin contributed the secretarial help that converted indecipherable scribbling to legible (if not always readable) text.

Finally, it is customary in acknowledging assistance to thank the author's wife and family for their understanding support and forebearance. I am indebted to my wife and daughter for their eager willingness to travel abroad during the critical months when the original text was being prepared. Seldom is a scholar given the opportunity for contemplation in peaceful solitude that was mine.

It probably is unnecessary to add that in spite of all the assistance of family and friends, responsibility for any errors of fact or judgment are wholly the author's.

Contents

V

Current Techniques of Treasury Finance
and Role of Investor Groups as Underwriters 153

VI

The Dealer Market for United States
Government Securities   197

VII

Federal Reserve Credit Policy
and Treasury Debt Management   228

VIII

Conclusions: Objectives and Techniques of Treasury Debt Management

Techniques of Treasury Debt Management

I

Introduction

Management of the huge public debt created by the depression of the 1930's and the Second World War has been a dominant, sometimes the dominant influence in the financial markets since the end of the war. In the early postwar years, an independent central bank monetary policy was subordinated to the preservation of low interest rates on the public debt, with inflationary consequences. In more recent years, since the Treasury-Federal Reserve "accord" of March, 1951, additional inflationary impulse has resulted from the seemingly irresistible shortening of the debt as the passage of time moved what had been funded debt into shorter and shorter maturity categories, and the Treasury considered itself unable to sell new long-term securities in the necessary volume to maintain the debt structure. Meanwhile, the need to refund rather than retire maturing debt, along with the recurring need to borrow new money, has brought the Treasury into the market several times each year in immense financing operations which often have had a jolting impact upon the smooth functioning of all securities markets.

Public debt management has not been a neglected area of study. A great deal of unsolicited advice has been available to the Treasury from the extensive literature on debt management policies that has blossomed in the postwar years. By and large, however, this literature has been directed toward the broad economic consequences of alternative debt policies or toward

1

developing the hypothetical role of debt management as one of the instruments of public economic policy. It has generally not recognized that the development of debt management as a positive policy instrument or, for that matter, the mere control of the debt to prevent its being a disturbing influence in the economy, must rest first upon the development of technical debt management procedures that enable the Treasury to control the structure and composition of the debt. The failure to develop techniques that would bring the debt under administrative control has been the most important deficiency in postwar debt management. Until this elementary deficiency is corrected, discussion of the economic policy role of public debt management is of only academic interest.

This study is narrowly focused upon the techniques of debt management; it is intended to fill at least part of the gap in the recent literature on this important subject. The opening chapters are devoted to a summary review of the technical history of the management of the public debt from the Civil War to the present. Although the problems of public debt management prior to the Second World War might appear to differ not just in degree but also in nature from the problems of the postwar years, the competence and ingenuity which earlier Treasury administrations brought to the management of the debt provide valuable lessons for the present. Subsequent chapters describe and analyze the differing interests of various investor groups in United States Government securities, the functioning of the dealer market in which Government securities are traded, and the technical procedures the Treasury has used in its financing. A separate chapter is devoted to the relationships between Federal Reserve credit policy and debt management and to the implications of an independent central bank policy for the objectives and techniques of Treasury finance. In the concluding chapter, the strands of analysis running through the earlier discussion are pulled together and changes in debt management techniques are suggested that might improve the Treasury's control over its debt, lessen the disturbing influence that the physical management of the

2

debt has had upon the financial markets and, by so doing, open the door for future experimentation toward developing debt management as a useful instrument of economic policy.

Although the study is limited to the technical aspects of managing the public debt, the author recognizes that the techniques selected, by themselves, have some influence upon the level of interest rates, the ownership of the debt, income distribution, private capital outlays, and so on. These subjects are not dealt with explicitly. Individual analysts, depending upon the weights they attach to various economic and social objectives, will find the techniques and technical objectives suggested here more or less acceptable. Whatever the broad economic purposes that might be assigned to or associated with the management of the public debt, however, there probably would be agreement that techniques should be developed which would make achievement of these objectives as simple as possible. Failure to develop techniques appropriate to the achievement of clearly stated objectives, as has been the case during much of the post-World War II period, should not be allowed to make debt management a source of disturbance to the economy.

The analysis concludes that demonetization of the public debt and lengthening of the debt, the two most frequently cited technical objectives of Treasury debt policy, are not appropriate or meaningful objectives of Treasury debt management. United States Government securities are one form of financial asset among many forms, and the responsibility for policies to regulate the monetization of financial assets clearly rests with the central bank. It is argued, therefore, that the Treasury need not allow itself to be distracted by concern for the ownership distribution of its debt. With respect to debt lengthening, the study concludes that changes in the maturity structure of the debt are means to the achievement of an economic objective and should not be pursued without reference to the broader objective sought.

With these "objectives" cleared away, the study proceeds to a discussion and recommendation of technical procedures designed, in the first instance, to routinize debt operations with a view to

3

achieving a stable maturity structure. Briefly, the techniques would: (1) place the short-term debt on a routine roll-over basis; (2) achieve a more orderly arrangement of maturities in the intermediate and long-term areas; and (3) refund intermediate and long-term obligations principally through a regular schedule of cash offerings, rather than exchange offerings, using the proceeds to call and repay outstanding issues before or at maturity. The proximate objective would be orderly debt management processes more nearly in step with modern procedures in the other capital and credit markets. Such technical processes would be calculated to lessen the disruptive influence of public debt management and, simultaneously, enable the Treasury to recapture control of its debt.

The detailed techniques for debt management suggested here are not the only nor necessarily the best combination of procedures for managing the debt. What is important is the emphasis upon the development of *some* set of techniques that will increasingly routinize and bring order to public debt management. Upon this base might then be built debt management policies that could contribute importantly to stability, growth, income distribution, or other policy objectives that might in time become popular.

II

Management of the Public Debt from the Civil War through World War II

The history of the public debt of the United States during the past one-hundred years reduces, in substantial part, to the record of the financial after-effects of the three major wars in which the nation has been involved. In the Civil War and the First and Second World Wars, public debt burdens were created which seemed, at the time, to place almost insurmountable obstacles in the way of a return to a state in which Government financing decisions were not dominant influences in the financial markets. Within a relatively brief period of years after both the Civil War and the First World War, however, the public debt had been brought under control through retirement out of surplus revenues and through refunding programs that were more or less wisely conceived. Whether or not wisdom prevailed in all cases is not so important as the fact that the debt was brought under control; policies and techniques were developed that enabled the Treasury to master the problems that had at first seemed so awesome. Treasury debt management since the Second World War, how-

5

ever, had not yet brought the war-created debt fully under control fifteen years after the war had ended.

Study of the history of an area of public policy is intended, principally, to supply guidance for current policy through analysis of the successes and failures of past policy action. There is danger, though, in any attempt to apply the lessons of the past uncritically to the problems with which Treasury debt policies have struggled for the past several years and will, in all probability, continue to struggle for some years to come. While the debt arose from the same source in all three instances of major debt creation—failure to provide tax revenues sufficient to pay for war-induced expenditures—and while many of the debt problems in all three postwar periods were similar, the sheer size of the post-World War II debt has given to it a significance and an economic role far more critical than was true in either of the earlier instances. Federal debt probably did not exceed one-half of national product at its highest point during the Civil War or one-third of national product at its peak in the First World War, and within twenty years of the end of the war in the first case and ten years in the second it had been reduced to about 15 per cent of national product. By the conclusion of World War II, on the other hand, gross Federal debt exceeded national product by nearly one-third, and fifteen years later, despite a rapid inflation-supported growth in the dollar value of economic activity, the Federal debt owned outside of Government trust accounts was still almost one-half as large as national product.

Perhaps the most important lesson for contemporary debt management to be learned from the record of past policies is that the debt managers have not, by and large, relied upon tradition or a well-established body of doctrine to supply them with the techniques for meeting new problems. In fact, with the exception of the debt repayment tradition, the management of the public debt in the United States over the past century has been remarkably free of the stultifying influence of tradition. The record, on the whole, has been one of intelligent adjustment of policies and

6

procedures to the problem to be met and to the institutional setting in which it was to be met. Decisions as to terms, techniques, and maturities ordinarily have been arrived at on the basis of careful analysis of alternative objectives, rather than because tradition had, in some fashion, made one course more virtuous than another.

A. The Civil War Debt

At its peak on August 31, 1865, the Civil War debt totaled approximately $2.8 billion. Of this total, only 40 per cent ($1.1 billion) represented securities with more than three years to run to maturity, 30 per cent ($0.8 billion) was in the form of short-term, interest-bearing notes, and the remaining 30 per cent ($0.8 billion) was in the form of legal tender notes or demand obligations. The debt had increased by some thirty-three times from its prewar level (a greater relative increase than in either World Wars I or II).

Most analysts have been harshly critical of the Civil War financing policies of Secretary Chase.[1] The catalogue of charges includes over-reliance upon legal tender issues (principally United States notes), failure to anticipate the duration of the war and thus to recommend adequate tax legislation, insistence in early financing upon settlement in specie, refusal to use banks as Government depositaries and to accept checks in payment to the Government, and refusal to sell Government securities below par, thus complicating an already difficult financing problem.

In evaluating the conduct of Civil War financing, it is im-

1. Cf. Paul Studenski and H. E. Krooss, *Financial History of the United States* (New York: McGraw-Hill Book Co., Inc., 1952); Robert A. Love, *Federal Financing* (New York: Columbia University Press, 1931) pp. 116–117; A. Barton Hepburn, *History of Coinage and Currency in the United States* (New York: The Macmillan Co., 1903), pp. 202–203; Wesley C. Mitchell, *A History of the Greenbacks* (Chicago: The University of Chicago Press, 1903), esp. Chap. X.

portant to keep in mind that the Treasury was called upon to raise sums of money vastly greater than had ever before been borrowed in the financial markets of the country, and to do this without the assistance of a central bank. The techniques that had been employed to finance the Government before the Civil War were sufficient for the small amount of borrowing undertaken by the Treasury, but they proved totally inadequate for financing the war. The occasional deficits the Treasury had incurred during the nineteenth century prior to the Civil War—principally during the War of 1812, the Mexican War, and the depressions of the late 1830's and 1850's—were financed largely through negotiated placement of securities with the banks and private banking houses in New York, Philadelphia and Boston.[2] These institutions then attempted to redistribute the Government securities to banks and other investors throughout the country. During most of the period prior to 1836 the Treasury had the assistance of the First and Second United States Banks, both in the initial placement of debt and in maintaining a market for Government securities, but after that date it acted as its own broker in its negotiated placements with the banks and in its efforts, usually futile, to place part of its securities with other investors on public offerings.

It had become evident by 1862 that the procedures of the pre-war period for placing debt with the big city banks would not serve to finance the Civil War, since these banks did not have the resources to underwrite the Government. At the same time, both legal and bureaucratic problems caused the Treasury to fail in its early attempts to place popular loans on direct public subscription. The result was that a disturbing proportion of the financing through the first three years of the war was in the form of noninterest-bearing United States notes, actually a forced loan, and short-term interest bearing obligations, some of which were legal tender.

2. The first private banking syndicate to underwrite the Treasury consisted of David Parrish, Stephen Girard, and John Jacob Astor, during the War of 1812.

8

In October, 1862, Secretary Chase appointed Jay Cooke, a private Philadelphia banker, as general agent for marketing United States Government securities. Prior to this time only small amounts of permanent debt had been sold. Cooke completely reorganized debt management techniques. Through hundreds of subagent banks and an extensive publicity campaign that stressed patriotism as a principal motive for investment in Government securities, he was successful in selling Government obligations to an estimated three million private investors. Under Cooke's direction, $500 million of 5–20 year, 6 per cent bonds were sold during 1862-63, the first important Civil War financing in longer-term securities. The Treasury again encountered serious difficulties during 1864 in placing its debt, and Secretary Fessenden reappointed Cooke as general agent. With Cooke's assistance, the Treasury successfully sold more than $800 million 7.3 per cent three-year notes in a space of seven months, thus completing Civil War financing.

The importance of Jay Cooke's operations during the Civil War was not limited to his activities as agent for the Treasury in the sale of new securities. Only $50 million to $60 million of United States Government securities had been outstanding before the war, held in large part by the leading Eastern banks. Consequently, at a time when the organization of financial markets of all types in this country was still rather rudimentary, the market organization for trading in United States Government securities probably was particularly primitive. There is no evidence that there were any firms or individuals specializing in Government securities before the Civil War—the small size of the debt would almost rule out the possibility of specialists—and the relatively small amount of market trading in Government securities apparently was handled as a side line by brokerage firms on the stock exchange.[3] One of Cooke's most important

3. The New York Stock Exchange (then known as the Regular Board) first opened a Government bond department to provide for continuous trading in United States Government securities in April, 1867. See: George Garvy, "Rivals and Interlopers in the History of the New York Security Market," *The Journal of Political Economy,* 52, 2 (June, 1944), 133.

contributions to Civil War finance was the assistance he gave to the creation of a broad market for Government debt. He established an office in New York that specialized in Government securities. Employing techniques that are still characteristic of the Government securities market, he entered into large commitments for his own account (sometimes he operated with Treasury funds on orders from the Secretary) to absorb blocks of securities pressing on the market, simultaneously selling for his own account to customers located throughout the country. On frequent occasions he supported the market for Government issues, sometimes on his own initiative and sometimes with Treasury funds, in order that below-par prices in the market would not interfere with his efforts to sell new Treasury securities. The development of a broad market in Government securities was a necessary precondition for successful financing on the scale required by the Civil War, and its creation was an important result of Civil War financing.

In brief, the financing of the United States Government during the Civil War required that new techniques be devised for selling Government securities and that an active and specialized secondary market be developed for these obligations. The successful placement of a large part of the Government's debt with a broad group of investors throughout the country under the popular loan techniques developed by Chase and Cooke provided a stability of ownership in the years immediately following the war that allowed the Treasury the time necessary to refund the debt into more orderly maturities. The development of a broader trading market in Government issues provided for price continuity as the redistribution of debt ownership took place. And the creation of the national banking system toward the end of the war brought into existence a group of institutions with a continuing demand for Government securities both to meet their charter requirements and to support their note issues. The relatively orderly refunding and consolidation of the Civil War debt between 1866 and 1880 owes much of its success to these innovations during the war.

B. Refunding and
Debt Retirement: 1865–1890

As noted earlier, the post-Civil War public debt at its peak, in August, 1865, had totaled $2.8 billion, of which $1.1 billion was "funded" in the sense that it had more than three years to run to maturity; the largest part of the funded debt consisted of the 6 per cent 5–20's. The remainder of the debt included $430 million of United States notes, $440 million of miscellaneous short-term issues (legal tender notes, temporary loans, and certificates of indebtedness), and $830 million of three-year, 7.3 per cent notes with staggered maturities running to July, 1868. By the time the last of the 7.3 per cent notes were refunded in fiscal 1870, the debt had been reduced by $400 million and the remainder had been fully consolidated in a form that would simplify subsequent refunding and redemption. Of a total debt of $2.4 billion, approximately $1.6 billion was in the form of 6 per cent 5–20's with first call dates staggered from 1869 through 1873, $400 million was in the form of United States notes and fractional currency, and $400 million was in longer-term bonds.

The initial refunding of the Civil War debt into the 5–20–year 6's was understood at the time to be a temporary expedient that would relieve the Treasury of the risk inherent in a large floating debt during the period of adjustment after the war and still place the debt in a form that could soon be called for redemption or more permanent refunding.[4] The Treasury was willing to pay a relatively high rate of interest to sell securities that would achieve these ends. The next stage of post-Civil War

4. It might be mentioned that the success of McCulloch's refunding operations was the more remarkable in view of the debate at the time on whether the United States should redeem its bonded debt in currency other than gold coin; uncertainty on this point caused United States Government bonds to trade at a 10 per cent basis on foreign exchanges. It was not until the Republican victory in 1868 and President Grant's firm pledge to pay principal and interest on United States Government bonds in gold that the uncertainty was finally resolved.

debt management began with the Loan Act of July, 1870, which was to provide for more permanent refunding of the debt at lower rates of interest. Incorporating in general form recommendations made by Secretary Boutwell, this legislation authorized the Secretary of the Treasury to issue up to $200 million (increased to $500 million in 1871) 5 per cent bonds redeemable 10 years from initial issue, $300 million 4½ per cent bonds redeemable after 15 years from initial issue, and $1,000 million 4 per cent bonds redeemable 30 years after initial issue. The new bonds were made payable in coin, were fully exempt from all Federal and other taxes (the first time fully tax-exempt bonds had been authorized for Federal finance), had to be sold at par or better or exchanged for 5–20's at par, and could be employed only for refunding purposes.

The second refunding of the Civil War debt was completed by the end of fiscal 1879. A total of approximately $1.4 billion of outstanding securities had been refunded under the Loan Act of 1870 into the following issues:

(in millions of dollars)

Funded Loan of 1881 — $500
Funded Loan of 1891 — $185
Funded Loan of 1907 — $710

An additional $96 million of these securities had been sold by the Treasury for gold in preparation for specie resumption, which took place in January, 1879. Of a total debt of $2.3 billion at the end of 1879, $1.5 billion consisted of the funding securities designated by the Loan Act of 1870, about $350 million was in the form of United States notes, $190 million was still outstanding in 6 per cent bonds not callable until 1881, and the remaining $250 million represented, in large part, a few other Civil War issues that were not yet callable. The Civil War debt had been almost completely consolidated, at a considerable saving of interest to the Treasury.

Later writers have characterized the Loan Act of 1870 and

1 2

the sale of the long-term 4 per cent and 4½ per cent bonds as a "major error" in debt management policy.[5] They argue that the sale of these bonds reduced the Treasury's control of its obligations in that there was not a steady volume of securities reaching maturity or call date, with the result that the large surpluses accumulated during the 1880's could be employed to retire debt only by purchasing outstanding securities in the market at substantial premiums. Patterson also suggests that the Act of 1870 which authorized the securities, and their subsequent sale, may have ". . . contributed to the perpetuation of a high tariff system . . . [and] lengthened the life of an awkward and inadequate banking and currency system."[6] Some contemporary financial experts held the view that the Act was dangerous, notably Senator (later Secretary) Sherman, but other thoughtful men, including Secretary Boutwell, favored the sale of long-term bonds, principally as a device for assuring that an adequate supply of United States Government bonds would remain outstanding to support the national bank notes.

It is difficult at this distance to form any judgment on whether the funding of the 1870's contained "errors." It should be recalled that the principal objective of the Act of 1870 was to reduce interest charges on the public debt. It is true that the 4's and 4½'s subsequently went to premiums, indicating that bonds could have been sold at still lower rates of interest at that time. But it would have been asking too much to expect Congress in 1870 or the Secretaries of the Treasury during the 1870's to have anticipated surpluses of the size that developed in the 1880's or to have guessed the extent to which national bank's demands for Government securities would subsequently depress the effective rate of interest for Treasury financing. Perhaps all that can be concluded about the episode is that it

5. Cf. Robert T. Patterson, *Federal Debt Management Policies, 1865–1879* (Durham: Duke University Press, 1954), pp. 83–92. D. K. Dewey, *Financial History of the United States* (New York: Longmans, Green and Co., 1928), p. 353.

6. Patterson, *op. cit.*, p. 83.

shows the desirability of Treasury debt planning that results in a maturity structure which allows the Treasury freedom to meet any contingency. Either a large floating debt or a fully funded debt can handcuff policy decisions.

Before leaving the discussion of post-Civil War debt consolidation and refunding, a word might be said about financing techniques. The Treasury prior to its 1879 operation in the 4's employed a banking syndicate to market its securities (a banking syndicate also was used to sell the 4's abroad during 1879). Before 1873 this syndicate usually was headed by Jay Cooke and Company, and in following years it was headed by August Belmont and Company in this country and the Rothschild firm in London. The post-Civil War syndicates took responsibility for selling the Treasury's securities at an agreed upon commission, and did not actually underwrite the Treasury offerings. In this respect, the arrangement differed significantly from the pre-Civil War practice, under which the larger banks, as Treasury underwriters, were sometimes in a position to dictate terms to the Secretary of the Treasury. During the period of recovery from the Civil War, with the disturbances in the capital market that characterized that period and the uncertainties resulting from debates in Congress on the greenbacks and silver, the Treasury clearly needed all the professional assistance it could command. Also, the need for a middleman to convert the various currencies into gold coin during the refunding program of the 1870's was an important *raison d'être* for the banking syndicate arrangement. These problems had largely been resolved by the time of specie resumption in 1879, however, and with the market for Government securities developed during the war and the generally broad financial markets that had emerged in the period of rapid industrialization after the war, the ground was laid for adoption of the practice of selling Government securities directly, on public advertisement and subscription. With rare exceptions, the practice of direct Treasury offering and public subscriptions has been employed to the present day.

After the completion of the debt funding program of the

14

1870's, debt management for a decade was concerned principally with the problems involved in employing a steadily large budget surplus to retire debt. It will be recalled that at the end of 1879 the principal interest-bearing debt issues consisted of $500 million of 5 per cent bonds first callable in 1881, $250 million 4½ per cent bonds callable in 1891, and about $740 million 4 per cent bonds that would not be callable until 1907. In addition to the 5's callable in 1881, some $280 million of miscellaneous debt issues bearing interest rates of 5 or 6 per cent matured or became callable by 1881. Consequently, the total of debt maturing or redeemable in the decade of the 1880's was of the order of $800 million; the debt actually redeemed during that period out of surplus revenues amounted to $1.2 billion. The debt management problem of the 1880's was one of acquiring sufficient securities to retire with the funds available in the Treasury.

In spite of urgent and continuing appeals from the Secretary of the Treasury to Congress to reduce taxes, the combination of high protective tariffs and a revenue system based almost entirely upon these tariffs produced surpluses year by year. By late 1887, the Treasury had called and retired all outstanding debt that had reached optional call date. With the complete elimination of the redeemable issues, further debt retirement until 1891 could be effected only through purchases of outstanding bonds in the market at substantial premiums. Beginning in fiscal 1888 and continuing through fiscal 1891 the Treasury steadily paid large premiums to buy its securities back in the market. At times, the premium on the longer-term 4 per cent bonds ranged as high as 29 points. By the end of fiscal 1891, two months before the 4½'s would reach first call date, only $50 million of the original $250 million issue remained outstanding and, in addition, some $180 million 4's, first callable in 1907, had been purchased and retired, reducing that issue to $560 million. The remaining 4½'s were called and retired in fiscal 1892.

The principal objectives of debt management between the end

of the Civil War and the completion of the postwar refunding program in 1879 were to consolidate and demonetize the debt and to reduce interest cost on the debt by refunding at declining rates of interest. Debt retirement was a continuing, longer-run objective, but there was no messianic fervor to retire the debt quickly. In fact, the more frequently expressed attitude on debt repayment was that it should proceed slowly so as to minimize its impact on the economy.[7] Therefore, the rapid debt retirement of the 1880's was an unplanned and, by and large, an unwanted development. The thorniest part of the Treasury debt retirement problem during the 1880's was the influence that Treasury purchases of outstanding bonds had upon the national bank note circulation. These purchases not only resulted in the retirement of instruments supporting the note circulation but also affected the willingness of national banks to hold United States Government bonds and to issue notes against them. With Treasury circulars offering to buy the 4's and 4½'s almost constantly in force (sometimes including prepayment of interest to a specified date to induce offerings of bonds), market rates of interest were driven down to the point where it became unprofitable or only marginally profitable (considering the one per cent circulation tax) for national banks to own the bonds for the purpose of currency issue. National bank note circulation was reduced from nearly $360 million in 1882 to less than $170

7. See: *Annual Report for 1881*, pp. 18–19; *Annual Report for 1882*, p. 27; *Annual Report for 1883*, p. 24. The following quotation is from the *Annual Report for 1881*, p. 19: "It is estimated that if the present ratio of receipt and expenditure is kept up the public debt now existing may be paid in the next ten years. In view of the large sum that has been paid by the present generation upon that debt and of the heavy taxation it now bears upon the industries and business of the country, it seems just and proper that another generation should meet a portion of the debt, and that the burdens now laid upon the country should be lightened. . . . Other considerations have been presented, such that if the public debt should be fully paid and all government bonds retired, the best and safest basis for the national banking system will be gone, and that a desirable mode of investment for savings banks, trust companies, and fiduciary representatives will be taken away, and that the return of the large sum paid to the holders of bonds, to seek reinvestment through other channels, will disturb the business of the country."

16

million by 1891. Various corrective measures were recommended to Congress by the Secretaries of the Treasury, year by year, during the 1880's, but no action was taken.

C. Defense of Gold and the Monetary System: 1890–1917

Treasury debt management between 1890 and the First World War was concerned principally with defense of the country's gold reserves and support of the monetary system. In addition, a relatively nominal amount of borrowing was necessary in connection with financing the Spanish American War and the Panama Canal. But monetary problems—international and domestic—were the major issues.

Financial disturbances abroad were principally responsible for starting an outflow of gold from this country in fiscal 1891 that continued almost without interruption through 1895. The gold reserve had fallen to slightly more than $80 million by late 1893, and in January, 1894, the Treasury sold $50 million of 5 per cent bonds at a price to yield 3 per cent. Payment was in gold and the proceeds were used to rebuild the gold reserve. The Treasury continued to lose gold, however, and by August, 1894, the gold reserve against United States notes had fallen to $52 million. Therefore, an additional offering of $50 million of the 5 per cent ten-year bonds was made in November for payment in gold. Bids totaled $179 million, including a winning bid for the full $50 millon from J. P. Morgan and Company at a 2⅞ per cent basis.

The second issue of bonds to raise gold was no more successful in maintaining the gold reserve than the earlier one had been. In fact, the Treasury's efforts appeared to be self-defeating, because the law required that the United States notes and the Treasury notes issued against silver be kept in circulation. Consequently, the sale of bonds for gold in the domestic market to replace gold lost through redemption of currency issues was followed by the reissue of the currency and the prompt return of this currency to the Treasury as the market attempted to rebuild its gold supply. In an effort to get off this merry-go-round, the Treasury in February, 1895 (when the gold reserve had fallen to $41 million), entered into a contract with a syndicate headed by J. P. Morgan and Company (marking the first time the Treasury had employed a syndicate since 1878) whereby the Treasury agreed to sell $62.3 million of thirty-year 4's for 3½ million ounces of gold having a value of $65.1 million. It was further stipulated that the syndicate would acquire at least one-half of the gold abroad (this did not prove to be feasible) and that the syndicate would

as far as lies in their power exert all financial influence and . . . make all legitimate efforts to protect the Treasury of the United States against withdrawals of gold pending the complete performance of this contract.[8]

Under the latter stipulation, Morgan and his associates conducted a private exchange stabilization program for six months until they had completed performance on the contract.

Gold reserves had again fallen to $61 million by January 1896, and an additional offering of $100 million of the 4 per cent, thirty-year bonds was made. In this operation the Treasury decided to bypass the syndicate and to offer the bonds on direct subscription. Bids totaling nearly $700 million were received, and the bonds were awarded at an average price of 111⅛. The loss of monetary gold was stopped during 1896 and a return flow of gold soon set in, so that the debt operations "in defense of gold" were concluded with the above-mentioned offering early in that year of $100 million 4 per cent bonds.

In June, 1898, Congress authorized the sale of $200 million of 3 per cent bonds to finance the cost of our participation in the Spanish-American War. The principal importance of this financing was that it initiated certain techniques of Treasury finance that have been employed to the present day. First, it was

8. *Annual Report for 1895*, pp. 69–70.

18

an offering of securities at a fixed price of par rather than at auction or on a negotiated basis; second, it specified that smaller investors should receive preference through a process of allotting smaller subscriptions in full. While offerings of securities for the previous twenty years had, in all but one instance, been handled on a popular subscription basis, the fact that they were offered at competitive bidding had made it difficult for less sophisticated investors to participate, and the large Eastern banks had, in fact, still been underwriting the Treasury. The legislation authorizing the bond sale, while a step forward, continued to tie the Secretary's hands, however, in that it specified not only interest rate and maturity but also that the bonds must be sold at par. It would be another twenty years before Congress, at last recognizing the impossibility of setting financing terms by legislation, would give the Secretary virtually full authority to determine terms.

During the first decade of the twentieth century the United States Treasury Department took two very realistic actions. First, it recognized explicitly that the prices and rates of interest at which Government bonds traded in the market wholly reflected their scarcity value as backing for national bank notes rather than their investment value, and the Treasury refunded debt to take advantage of this circumstance. Second, the Treasury Department under Secretary Shaw recognized by its actions that, in the absence of a central bank and with the type of monetary system under which the American economy was attempting to operate, the Treasury had no alternative but to attempt to perform a central banking function. The attempt to maintain a viable monetary system was the most important influence on debt management during the decade.

In the *Annual Report for 1892,* the Secretary of the Treasury had mentioned that the Treasury might offer long-term bonds bearing 2 per cent interest in optional exchange for the 4 per cent bonds callable in 1907, and by so doing create a bond issue which, by trading closer to par, would be more useful for assuring an adequate national bank note circulation. No action

19

was taken by Congress on the suggestion at that time, but in the Financial Act of March, 1900, Congress adopted a measure that closely approximated the earlier suggestion. The Secretary was authorized to offer holders of the 5 per cent bonds callable in 1904, the 4 per cent bonds callable in 1907, and the 3 per cent bonds callable in 1908 (the Spanish-War bonds) optional conversion into a consolidated 2 per cent issue callable after thirty years and with no fixed maturity. The Act also provided that national banks should be allowed to circulate notes in a face amount equal to the par value of the 2 per cent consols pledged (the limit was 90 per cent on outstanding bonds), and the annual tax on note circulation was reduced from one to one-half per cent.

Upon completion of the full consolidation operation at the end of fiscal 1907, nearly $650 million of 2 per cent consols of 1930 were outstanding. The unexchanged 4 per cent bonds of 1907 and 5 per cent bonds of 1904 either were purchased before call date for the sinking fund or redeemed at call date; the Spanish-War 3 per cent issue had been reduced by conversions to $64 million from $200 million. Therefore, of the original $860 million bonds of the three issues, nearly $650 million were converted, $145 million were retired, and fewer than $65 million were still outstanding at the end of fiscal 1907. Meanwhile, in the period between March, 1900, and June, 1908, national bank note circulation almost tripled, increasing from $250 million to nearly $700 million. The Secretary, Mr. Cortelyou, concluded in his *Report for 1908* that this expansion of the money supply had reflected principally the liberalizing provisions in the act of March, 1900, with respect to national bank note issues.

The other major financing operation prior to the First World War was to finance construction of the Panama Canal. Total expenditures on the Panama Canal between 1904 and 1916 amounted to approximately $400 million, of which $135 million was financed through the sale of bonds. The first $85 million of these bonds, sold as needed in fiscal years 1907-09, carried a 2 per cent rate of interest, were redeemable in ten years and matured in thirty years, and were eligible as a basis for national bank note circulation. The bonds were sold at auction rather than at a predetermined price and brought an average price above par. The last $50 million of Panama Canal bonds, sold in May, 1911, did not carry the note circulation privilege and therefore required a 3 per cent coupon for a first call date fifty years in the future.

The sale of the 3 per cent Panama Canal bonds was the last item of Treasury financing prior to the financing of the First World War. At the end of fiscal 1916, the last fiscal year not affected by war financing, the total public debt was $1,225 million, of which $971 million represented interest-bearing securities. The Federal Reserve System had come into existence just three years earlier and, though still uncertain of the principles by which its operations should be guided, it would prove to be invaluable in the unprecedented war-finance job ahead. Government finances were in strong condition, the tradition of popular subscription for Treasury securities had been established, and at least the nucleus of a specialized market for Government securities existed.

If it may be said that public debt management in the United States came of age during the First World War, it is equally true that the period from the Civil War through 1916 was one in which debt management passed through the experimental adjustments of adolescence. By and large, the record made was quite satisfactory. From a condition in 1860 in which the poor credit standing of the Federal Government required Government bonds to carry higher rates of interest than the bonds of some State governments, the long record of sound financial policy after the Civil War had, by 1916, created the highest credit rating for United States Government debt. Some inadequacies in debt management procedures remained to be corrected, of course, and new problems in subsequent years were to develop other inadequacies. For example, as the period of World War I finance opened, Congress still retained authority

21

to establish rates of interest, maturities, and other details of new security issues; the need for greater administrative discretion in this area had long been apparent. Also, the bulk of the interest-bearing public debt was still owned by the national banks in 1916, and the creation of the structure for a new currency system with the establishment of the Federal Reserve System would soon have required the development of techniques and instruments to achieve broader ownership of the debt even if World War I financing had not made such action immediately necessary. Finally, the adoption in 1913 of an income tax system for Federal finance created a series of questions as to the proper tax status for Government securities that would not finally be resolved until the 1940's. These remaining deficiencies, however, should not obscure the progress in Federal debt management that had been made, from the condition of hat-in-hand borrower from the big city banks in 1860 to a preferred-risk borrower able to sell its debt instruments in a broad market in 1916.

D. Financing World War I

Two fortuitous circumstances helped to make the management of the Government's finances during the First World War a simpler task than it had been during the Civil War; these were the establishment, only a few years earlier, of an income tax system and of a central banking system. The existence of an organized income tax program by the time the United States became involved in the war provided the foundation upon which a much enlarged revenue system could be rapidly built. And the existence of a central bank supplied a mechanism for money creation that assured an almost unlimited market for Government securities to cover expenditures not provided for by taxes.

Approximately one-third of the more than $35 billion of Federal Government expenditures between April, 1917, and

October, 1919, was covered out of tax revenues, and the balance was raised through borrowing. Treasury policy was directed toward financing at least one-fourth to one-third of expenditures from tax revenues; more aggressive tax programs were eschewed for fear of their effect on business confidence and initiative. The total gross public debt, which had been $1.2 billion at the end of fiscal 1916, had increased to $25.5 billion by the close of fiscal 1919.

Financing techniques employed during the First World War were similar in many respects to those developed by Jay Cooke to finance the Civil War. With the assistance of the Reserve Banks, which served as fiscal agents in handling the sale of securities, "Liberty Loan" committees were set up in each Federal Reserve District, and intensive publicity campaigns, based almost wholly on an appeal to patriotism and buttressed by coercive moral pressure, were employed to stimulate subscriptions. These appeals for public subscriptions were, to all appearances, strikingly successful, but the pressure on citizens to buy Liberty bonds resulted in an unstable distribution of the debt and led to severe postwar congestion in the market as the redistribution of the debt took place. During the First Liberty Loan operation in May, 1917, some four million separate subscriptions were received; by the time of the Fourth Liberty Loan in September, 1918, the number of subscriptions had increased to 21 million. In addition to the wide ownership distribution of marketable securities achieved through appeals to patriotism at the time of each of the Liberty Loan drives, the Treasury also employed nonmarketable War Savings Certificates and Thrift Stamps in denominations as small as twenty-five cents. More than $1 billion maturity value of these certificates and stamps were outstanding in June, 1919.

The ability of the Treasury to sell more than $24 billion of new interest-bearing securities, net, in the short space of little more than two years can be traced to the role played by the Federal Reserve Banks and the commercial banks. Several innovations were adopted to stimulate the use of bank credit to support Treasury financing. First, by Act of April, 1917, the Secretary was specifically authorized to redeposit with selected depositary banks amounts of money equal to their own and their customers' subscriptions to Liberty bonds and certificates. By November, 1917, 1,900 national banks and 1,300 state banks and trust companies had been designated as depositaries. While redeposits of the proceeds of financing with the subscribing banks had been employed from time to time during the nineteenth century, the practice was not formalized or used extensively until the First World War. Second, subscribers to new Treasury securities were encouraged to "borrow and buy," and commercial banks were given every encouragement to lend against Government security collateral. As a result of these policies toward the banks, the World War I public debt expansion was accompanied by a burst of bank credit creation. Demand deposits adjusted and currency in circulation grew by $7 billion, or 44 per cent, in the three years between June, 1916, and June, 1919.

The securities offered by the Treasury in the four Liberty Loan operations undertaken during the First World War were, in all instances, intermediate to longer-term bonds. In the First Liberty Loan, in April, 1917, investors were offered $2 billion of 3½ per cent bonds of thirty-year maturity, callable after fifteen years. The Second Liberty Loan was conducted in October, 1917. Three billion dollars of 4 per cent bonds were offered for public subscription, with the Secretary retaining the privilege to overallot; these bonds carried twenty-five year maturities and were callable in ten years. A total of $3.8 billion bonds was allotted. The Third Loan was offered for public subscription in April, 1918, and consisted of $3 billion (subject to overallotment) of 4¼ per cent bonds bearing a fixed ten-year maturity. Some $4.2 billion of subscriptions were received and were allotted in full. The Fourth Liberty Loan followed closely upon the Third. In October 1918, the Treasury invited subscriptions for $6 billion, or more, of 4¼ per cent bonds due in twenty years and redeemable in fifteen years. Subscriptions totaling $7.0 billion were allotted in full.

These four Liberty Loans completed the Treasury's permanent financing in the First World War. However, expenditures continued to exceed receipts during the remainder of fiscal 1919, and it was necessary for the Treasury to return to market in April, 1919, for additional money. It was decided that this financing should be in the form of Treasury notes maturing within five years in order that maturing securities would be available for retirement in the early postwar years, thus avoiding the frozen debt position that had plagued the Treasury in the 1880's after the Civil War debt had been completely refunded into longer-term maturities. The Treasury, therefore, offered $4.5 billion of three- and four-year notes for public subscriptions; the securities were offered in two issues bearing coupon rates of 4¾ per cent and 3¾ per cent, the latter issue being fully tax-exempt and the former subject to surtax levies. This offering also was oversubscribed, but the Treasury limited allotments to $4.5 billion.

Throughout the First World War the Treasury employed short-term (thirty- to ninety-day) tax-anticipation and bond-anticipation certificates of indebtedness as part of its over-all financing program. Certificates of one sort or another had been used in the War of 1812, the Mexican War, the Civil War, and in the various financial crises of the nineteenth and early twentieth centuries, but in all cases such short-term financing had been turned to as a last resort when longer-term financing did not appear to be feasible. Certificates of indebtedness were employed in the financing of the First World War, on the other hand, as an orderly method for bridging the gap between the steady flow of expenditures and the periodic large flow of receipts at the quarterly income tax dates and at the settlement dates for the various Liberty Loans. The total of certificates outstanding (tax anticipation and bond anticipation) reached a peak for the period of war finance in early May, 1919, at $6.5 billion, but receipts from the Victory Liberty Loan financing

25

and from June tax payments had reduced this total to $3.6 billion by the end of fiscal 1919.

At the close of fiscal 1919, which may conveniently be used as the terminal date for the period of World War I financing, the maturity structure of the debt was as indicated in Table 1.

Table 1—Treasury Debt Structure, June 30, 1919

Maturity or First Call Date	Amount, in Billions of Dollars
Debt maturing within	
1 year	$3.6 (Certificates)
Debt maturing	
3 to 4 years	3.5 (Victory notes; $1 billion still not paid in by 6/30/19)
Bonds callable in 1925	0.1 (4's of 1925)
Bonds callable in 1927	0.7 (Second Liberty 4's)
	2.9 (Second Liberty Converted 4¼'s)
Bonds maturing in 1928	4.0 (Third Liberty 4¼'s)
Bonds callable in 1930	0.6 (Consol 2's)
Bonds callable in 1932	1.4 (First Liberty 3½'s)
	0.2 (First Liberty Converted 4's)
	0.4 (First Liberty Converted 4¼'s)
Bonds callable in 1933	6.8 (Fourth Liberty 4¼'s)
Nonmarketable debt due	
1922, 1923	1.0 (War Savings Certificates)
Miscellaneous debt	0.4
Total debt	$25.5 billion

Source: United States Treasury Department.

As Table 1 shows, only $3.6 billion of marketable debt, or 14 per cent of total debt, was scheduled to mature within one year, and a total of only $8.1 billion (including War Savings Certificates), or 32 per cent, would mature within five years.

The financing of the First World War under Secretary McAdoo has received only slightly more gentle treatment in the literature than the financing of the Civil War under Chase. In particular, the encouragement given to the use of bank credit to finance bond purchases has been severely criticized. The criticisms directed toward the use of bank credit in financing World War I are, perhaps, well taken, but one is driven then to ask what the alternative might have been, given the apparently inevitable lags in adjusting taxes to the rate of spending in a

major war. To the extent that taxes, because of unrealistic taxing policies, have in each of our major wars left a margin of
expenditures to be covered by borrowing in amounts that were
completely unprecedented, creation of vast amounts of new
money, either in the form of currency or of bank deposits, probably was unavoidable. There is no evidence to support the conclusion that any level of interest rates, however high, could have
expanded the voluntary flow of savings into Government securities at a rate sufficiently rapid to have met the Government's
requirements in any of our major wars.

Perhaps the most valid criticism that can be made of World
War I financing is not that massive creation of new bank credit
was employed to finance the Treasury but that this credit was
largely in the form of loans to customers against Government
securities rather than direct additions to bank portfolios of
Governments. The placement of a major part of the World War
I debt with individual and business investors, who had financed
their purchases with bank credit, created an unstable ownership
pattern that led to the subsequent collapse in the capital markets
and contributed to the severity of the postwar recession. Even
this criticism, however, must answer the question of whether, by
ultimately being less inflationary, the policies followed and the
sharp market shake-out that resulted were not preferable to the
more permanent increase in the money supply that would have
resulted if the securities had been sold directly to banks.

E. Orderly Debt Retirement: 1920–1930

The decade of the 1920's witnessed what is probably the most
effective execution of debt management policy, in a technical
sense, in the history of the country. Without regard to the other
economic and financial excesses of this decade or the extent to
which Treasury debt retirement might have contributed to these
excesses, debt management policies under Secretary Mellon were

successful in the sense that the policies that were defined at the beginning of his term of office were then executed methodically through techniques that made their execution as simple as possible.

In his first address to Congress, President Harding described the objectives of debt management under his administration as "orderly funding and gradual liquidation."[9] Secretary Mellon directed his policies, first toward gradual reduction of the high level of taxes imposed during the war, consistent with, second, orderly retirement of the war-created debt through purchases or retirement of maturing securities for the sinking fund. He explained his policy of debt retirement as follows:

Since 1919 . . . the Treasury has been paying its debts and the retirement of outstanding obligations has been greatly in excess of new issues, so that the net effect of the Treasury's operations during this period has been a tendency to bring about lower rather than higher money rates. . . . The effect of this policy of debt repayment on money rates is more apparent when it is considered that the principal reduction in the debt has taken place through the retirement of certificates of indebtedness and other short-term securities which are largely held by banks and financial institutions. . . . The repayment of our public debt involves a collection of taxes from all taxpayers and turning over the proceeds to holders of Government securities. Whether or not this process has any effect upon savings and upon short and long-term interest rates depends in some measure upon how the taxes are collected and upon the type of securities retired. If a large proportion of the taxes with which debt payments are made is collected from persons who would have saved the amounts paid in taxes, the volume of investment funds will not be materially affected. . . . On the other hand, whenever tax collections result in a reduction of personal expenditures the result is a net increase in the supply of capital and consequent reduction in general interest rates. In either case, however, there may be some influence upon the rate structure . . . that is, the relation between short-term and long-term rates. When, for example, the Government pays off the short-term debt, such as certificates of indebtedness and Treasury notes, a larger proportion of which is held by financial institutions, it releases bank credit for other uses and money rates tend to decline. As the process goes on,

9. Andrew W. Mellon, *Taxation: The People's Business* (New York: The MacMillan Company, 1924), p. 31.

surplus funds may gradually be drawn into the long-term investment market but the first effect of such payments is on short-term rates.

. . . The heavy volume of savings during recent years, both corporate and individual, has also been a material factor in the decline of general interest rates . . . It is clearly demonstrable moreover, that the Government's program of debt retirement has been a material factor in bringing about the improved credit conditions which now prevail, and the improvement in credit conditions in turn is a prime factor in the present prosperous condition of industry.[10]

In short, Secretary Mellon had a clearly defined philosophy of debt management, and of the relationship between debt management and the economy. Policy actions of the 1920's were directed toward specific, clearly-stated objectives. Maturing securities were redeemed if funds were available in the sinking fund or from surplus; if not, they were refunded to a carefully selected niche in the debt structure where, when they matured, funds might be expected to be available to redeem them. Longer-term obligations were employed infrequently in this refunding, and only when there was no near-term probability that the debt component could be retired. The "average maturity of the debt" shortened considerably during Mellon's administration, but this was a natural result of his policy of short-term refunding with an eye constantly on the prospect for orderly debt retirement, and there is no reason to think he was in the least concerned with a concept as vague as "average debt maturity."

A detailed description of the retirement and refunding of the Second Liberty Loan 4¼'s, callable in 1927, and Third Liberty Loan 4¼'s, maturing in 1928, would help to illustrate the careful planning of debt management operations in the 1920's under Secretary Mellon. These two issues were outstanding in amounts of $2.9 billion and $4.0 billion, respectively, and refunding in amounts of this size would have over-strained the market. Consequently, the Treasury began its refunding operations in small amounts well before call or maturity dates.

The first step was taken in December, 1924, when the Treas-

10. *Annual Report for 1925,* pp. 45–48.

ury offered $200 million of 4 per cent 20–30 year bonds for cash subscription and, simultaneously, offered an unspecified additional amount of the same issue on optional exchange to holders of the Third Liberty Loan 4¼'s. A second optional exchange offering of the same issue was made to holders of the Third Liberty Loan 4¼'s in March, 1925. Meanwhile, the Treasury's debt retirement efforts were also directed toward the Third Liberty 4¼'s, and $400 million of these bonds were retired during fiscal 1926 through direct purchases for the sinking fund. Part of these purchases were made through a direct offer from the Treasury to owners of the bonds who might wish to sell them to the Treasury at the announced price. Additional purchases of Third Liberty 4¼'s were also made during fiscal 1927, totaling some $340 million. During the two fiscal years combined, therefore, total retirement of the Third Liberty 4¼'s amounted to almost three-quarters of a billion dollars which, together with the earlier exchanges, reduced the total outstanding to slightly more than $2 billion.

Having reduced the amount of Third Liberty bonds outstanding to a manageable total, the Treasury turned its attention to the Second Liberty Loan 4¼'s (converted from the 4's initially issued in the Second Liberty Loan), which would reach first call date in November, 1927. Although this issue actually was the first of the Liberty bonds scheduled to be refunded and retired, the Treasury had, until 1927, concentrated its efforts toward reducing the size of the Third Liberty 4¼'s, since the latter issue had a fixed maturity in early 1928 and would have to be refunded at that time, while the Second Liberty 4¼'s were callable for fifteen years after 1927 before reaching maturity. Beginning in March, 1927, a series of refunding operations and cash purchases were employed to retire the Second Liberty Loan bonds, and only a fraction of the issue remained to be redeemed at the call date in November, 1927.

In a major effort to refund the Second Liberty 4¼'s, first callable in November, 1927, so as to take advantage of the lower rates prevailing in the market, the Treasury in March, 1927, offered holders of these bonds an optional exchange at par into 3½ per cent notes that would be callable in three years and mature in five years. Inducement to accept the exchange offer consisted of a provision that interest would be paid on the 4¼'s for two months after the exchange, representing a bonus of two months' interest. A total of $1.3 billion subscriptions was received and allotted. This operation reduced the amount of the outstanding Second Liberty Loan to $1.7 billion, a manageable amount, and in May the Secretary announced that the remaining bonds were called for redemption in November. The next step in refunding the Second Liberty 4¼'s was taken in June, when holders of the bonds were given an opportunity to exchange at par for an issue of 16–20 year, 3⅜ per cent bonds that were, simultaneously, being offered at 100½ to raise about $250 million cash. Some $250 million exchange subscriptions were received. The final step in refunding the Second Liberty Loan was taken in September, 1927, when bond-holders were offered an exchange into an additional amount of the 3½ per cent notes issued in March, at a ⅛-point premium on the notes and with interest on exchanged bonds prepaid to November. Approximately $600 million of the notes were issued on this combined cash-exchange offering, of which $360 million were on exchange for called bonds. These operations, in combination with purchases in the market for the sinking fund, left only $500 million of Second Liberty bonds to be retired in November, 1927.

With the refunding of the Second Liberty Loan out of the way, the Treasury turned its attention during fiscal 1928 to the job of refunding the balance of the Third Liberty 4¼'s, scheduled to mature in September, 1928. As noted earlier, purchases out of surplus and for the sinking fund had centered in this issue for some years, with the result that by June, 1927, it had been reduced in size by more than $2 billion from the $4.2 billion that had been sold originally. An offering of 3–5 year, 3½ per cent notes in January, 1928, attracted about $600 million exchanges out of the Third Liberty 4¼'s; interest was again prepaid for two months to compensate bond-holders for the premium at which their securities were quoted in the market. In July, 1928, the Treasury offered holders of the Third Liberty Loan another exchange option, this time on a par-for-par exchange, with two months interest bonus, into 3⅜ per cent, 12–15 year bonds which were simultaneously offered at par to raise $250 million cash. Exchange subscriptions totaled only slightly more than $100 million. The decision to sell bonds was taken since the three issues of 3–5 year Treasury notes that had been sold during the preceding year provided adequate maturities to meet the requirements of the debt-reduction program between the maturity of the Third Liberty bonds and the earliest redemption date of other outstanding Liberty bonds. In addition to these two refunding offers, the Treasury had purchased nearly $500 million of the Third Liberty 4¼'s for the sinking fund between the end of fiscal 1927 and the maturity of the bonds in September, 1928, so that the balance to be redeemed at maturity was approximately $950 million. Two issues of certificates were sold for cash in September and October to provide funds for retirement of the Third Liberty bonds as they were presented to the Treasury.

Summarizing the refunding of the Second and Third Liberty Loans, there had remained outstanding at the end of February, 1927, approximately $5.3 billion of Second and Third Liberty 4¼'s. Between February, 1927, and October, 1928, approximately $2.8 billion of this total was exchanged directly for other issues, $0.7 billion was purchased for the sinking fund, and $0.6 billion was purchased out of surplus. The remaining $1.2 billion was discharged with the proceeds from other issues—certificates, notes, and bonds—sold for cash.

The retirement and refunding of the Third Liberty Loan by September, 1928 completed the important Treasury financing operations of the 1920's. During the balance of fiscal 1929 and through fiscal 1930 the only new public securities issued by the Treasury were tax certificates sold to replace maturing issues and, beginning in 1929, Treasury bills. Treasury revenues continued to cover sinking fund requirements during these two fiscal years and to provide a small additional surplus for debt retirement. The total gross debt had been reduced to $16.2 billion by the end of fiscal 1930, down $9.3 billion from the end-of-the-war total in June, 1919. The $16.2 billion of public debt included $1.4 billion of Treasury bills and certificates maturing within one year and $1.6 billion of Treasury notes maturing within two years. The funded debt included approximately $1.8 billion of special issues and prewar obligations, $8.2 billion of First and Fourth Liberty Loan bonds, and $3.1 billion of the five issues of bonds that had been issued during the refunding programs of the 1920's. Of the total marketable debt, only $4.6 billion carried maturities more than ten years in the future and only $2.8 billion neither matured nor became callable during the 1930's.

In June, 1929, Congress adopted two important amendments to the Second Liberty Bond Act (which had authorized the use of certificates of indebtedness in World War I finance). [11] First, the Secretary was authorized to sell discount Treasury bills. Second, it was provided that the interest or discount earned on certificates of indebtedness and Treasury bills should be exempt from all taxes except estate and inheritance taxes. The full tax exemption extended to Treasury bills and certificates was in line with recommendations made by Secretary Mellon on several occasions. The Secretary had first recommended a constitutional amendment to prohibit tax exemption on all securities, Federal and other. Failing in this, he had urged that Congress approve full tax exemption on Federal securities to make them competitive with state and municipal obligations and to encourage a broader ownership of United States Government obligations. The taxable status had been quite confused since the First World War. The Secretary had authority to issue fully tax-exempt Treasury notes, but not bonds or certificates. Moreover, the tax at issue in the discussion was the income surtax, as all Government obligations were already exempt from normal income

11. *Annual Report for 1929*, pp. 40–42.

taxes; and since there were no surtaxes levied against corporations, a tendency had arisen for United States Governments to be popular investments for corporations but not for individuals. The action of Congress in 1929 clarified the matter for bills and certificates by exempting them from all taxes, but it did not apply to bonds. In spite of subsequent requests that full tax-exemption be extended to Treasury bonds, Congress never acted on the matter.

At a purely technical level, the job done by Secretary Mellon during the 1920's was superb. Each operation, whether intra-year certificate financing or refunding the Liberty and Victory loans, was carefully planned and conducted through a series of steps that at no time overstrained the market's absorptive capacity. The program was orderly, with ample advance notice to the market before each step, and predictable, in the sense that the Secretary's program and intentions were clearly understood. In short, the Treasury had complete control of the debt at all times, and there was never a suggestion that securities were designed to fit what the market wanted rather than what was called for by the Treasury's program. Moreover, Secretary Mellon did not hesitate to adapt techniques to fit the Treasury's requirements. Maturing debt was paid off if funds were available, or refunded at longer-term if there was no near-term prospect that funds would be available to retire the debt. New issues were sold at par or at a price on either side of par, or sometimes at two different prices on a simultaneous cash and exchange offering. Interest was prepaid for lengthy periods to encourage exchanges or, when the Treasury did not particularly care whether exchanges were large, virtually no incentive bonus of any sort was offered. New issues were priced liberally when liberal pricing was necessary, but at most times new securities were offered at rates only a few basis points away from market yields for comparable maturities, and on at least one occasion the Secretary took advantage of a declining rate trend to offer bonds at rates below current market yields, thus anticipating the direction of market movement. Debt management in the 1920's was effective, in large part, because it was well planned and because it was not hamstrung by being bound to "traditional techniques."

F. Deficit Financing: 1931–1941

Early depression financing. The decline in Treasury revenues resulting from the depression that began in the last half of 1929, along with enlarged expenditures to combat the depression, created a deficit of some $900 million in fiscal 1931. Deficits resulting from the depression were subsequently incurred in each year through fiscal 1941. The total gross debt during this eleven-year period, from June, 1930, to June, 1941, increased by $32.8 billion. The increase in the debt was financed by the net sale of $22.6 billion public marketable securities and $4.3 billion non-marketable savings bonds sold to the public, and by an increase of $5.6 billion in the special issues to Treasury trust funds. Within the total $22.6 billion change in marketable debt outstanding, bonds were enlarged by $18.3 billion, notes by $4.1 billion, certificates reduced by $1.3 billion, and Treasury bills increased by $1.5 billion. No fewer than twenty-seven separate bond issues were marketed during the eleven-year period, in a total amount of nearly $30 billion, while seven bond issues amounting to $10.6 billion were retired. Altogether, for both cash and refunding purposes, some $49 billion of bonds and notes were issued by the Treasury during the eleven years.

The foregoing data clearly indicate that the depression-generated debt of the 1930's was financed almost entirely in a funded form; the proportion of longer-term obligations in the total publicly-held interest-bearing debt increased from 65 to 80 per cent during the depression years.

The bulk of the funding of the Treasury debt during the 1930's occurred after 1933, under Secretary Morgenthau. Disturbed market conditions during the years of financial crisis in the early 1930's made it virtually impossible to finance outside the short-term area. A strong drive for liquidity on the part of virtually all investors was clearly at the bottom of the weak bond markets in the 1931–33 interval, since short-term rates of interest on Government securities at times almost reached the vanishing point. In any event, the maturity structure of the publicly-held Treasury debt continued to shorten during the last three years of Republican administration of the Treasury, fiscal 1931 to fiscal 1933, inclusive. Between June, 1930, and June, 1933, the total gross debt increased by $6.2 billion, and the public debt by approximately $6.6 billion. This public debt increase was financed by net additions of $800 million to certificates of indebtedness, $2.9 billion to Treasury notes, and $2.1 billion to bonds. Only 32 per cent of the new debt was in a funded form, 44 per cent was represented by 1–5 year notes, and nearly one-fourth was financed through additions to the floating debt.

The immediate problems confronting the new Treasury administration when it took office in March, 1933, grew out of the collapse of the banking system and the resulting national "bank holiday" declared on March 9. An issue of Treasury bills sold at the time of the bank holiday, while funds were virtually immobilized, was awarded at an average rate of discount of 4¾ per cent, a record rate for Treasury bills that was not exceeded for more than a quarter of a century. Pressing needs for cash also forced the Treasury into the market at the time of the bank holiday to sell two issues of certificates for cash in a total amount of nearly $1 billion. Whereas the Treasury had successfully marketed one-year certificates of indebtedness on a ¾ per cent coupon only three months earlier, the certificates sold in March, 1933, carried a 4 per cent coupon for five months and 4¼ per cent for nine months. The effect of the crisis on Treasury financing passed quickly, however, and by June, 1933, the rate for one-year certificates had returned to ¾ per cent.

Market rates of interest at all maturities and on obligations of all types declined almost without interruption during the

3 6

remaining years of the 1930's. The steadily greater store of excess liquidity in the economy, resulting both from positive Federal Reserve action and from international money flows, created a setting which simplified the Treasury's task in financing large yearly deficits. Moreover, the damage to investor confidence after 1929 drove investment funds into riskless Government securities. Spreads of a full point and more developed between United States Government and high-grade corporate bond yields during the early 1930's, and the spread remained more than one-half point through the latter 1930's in spite of the heavy issue of Treasury bonds and the steadily short supply of investments of other types.

The financing problem with which the Treasury had to deal during the 1930's was a steady need for new cash and the prospect that funds for the retirement of this debt would not be available for an indefinite period in the future. In view of this prospect, it would have been pointless to finance at short-term, since the funds would not be available to retire the securities at maturity and they would have to be refunded. The financing of the depression deficits, therefore, was effected principally in securities of ten- to twenty-year maturity. Short-term debt instruments were employed in minimum amounts to provide intra-year flexibility in the flow of receipts and expenditures. The combined total of Treasury bills and certificates outstanding varied from $2 to $3 billion until fiscal 1935, when the use of certificates of indebtedness was abandoned and all subsequent short-term financing prior to World War II was arranged through discount bills sold at auction. In fiscal 1938 a regular schedule of thirteen weekly issues of three-month bills was established, each issue totaling $100 million, and this schedule was maintained with only minor adjustments through fiscal 1941. Intermediate financing was conducted through Treasury notes. Three or four note issues were sold each year, usually bearing a five-year maturity and scheduled to mature on quarterly tax dates. New notes were issued both for cash and in exchange for maturing bonds, notes, and certificates; in turn, maturing notes were

3 7

offered exchange options into either new notes or bonds, or both. Heavy reliance was placed on note issues in the earlier years of depression financing under the Roosevelt administration, and by June, 1936, the total of Treasury notes outstanding had been increased to $11.3 billion from $4.5 billion three years earlier. Subsequently, however, financing through note issues was reduced, and by June, 1941, the total outstanding had dropped to $5.7 billion, only $1.2 billion more than the total in June, 1933. Since certificate and bill issues, combined, were reduced by $1.4 billion between June, 1933, and June, 1941, it is evident that the depression-induced prewar deficits of the "New Deal" were financed in their entirety in the most conservative form, through bond issues.

Financing techniques were evolved gradually, through an experimental process, under Secretaries Woodin and Morgenthau (who entered office January 1, 1934). Thus, the heavy padding of cash subscriptions that emerged as a characteristic of depression financing initially led the Treasury to make only partial allotments on exchange as well as cash subscriptions so as to avoid ridiculously low cash allotment ratios, but full exchange allotments were made after 1933. Also, in the earlier years of Secretary Morgenthau's administration of the Treasury, new securities customarily were offered simultaneously for cash and exchange. Of the twelve new bond issues marketed by the Treasury between March, 1933, and December, 1937, ten were offered simultaneously for cash and to refund maturing obligations; of the ten bond issues marketed between January, 1938, and June, 1941, on the other hand, only four were offered simultaneously for cash and exchange. Through 1935, refunding offerings of bonds were made for maturing certificates, notes, and for the First and Fourth Liberty Loan bonds. But the elimination of certificates as an instrument of Treasury finance in 1935 and the absence of any bond maturities or call dates from October, 1935, until March, 1940, meant that maturing issues to be refunded were exclusively Treasury notes. These note issues, of which three or four matured each year, usually were offered new bonds in exchange and, frequently, an option of either new bonds or new notes.

Practices with respect to the pricing of new issues also underwent modification with the passage of time. Through 1935, several variants in pricing techniques were experimented with. For example, the bonds offered in par for par exchange for the first-called Fourth Liberty bonds in October, 1933—3¼ per cent bonds that paid 4¼ per cent interest for the first year—were simultaneously offered for cash subscription at a price of 101½. In effect, holders of the Liberty bonds that had been called for the following April were offered one and one-half points premium to tender their securities in the October refunding. Then, beginning in May, 1935, and extending through August of that year, the Treasury experimented with the sale of bonds at competitive auction. The first issue of bonds offered at auction was the 3's of 1946–48, which had first been issued in June, 1934, in an amount of $825 million. Two additional offerings of these bonds were made at auction in May and June, 1935, each for $100 million. Subsequently, the Treasury reopened the 2⅞'s of 1955–60, which had first been issued in March, 1935, in an amount of $1.6 billion, on three occasions in July and August, 1935, for additional amounts of $100 million on each offering. This procedure of frequent small bond offerings for competitive bidding was abandoned after the August, 1935, issue of 2⅞'s because of the disturbing effect it had on the market. In later financing during the period through June, 1941, bonds were offered at par in each operation, with the exception of two occasions when additional amounts of bonds that had been issued earlier were offered by the Treasury for exchange subscriptions at a premium from par.

By 1937 a pattern of Treasury financing practices and techniques had developed which was followed with few variations up to the Second World War and which, in fact, has been followed as the "traditional" technique of Treasury finance throughout much of the post-World War II period. These practices and techniques were peculiarly well adapted to the circumstances of constant deficits and of financial markets awash with surplus funds that characterized the 1930's. Because of the yearly deficits to be financed it would have been pointless to approach debt management with a view to scheduling maturities to provide for orderly near-term debt retirement, as Secretary Mellon had done in the 1920's, and the practice was to place debt maturities ten years or more in the future. Maturing securities, in most instances Treasury notes, were offered attractive opportunities for exchange into intermediate to longer-term bonds, and the almost certain knowledge that such an exchange offering would be made resulted in an orderly redistribution of "rights" (maturing securities) over the months preceding the exchange to investors with funds available to place in longer-term obligations.[12] New issues of Treasury notes were then sold on cash subscription to rebuild the total of notes so as to provide maturities of approximately equal size at each of the quarterly tax dates over the ensuing five years. Cash offerings of Treasury bonds also were made, but usually in relatively small amounts of $300–$600 million in order to avoid straining the market's redistributive machinery.

Meanwhile, the dearth of competitive investments and the huge supply of funds available for investment, both from commercial banks and from nonbank investors, made it possible for the Treasury to sell its longer-term obligations without difficulty and thus avoid piling up a floating debt that might have created greater refunding problems. In fact, the Treasury was in such a favorable position that it needed to give little attention to the problems of scheduling securities to fit market wants and of making its offerings sufficiently attractive to stimulate a good reception—the problems with which debt managers have wrestled since the Second World War. The process of deciding upon financing terms usually involved nothing more than selecting a niche in the maturity schedule that was not already oc-

12. A corollary of this was the tendency for securities to develop a "rights value" as they approached maturity that usually resulted in negative rates of interest.

cupied and a rate of interest that was as close as possible to prevailing market yields for similar maturities. The new security was then "thrown up for grabs" with complete confidence that it would be a success.[13] Cash offerings were consistently over-subscribed by ten or fifteen times, and the unexchanged portion of maturing issues was consistently very small. The technical aspects of the offerings—nearly all offerings at par, subscription books open only one day for cash and three days for exchange, the general lack of concern about the secondary distribution of speculative subscriptions, the confident assumption that long-term funds were available to be tapped by the Treasury when it chose—were all indicative of a situation in which the Treasury was able to call the tune.

An important innovation in Treasury financing practices during the 1930's was the initiation of the savings bond program in 1935. In February, 1935, Congress adopted an amendment to the Second Liberty Loan Act which, among other changes, authorized the Secretary of the Treasury to sell nonmarketable bonds to the nonbank public on a discount basis, redeemable at the option of the holder, carrying maturities of not less than ten nor more than twenty years, and at an issue price calculated to yield not more than 3 per cent interest compounded semi-annually. The new savings bonds, designated Series A, were placed on sale beginning March 1, 1935. In nearly all respects,

13. Serious pressure on the Government securities market that impeded Treasury financing developed briefly on two occasions, in the spring of 1937, following the second increase in member bank reserve requirements and a consequent wave of commercial bank liquidation, and in September, 1939, upon the outbreak of war in Europe. On both occasions, the Federal Reserve System's open market account engaged in a program of purchases aimed at steadying the market. Referring to the latter episode, the *Annual Report of the Board of Governors of the Federal Reserve System for 1939* (p. 5) has this to say: "While the System has neither the obligation nor the power to assure any given level of prices or yields for Government securities, its policy insofar as its powers permit is to protect the market for those securities from violent fluctuations of a speculative or panicky nature." In both cases, the market quickly reversed its movement and yields resumed the downward trend that characterized the decade.

the Series A Savings bonds first offered in 1935 were identical to the Series B through D bonds offered before the Second World War and the Series E bonds sold during the war and throughout the postwar years. As in all subsequent issues, the yield in the earlier years was small and increased year by year to give the effective yield in ten years. This yield arrangement was adopted both because it conformed roughly with the shape of the yield curve for marketable securities and as a means of encouraging investors to hold the bonds to maturity.

Other important legislative changes were made during the years leading up to the Second World War. Beginning with the Victory Liberty Loan Act of 1919, Congress had steadily relinquished its control over the Secretary's authority to set terms on new securities issued to finance the Government. Prior to 1935, Congress had specified the total amount of Treasury bonds the Secretary could issue, although not specifying the rate of interest and maturity at which they might be issued, and the maximum amounts of notes, certificates, and bills that could be outstanding at any one time. The amendments to the Second Liberty Loan Act adopted in 1935 changed this authorization to read that a maximum amount of $25 billion Treasury bonds might be outstanding at one time, thus providing for a revolving total that allowed the Secretary to issue new bonds to replace bonds that had been retired. The amendments also combined the authority to issue notes, certificates, and bills into a single $20 billion total that might be outstanding at any one time. Then, in the Public Debt Act of 1941, a single debt ceiling of $65 billion was adopted that did not specify maximum amounts of any type of security that might be outstanding. With this action, Congress reduced its role in debt management to the two functions of establishing a ceiling on the direct and guaranteed public debt and a maximum rate of interest on Treasury bonds.

Still another important action affecting debt management was contained in the Public Debt Act of 1941, approved in February, 1941, which made interest on future issues of securities of the Federal Government subject to all Federal income taxes. It will be recalled that the financing legislation adopted in 1929 had made certificates of indebtedness and Treasury bills fully tax-exempt, and that the Secretary already was authorized to issue Treasury notes on a fully tax-exempt basis, but that Treasury bonds had remained subject to income surtaxes. As a result of the 1941 legislation all United States Government securities, including Savings bonds, were brought to parity as regards the tax treatment of their interest income.

The foregoing comments, calling attention to the favorable market circumstances in which debt management was conducted in the 1930's, are in no sense intended to derogate the job done by Secretary Morgenthau. In facing up to the problems to be solved and in devising the most effective techniques to meet those problems, the record of debt management in the 1930's was, in its way, as impressive as the record compiled by Secretary Mellon, under different circumstances and dealing with different problems, in the 1920's.

G. Financing World War II

On June 30, 1941, the total gross United States Government debt amounted to $49.0 billion; by the time it had reached its immediate postwar peak in February, 1946, it had nearly sextupled, totaling $279.8 billion. Total Government expenditures in the five fiscal years of full defense effort, 1942 through 1946, inclusive, amounted to some $368 billion, of which $164 billion, or 45 per cent, was covered through taxes and other receipts. The low point was reached in fiscal 1943, before the wartime tax program got into full operation, when only 28 per cent of expenditures was covered by receipts from sources other than borrowing. In fiscal 1946, as the tax schedule continued to pour funds into the Treasury while expenditures were reduced sharply, approximately two-thirds of expenditures were financed out of ordinary receipts.

43

Three principles guided the Treasury in its conduct of borrowing to finance expenditures not covered from ordinary revenues during World War II. As stated by Secretary Morgenthau in his 1945 Special Report, these were:

(1) The necessary funds should be raised in such a manner as to minimize the risk of inflation; (2) the securities offered should be those best suited to the needs of the investors to whom they are sold; and (3) the cost of financing the war should be kept at a reasonable level.

The first of these principles was reflected in strenuous efforts to place as large a part of the debt as possible with nonbank investors, and particularly with individuals, the second through the inclusion in each financing campaign of a "basket" of securities designed to appeal to all potential investors, and the third through the assistance of the Federal Reserve System in maintaining throughout the war the historically low pattern of interest rates prevailing at the outset of the war.

During the First World War, it will be recalled, the Treasury's efforts to encourage additional saving were reflected in the slogan "borrow and buy." It was hoped that individual investors who had incurred indebtedness to buy Liberty bonds would then be under pressure to save to repay this indebtedness and that, by this process, savings would be increased. These hopes were not fully realized, and the inevitable redistribution of Liberty bonds and Victory notes that occurred when the loans to purchase the securities matured took place at large discounts and was an influence in the recession of 1920. Treasury planning in the Second World War was directed toward avoiding this outcome. Two alternatives were open to the Treasury: a compulsory savings program or a voluntary savings program. The policies settled upon relied principally upon voluntary savings. Early in the defense effort, considerable thought had been given to adoption of a compulsory savings (or lending) program, in the form of a special tax that would be rebatable at the end of the war, but public opposition to the plan was aroused, and by the end of 1942 it had been decided that the war borrowing

44

program would rely upon voluntary purchases of Treasury securities. The compulsory—or at least involuntary—aspects of World War II financing were confined to the social pressure to buy savings bonds, the product rationing that distorted normal consumption/saving relationships, and the war and postwar inflation of prices.

The efforts to minimize the inflation threat of World War II financing through encouragement of voluntary saving and lending to the Government took several forms. First, all publicity media were employed intensively to promote sales of securities, particularly savings bonds to individuals, emphasizing the patriotic motive principally but also stressing the income to be earned by such investment. Second, a broad range of securities was offered for sale intended to appeal to the needs and the tastes of all potential investors. Third, offerings of securities for commercial bank subscription were made only after all available nonbank funds had been tapped. Finally, the Treasury encouraged banks to finance purchases of Government securities by nonbank investors, but attempted to avoid the errors of the First World War by specifying that such loans should be on an amortized basis and should be repaid within six months.

The efforts to minimize the inflation potential of World War II finance by encouraging saving and by selling maximum amounts of securities to nonbank investors were not entirely successful. Of a total increase in the United States Government debt amounting to $204.2 billion between June, 1941, and December, 1946, $75.9 billion, or 37 per cent, represented purchases by commercial banks and the Federal Reserve System. Of the remainder, 11 per cent went to Government agency and trust fund accounts, 13 per cent to insurance companies and mutual savings banks, and 39 per cent to "others," principally individuals.

Another measure of the extent to which the Treasury was successful in conducting its World War II financing so as to minimize its inflation potential is the growth in total bank assets and the money supply over the war years. Between June 30,

1941, and December 31, 1946, total loans and investments of all commercial banks increased from $47.6 billion to $114.0 billion, or by 140 per cent, while the money supply[14] grew from $45.5 billion to $110.0 billion, or by 141 per cent. That is to say, the $204.2 billion increase in the total gross debt of the United States over this five-and-one-half year interval was accompanied by a $64.5 billion expansion in the money supply. The growth in the money supply, therefore, was equal to about 31 per cent of the increase in the debt, roughly equal to the change in money supply relative to the change in debt during the First World War. There are no wholly satisfactory criteria for measuring the success of the Treasury's World War II financing program in achieving its anti-inflationary objective, but these data would suggest that the policies followed were no less successful than those followed in World War I. At the same time, the appearance of successful stimulation of savings and of success in financing outside the banking system were achieved by giving virtually the status of money to the entire debt and, in its ultimate effects, this policy created the most serious inflationary problems.

The most important changes made by the Treasury in its offerings of marketable securities for the purpose of tailoring securities to investors' requirements were those designed to limit maturities, rates of interest, and the total of new securities available to commercial banks. In May, 1942, the Treasury made its first offering of bonds not eligible for bank ownership during the first ten years of their life (these were the 2½'s of 1962–1967), and this offering set the pattern for the Treasury's financing at long-term during the balance of the war. The following quotation outlines the Treasury's war-time policies with respect to securities to be sold to commercial banks and explains the reasoning behind these policies:

the commercial banks will be called upon to finance a large share of the deficit . . . [and] it is important that the banks preserve a maximum of liquidity. To help them do so, we have decided that securities sold to

14. Defined as demand deposits adjusted and currency outside banks.

46

the banks should have a range of maturities running from 3 months, in the case of Treasury bills, to 10 years, in the case of Treasury bonds. . . .

In securities of over 1-year maturity, we have continued to offer the banks Treasury notes, and Treasury bonds with a term of not over 10 years. This means a maximum interest rate of 2 per cent on Treasury bonds sold to commercial banks.

It may seem at times that banks are being discriminated against in not being permitted to subscribe for longer-term securities which bear higher interest rates than 2 per cent; but this is not the case. . . . I think all of you will agree that a frozen banking system trying to become unfrozen after the war by selling long-term Government securities might create a bad situation.

It should be noted that a large part of the securities which will be bought by banks will be financed by increases in deposits for the banking system as a whole. It seems reasonable that the interest rate on securities financed in this manner should be kept down to a maximum of 2 per cent. . . .[15]

In brief, therefore, bonds eligible for bank purchase carried maturities no longer than ten years, bore rates of interest not in excess of 2 per cent, and were offered to commercial banks only after it appeared that all other sources of funds had been fully tapped.

In its efforts to minimize commercial bank purchases of United States Government securities, the Treasury did not accept commercial bank subscriptions in the last six of the eight War Loan and Victory Loan drives. At the same time, each of the loan drives included ⅞ per cent certificates of indebtedness in the basket of securities offered to investors, and the Fifth and Sixth War Loan drives included Treasury notes, two types of securities that were eligible for commercial bank purchase in the market. Also, bonds that were eligible for bank ownership were included in the Third, Fifth, Sixth, and Seventh War Loan drives, although commercial banks were not allowed to subscribe for them on direct issue from the Treasury. It is interesting to note that of these four bank-eligible bonds offered exclusively to nonbank investors, by February, 1946, at the conclusion of

15. From an address by Under Secretary Bell to the Investment Bankers Association, October 19, 1942, reprinted in the *Annual Report for 1943*, p. 390.

World War II financing, commercial banks owned $16.3 billion, or 65 per cent of the $25.1 billion outstanding. The technique of including bank-eligible bonds in the War Loan drives but forbidding commercial bank subscriptions apparently did not limit the extent to which the war was financed through commercial bank credit but simply created a situation in which "free riding" and profits for speculators were encouraged.

The Treasury's efforts to design marketable securities to fit the needs of nonbank investors actually consisted of offering the widest possible range of maturities. Whatever the investor's requirements might be, there almost certainly would be a Treasury security available of appropriate maturity to meet these requirements. In addition to the wide range of nonmarketable securities available for investment of funds of different maturities, there were issues of Treasury bills maturing each week out to three-months maturity, issues of certificates of indebtedness maturing each month out to one-year maturity, issues of Treasury notes maturing at the quarterly tax dates out to five-years maturity, and dozens of bond issues bearing staggered maturities as much as twenty-five or thirty years in the future.

The third leg of World War II financing policies was the maintenance of a low and stable pattern of interest rates. By and large, the pattern of interest rates on United States Government securities maintained throughout the war was that which prevailed at the outset of World War II financing. This pattern of rates involved a steep, positively-sloped yield curve, with three-month Treasury bills at ⅜ per cent, one-year certificates at ⅞ per cent, ten-year bonds at 2 per cent, and long-term bonds at 2½ per cent. Principal responsibility for maintaining the wartime interest rate pattern rested with the Federal Reserve System, and there was little question among market professionals of the ability of the Federal Reserve System, through its open market operations, to maintain stability in the Government securities market at whatever pattern of rates was selected for the Treasury's wartime financing. The groundwork had been laid for this type of market support operation on two previous occasions when the market had suddenly weakened, in the spring of 1937 and upon the outbreak of World War II in September, 1939, and on both occasions the System had proved itself able to stabilize prices by mass purchases of securities overhanging the market.

It was not necessary for the System Open Market Account to buy Treasury bonds to support long-term rates of interest—in fact, System holdings of Treasury bonds were reduced between June, 1941, and the end of the war—it was necessary only that the banking system and the money market be kept flooded with funds and that the channels through which these funds flowed into United States Government securities of various maturities remain open. Member bank excess reserves, which had climbed to the ridiculously redundant level of nearly $7 billion at the end of 1940, were allowed to decline as required reserves and currency in circulation rose, and from late 1943 through the balance of the period of war financing excess reserves held in a range slightly above $1 billion. At this level, commercial banks were sufficiently liquid to absorb all new Treasury debt not readily placed with other investors at the interest rates employed by the Treasury. It is appropriate to note at this point that the volume of bank-restricted bonds sold by the Treasury during the Second World War, in combination with the large awards to speculative subscribers that had to be redistributed to other investors, might well have caused a market bottleneck that easy bank reserve positions could not have unwound, thus calling for direct Federal Reserve bond purchases, if it had not been for one factor. That factor was the volume of bonds eligible for bank ownership that were outstanding at the outset of the war-finance program. These bonds were sold by other investors to raise funds to buy new Treasury bonds, and purchased by banks with the abundant funds at their command. Commercial bank ownership of Treasury bonds which had been issued prior to June, 1941, amounted to $14.5 billion in February, 1946, up from $10.4 billion of these specific issues held by commercial

49

banks on June 30, 1941, and equal to 60 per cent of all such issues outstanding.

Various actions were taken by the Federal Reserve System to assure abundantly easy money to facilitate World War II Treasury financing on the established rate curve, but the purchases of Treasury bills at a "posted rate" and certificates of indebtedness in the market were clearly the most important actions. Reserve requirements at central reserve city member banks were reduced in three steps from 26 per cent in August, 1942, to 20 per cent by October of that year, at which level they were equal to requirements for reserve city banks. Also preferential rates were established on advances secured by United States Government securities. The nominal discount rate remained at one per cent throughout the war, but the rate on advances secured by Government securities within one year of maturity was lowered to ½ per cent in October, 1942, and remained at that level until early 1946. Finally, commercial banks were allowed to pay for their direct allotments of Treasury securities through credits on their books to Treasury "war loan deposit accounts" and, by act of Congress on April 13, 1943, these deposits were fully exempted from both reserve requirements and FDIC assessments. Through this battery of central bank actions, the Treasury was assured of ample funds to finance the Second World War and of being able to borrow these funds at predetermined rates of interest.

Techniques for financing the war developed rather slowly. The First War Loan drive did not occur until November, 1942, and in the period prior to that time the selling techniques developed during the 1930's were gradually adapted to the needs of war finance. Between June, 1941, and the First War Loan drive in November, 1942, the Treasury marketed eight separate bond issues for cash or cash and exchange in a total amount of $13.2 billion. Of these, seven were eligible for commercial bank subscriptions and only one (the 2½'s of 1962–67, first offered in May, 1942) was restricted as to commercial bank ownership. The seven cash flotations of bonds open to all subscribers employed the techniques of the 1930's with almost no variation.

It had become apparent before the end of calendar 1942, however, that the financing techniques employed thus far in the war would not suffice to sell the volume of debt instruments the Treasury had to sell and to do this in a way that would stimulate saving and minimize financing through the commercial banks. Therefore, at the end of November, 1942, the Treasury launched its first formal loan drive. The principal characteristic of the loan drives was the publicity campaigns, reminiscent of the tactics used by Jay Cooke in the Civil War and Secretary McAdoo in World War I, that accompanied them. War Finance Committees were established in each state under the direction of the War Finance Division in the Treasury, and sales efforts in all types of Government securities, marketable and nonmarketable, were handled by this organization. The composition of the "baskets" of securities offered varied somewhat from one drive to the next, but the principle throughout was that there should be "something for everyone" (with the notable exception of the commercial banks after the Second War Loan drive). In order to allow time for full publicity campaigns, subscription books remained open for three to four weeks in the first six drives and, in the Seventh War Loan Drive and the Victory Loan, for six to seven weeks on subscriptions of individuals and one to two weeks on all other subscriptions. All subscriptions were allotted in full; despite this fact and the frequency of the drives, the new issues regularly moved to premiums immediately upon issue. During the eight War and Victory Loan drives, a total of $114 billion marketable securities was sold and $43 billion nonmarketable savings bonds and notes were sold during the period in which sales of these obligations were included in the drives.

The procedure followed in the preceding discussions of Civil War and World War I finance has been to avoid judgments upon the financing policies adopted in war periods when the increase in borrowing needs has been so unprecedented as to be a change in degree that becomes a change in the nature of the problem. That precedent will be followed with respect to

51

World War II finance. Certainly, mistakes were made. The maintenance of a yield curve with a steep, positive slope, since the fact of its maintenance gave equal liquidity status to all United States Government securities, resulted in wholesale dumping of short-term issues upon the central bank and a scramble for the higher-yielding bonds. The discrimination against commercial banks probably, and in logic, had little influence upon the portion of new debt absorbed into the banking system, so that the net result of barring commercial banks from the war loan drives probably was principally to create speculative profits for non-bank "free riders" rather than to limit appreciably the increase in the money supply. Also, the record of developments since interest rates were freed in 1951 suggests that undue reliance was placed upon nonmarketable redeemable securities in World War II finance, and that the over-use of these securities proved ultimately to be a barrier to the return to free markets and, once free markets were re-established, a source of irritation to orderly debt management procedures. Finally, all that was written and spoken in the official and semiofficial records of the period suggests that debt management discussions were influenced by an obsessive fear of postwar underemployment and by an inclination to control rather than to allow scope for market processes; while understandable in their historical context, these attitudes appear singularly naive from a latter-day viewpoint.

On the positive side, the Treasury successfully raised greater sums of money than had ever before been borrowed, to finance a military effort that was more costly than anyone would have thought possible at its outset. Also, these sums of money were borrowed with a net reliance upon new money creation that did not compare unfavorably with the experiences in the two previous major wars, relative to the volume of funds borrowed and to the economic base upon which the debt was imposed. Also, the efforts to induce a higher rate of saving than would have obtained in the normal course, principally through the strenuous efforts to sell savings bonds to individuals, probably met with some success, although it is not possible to estimate the extent to which real savings—as distinct from deferred spending—was achieved through the publicity campaigns. The distinction between real saving and deferred spending might not have appeared too important at the time, in the face of the postwar recession fears, but the inflationary conditions of the postwar period have made it a most important consideration.

The most controversial aspect of World War II financing was the policy of pegging interest rates at the low levels resulting from a decade of depression. As noted earlier, the shape of the yield curve adopted was completely unrealistic. A combination of influences during the late 1930's had created a market yield curve with a steep positive slope. But the rationale for a curve of this shape immediately disappeared as soon as the curve was pegged; in fact, the administrative pegging of the rate at any given maturity should, in a competitive market, bring all rates on shorter maturities to a level with this rate. Beyond the question with respect to the shape of the rate curve is the question of whether a higher level of interest rates would have significantly increased the volume of saving, or whether freely moving rather than pegged rates would have had this effect. On the latter question, the answer probably is no. With the Treasury forced to allot all subscriptions in full, on open-end offerings, interest rate uncertainty would probably have reduced subscriptions. The answer to the first question also probably is no. Treasury debt placed with nonbank investors probably exceeded the volume of actual saving by a considerable margin, including funds allocated by both businesses and individuals for deferred spending programs, and it appears most unlikely that higher interest rates, as such, would have had any further limiting effect upon a volume of consumption already sharply limited by supply shortages.

One final word might be added on World War II financing. The pegged interest-rate policy adopted by the Treasury and the Federal Reserve System has been criticized principally because it was "inflationary." To the extent that this criticism implies that a different policy would have resulted in a smaller increase in the money supply, it would appear to have little foundation.

53

Given the gap between expenditures and tax receipts to be financed through borrowing, the level of income, the availability of consumer goods, consumption habits, etc., the supply of non-bank funds available to the Treasury probably was determinant within rather narrow limits. The balance of the Treasury's needs necessarily would be financed through bank credit, whatever the central bank's policy. However, the pegged rate policy was inflationary in other ways. First, it made United States Government securities of all maturities completely liquid so that, in effect, the entire war-created debt was in the form of interest-bearing near-money. Second, the pegging of the curve at the time the debt was created implied that it would continue to be pegged, and this implication was confirmed by official statements. The assurance given to investors that the marketable bonds they had purchased would continue to have full liquidity at stable rates of interest was, in all probability, an important consideration in shaping the Treasury's resistance to freeing market rates of interest after the war.

III

Management of the Debt: 1946–1960

A. Immediate Postwar Financing: 1946–1951

In the five years immediately following the Second World War, the principal developments in Treasury debt management were related to the Treasury's policy of stabilizing market rates of interest and to the conflict with the Federal Reserve System that resulted from this policy as the central bank became increasingly alarmed at the inflationary implications of its actions to stabilize interest rates. The actual debt operations during the period from the end of calendar 1945 through the "accord" reached between the Treasury and the Federal Reserve System in March, 1951, were largely routine.

The Treasury continued to sell nonmarketable Series E, F, and G Savings bonds; and Series C Savings notes were employed until September, 1948, when they were replaced by the somewhat higher-yielding Savings Series D notes. On a current redemption value basis, nonmarketable savings bonds outstanding were increased over these five years by $8.2 billion to $58.0 billion, and savings notes outstanding were increased by $2.9 billion to $8.6 billion on December 31, 1950. One other development in financing through nonmarketable securities was the sale for cash in September–October, 1947, of nearly $1 billion Investment Series A bonds. These bonds paid interest at a rate of 2½ per cent, were nonmarketable and noncallable before maturity in 1965, but were redeemable on the first day of any month upon thirty-days notice at a schedule of redemption values that yielded an effective return equivalent to the pattern of rates on various maturities prevailing in the market at the time the bonds were sold.

With the exception of these net sales of nonmarketable securities, the Treasury did not find it necessary to make any cash offerings of new securities in the five calendar years 1946–1950, inclusive. Financing in marketable obligations was composed of two elements: (a) retirement of maturing securities out of cash surplus and through reduction of deposit balances; (b) refunding of maturing securities that could not be retired, for which purpose short-term securities were used almost exclusively.

Cash redemption of maturing or called marketable debt was concentrated in calendar years 1946 and 1947. The total of maturing or called obligations in 1946 (excluding Treasury bills) was $53.3 billion, of which $41.5 billion were certificates of indebtedness, $9.5 billion were Treasury notes, and $2.4 billion were partially tax-exempt bonds. All of the bonds (four issues) were retired without an exchange offering, two of the three issues of Treasury notes (totaling $4.6 billion) were retired without an exchange offering, and one issue of certificates (amounting to $1.6 billion) was thus retired. Of the remaining ten issues of certificates and one issue of notes, all but three of the maturing certificate issues were offered only partial exchange into new securities. In total, $29.8 billion of new marketable securities were issued in calendar 1946 in exchange for the $53.3 billion of matured or called obligations, resulting in a net reduction of $23.5 billion in the short-term coupon-bearing marketable debt. During calendar 1947, maturing and called obligations (exclusive of bills) totaled $34.5 billion, of which $26.7 billion were certificates of indebtedness, $6.3 billion were Treasury notes, and $1.5 billion were bonds. One partially tax-exempt bond issue and a note maturity were retired in full, four certificate maturities were offered only partial exchange, and public holdings of the remaining nine maturities were offered full exchange. However, beginning in November, 1947, and effective in six refunding operations through March, 1948, all or part of Federal Reserve System holdings of maturing coupon securities were redeemed for cash. A total of $28.3 billion new marketable securities were issued during 1947 in exchange for the $34.5 billion of maturing obligations, thus providing for $6.2 billion redemption of short-term marketable debt. In addition to these operations in coupon securities, the Treasury reduced Treasury bill maturities outstanding by $1.9 billion.

The Treasury continued to accumulate funds from cash budget surpluses and/or from net sales of nonmarketable securities during the three calendar years 1948–1950, and these funds were employed to retire maturing or called marketable debt. Marketable public issues outstanding were reduced by $13.3 billion during these three years, while the total gross debt, after falling in 1948, increased in 1949 and 1950 and closed the three years almost unchanged on balance. However, the substitution of nonmarketable public securities and special issues for marketable obligations resulted in a further $8.7 billion decline in the combined holdings of United States Government debt by the commercial banking system and the Federal Reserve System. With the exception of the direct retirement of some Federal Reserve holdings of maturing securities in early 1948 and 1949, mentioned above, and the cash retirement of a small bond issue in September, 1948, the Treasury made exchange offerings for all of its maturing marketable securities in the three calendar years 1948 through 1950 and made 100 per cent allotments on all exchange subscriptions. Total matured and called marketable securities (excluding bills) during these three years amounted to $118.4 billion. New securities were issued in exchange by the

5 7

Treasury in an amount of $106.3 billion. All of the new securities issued by the Treasury were certificates of indebtedness or Treasury notes, and most of the notes were of short maturity. Of the $106.3 billion total new issues during the three years, only $22.1 billion carried original maturities in excess of two years, and of these, $12.1 billion were issued in the closing months of 1950. In addition to the net retirement of $12.1 billion interest-bearing marketable securities as a result of these operations in the years 1948–1950, the Treasury also reduced the total of Treasury bills outstanding by $1.5 billion.

B. Treasury-Federal Reserve Relationships: 1946–1951

As indicated earlier, it would be difficult to establish a logical case in support of the proposition that the results of World War II financing would have been significantly different if the Federal Reserve System had not maintained the rate curve and if market rates of interest had been allowed to rise in response to the Treasury's demands for funds. Assuming that patriotic necessity would have required the central bank to supply reserves for commercial bank underwriting of Government debt that could not be placed with other investors, it is likely that provision of these reserves on a rising pattern of rates would have resulted in a distribution of the debt as between bank and nonbank holders and as between short and long maturities roughly comparable to the distribution actually achieved at a stable pattern of rates. In other words, during the war the central bank through its support of the Treasury probably did not sacrifice any significant element of control over money and credit that it could reasonably have expected to retain, considering the circumstances, under any alternative policy.

Once the financing of the war was completed, however, and the Treasury actually began retiring debt, retention of the policy of supporting a pattern of interest rates did involve a sacrifice of the central bank's responsibility for regulation of money and credit that could no longer be justified in terms of patriotic necessity. The maintenance by the central bank of a rigid pattern of market rates of interest implied two consequences. First, with respect to the liquidity characteristics of financial assets, the entire marketable Government debt, regardless of nominal maturity of the instruments, was only slightly less liquid than money, with all that this implied for spending decisions and for the *ex ante* availability of credit and capital to finance private investment. Second, with respect to the money supply, the availability of money was regulated by the spending and investing decisions of Government bond holders, with the central bank impotent to maintain any degree of effective regulation. The inflation potential thus created naturally and inevitably led the Federal Reserve System to seek means whereby it could recapture the authority it required to establish a regulatory influence upon money and credit. The record of the postwar years, therefore, gradually became one of Treasury-Federal Reserve struggle as the Treasury fought to retain the market support policies it considered essential for the orderly management of the war-created debt and the Federal Reserve System fought for freedom to take effective action to control the inflation threat that the creation of this debt had, initially, brought into being.

Changes in market prices and ownership of United States Government securities during the years immediately following the Second World War formed an interesting and informative pattern. Beginning shortly after the Victory Loan campaign, prices of longer-term, bank-restricted bonds began to advance sharply, presumably reflecting the knowledge that, with war financing completed, there would be no large additional offerings of Treasury bonds in the near future and the fact that new bond issues by other borrowers had not yet expanded to fill the gap. The brief postwar bull market had run its course by April, 1946, and, while prices of Government bonds at no time approached par, market rates rose rapidly through the third quarter of 1946. Bond prices then fluctuated in a narrow range well above par until October, 1947. During this initial period of postwar debt absorption, relatively little liquidation of Treasury securities developed.

The first serious test of the long-term 2½ per cent rate occurred in the last quarter of 1947. Prices of Treasury bonds began to fall in early October, in response to rising rates in the corporate bond market, and by mid-November the price of Victory bonds (2½'s of December, 1967–72) had dropped to within one point of par. At this point both the Federal Reserve System and the Treasury, for its investment accounts, began buying Treasury bonds. These purchases were made "reluctantly," however, absorbing only part of the bonds being offered by dealers, and a backlog of securities piled up in the market. In this unstable setting, the Federal Open Market Committee decided to reduce its buying price on the Victory bonds to 100¼ and to stand ready to purchase all taxable Treasury bonds offered at prices in line with that price for Victory bonds. The announcement of this policy on Christmas Eve, 1947, touched off a deluge of selling of bank-restricted Treasury bonds to the Federal Reserve System that continued, with only brief interruptions, through calendar 1948. While the "pegs" held, this result was achieved only through net System purchases between December 24, 1947, and the end of 1948 of $8.3 billion bonds more than five years from maturity.

The wave of investor liquidation of Treasury bonds that began in November, 1947, and continued through 1948 may be ascribed to several initiating causes. In the first place, by the last half of 1947 new security offerings of corporate and tax-exempt borrowers had risen to a level in excess of the flow of liquid savings available to absorb them, and investing institutions relied upon Treasury bonds as a source of liquid funds to meet these demands. Secondly, the increase in short-term market rates of interest during the last half of 1947 had reduced the yield differential between short and long maturities, thus reducing the incentive to "play the pattern of rates" by making short-

60

term securities relatively more attractive investments. Finally, and perhaps most important, developments in the last half of 1947 and in 1948 raised questions about the permanence of market support.

In retrospect, it appears that a substantial part of the shift in the Federal Reserve System's portfolio during the closing weeks of 1947 and through 1948, consisting of a substitution of long-term bonds for short-term securities, represented a reversal of the process of "playing the rate pattern" that had characterized investor behavior during the war and earlier postwar years. Both because of the reduced yield differential between short and long maturities and because of the uncertain future liquidity status of longer-term bonds, investors sold bonds and purchased short-term Governments to maintain desired portfolio liquidity.

Economic recession was the dominant influence in the United States Government securities market during 1949 and the first half of calendar 1950. Prices of the bank-restricted bonds rose from the support levels at which they had remained at most times during 1948, and the price increase would have been even more pronounced if the Federal Reserve System and the Treasury, principally the former, had not sold large amounts of bonds to prevent the long-term Treasury rate from falling too far away from the 2½ per cent level. In spite of this "breather," it was during this period that the underlying conflict of purpose between the Federal Reserve System and the Treasury began to come more clearly into the open in official statements. The hearings conducted by the Douglas subcommittee in December, 1949, elicited replies from leading Federal officials indicating strong dissatisfaction with the weakened condition in which the commitment to maintain rates of interest on Treasury bonds left the Federal Reserve System, while the statement by Secretary Snyder indicated an unwavering intention that the 2½ per cent long-term rate on Treasury bonds should be maintained.

The conflict developed into open warfare during the summer of 1950. With the outbreak of fighting in Korea, Secretary Snyder's principal concern was that a broad and stable market for Government securities should be maintained to assure an ample availability of funds for financing the war. The Federal Open Market Committee was prepared to assure the Treasury of access to the funds required to finance the Korean War, but it was anxious to avoid repetition of the World War II mistake of being frozen into a low and steeply-sloped yield curve. On August 18 (Friday), 1950, in pursuit of its policy of rate stability, the Treasury announced an offering of two issues of thirteen-month 1¼ per cent Treasury notes in exchange for $13.6 billion of securities maturing September 15 and October 1; this rate of interest and maturity were the same as those employed in the May and June, 1950, refinancings. Three days later, on Monday, August 21, 1950, the Board of Governors approved an increase in the discount rates of the Federal Reserve Banks of Boston and New York to 1¾ per cent from 1½ per cent. Market rates of interest immediately adjusted toward the new discount rate, the "rights" value on the maturing issues evaporated, and the System Open Market Account purchased no less than $8.0 billion of the maturing securities in order to prevent astronomical attrition on the refunding.

There were no maturities of Treasury securities scheduled for the first five months of calendar 1951, and it was during this open period in the Treasury's financing schedule that the Treasury and the Federal Reserve System reached agreement on their relationship. Following a series of meetings among public officials, in two of which the President of the United States participated, and a barrage of press releases by the two agencies, the Treasury and the Federal Reserve System issued a joint announcement on March 4, 1951, to the effect that they had

reached full accord with respect to debt management and monetary policies to be pursued in furthering their common purpose to assure the successful financing of the Government's requirements and, at the same time, to minimize monetization of the public debt.[1]

The "accord" ended the period of subordination of central bank policy to Treasury interest rate policy and, by so doing,

1. *Annual Report for 1951*, p. 271.

converted the public debt from an extension of the money supply to a body of financial assets of varying degrees of liquidity. It is tempting to seek "heroes" and "villains" in appraising the course of debt management and monetary policies during the five years following the conclusion of World War II financing, when, in spite of considerable lip service to combatting inflation, these policies supported the most extreme inflation potential. In fact, however, the principal officials of the two agencies were in substantial agreement on basic policies through most of the first four postwar years, differing principally on the levels of interest rates that should be maintained not on the root question of whether *any* level of rates should be maintained.

What appears now to have been a peculiar type of blindness affected the policy officials on the matter of interest rate levels and on the market process as an allocator of funds of various maturities among different purposes. Debt management and credit policies were based on the conclusion that higher rates of interest, as such, would have little influence on credit demand unless they rose to a point where they would become economically disruptive, and that higher rates would bring with them a chain of unfortunate consequences. Specifically, it was feared that unless longer-term rates were regulated and "orderly" markets maintained, a volume of selling of "loosely held" bonds would develop that might drive prices of Treasury bonds to a discount, impair confidence in the credit of the United States, entail substantial capital losses for many commercial banks and other investors, impede economic growth, add to the interest burden of the debt, lead to mass redemptions of savings bonds, and disrupt trading processes in the market for United States Government securities. And, as the reasoning ran, all of these disadvantages would be incurred with little prospect of substantial offsetting advantage. At the same time, it was recognized that further monetization of the debt in the form of bank purchases of Government securities would constitute an inflationary development; a principal stated objective of debt management was to avoid such a development and, if possible, reduce

63

commercial bank-held debt. Various plans, all of them based upon attempts to bypass the market and to regulate the distribution of Treasury debt directly, were suggested or employed. Debt retirement in 1946–1948 was concentrated on maturing issues held principally by commercial banks or the Federal Reserve Banks so as to achieve a direct reduction in Reserve Bank credit and commercial bank deposits. Securities were "tailored" to the investment needs of various investor groups so as to tap directly the maximum amount of nonbank funds. Several plans for immobilizing commercial bank holdings of Government securities were studied, and one such plan, which would have established secondary reserve requirements in Government securities for commercial banks, actually was recommended by the Board of Governors of the Federal Reserve System in December, 1947, in a memorandum to the House Banking and Currency Committee.

These various actions and plans were almost wholly irrelevant to their object, *i.e.*, to prevent the war-created debt from being an inflationary influence. So long as the central bank was committed to maintain the rate of interest on any marketable Treasury securities and so long as there was a substantial volume of these securities in investors' hands, no amount of effort to control the ownership of the debt could make it anything but what it was, a body of financial assets only slightly less liquid than money. It would not be a gross exaggeration to conclude that the postwar policy of maintaining the long-term rate of interest through central bank open market operations meant that the entire World War II deficit was financed through addition to the money supply. The intermediate and longer-term marketable debt created during the Second World War represented an unequivocal commitment of funds that could not be withdrawn on demand (as in the case of savings bonds) and that did not lend itself to conversion into spendable funds through an increase in the velocity of money. By making these obligations redeemable on demand in the market at an assured minimum price through the intermediation of the central bank, the entire debt was made perfectly liquid and investors were enabled to view their holdings of Government securities, of whatever term, as reserves to be liquidated as needed to support other spending or investing programs.

The attempts to repress inflation through control of commercial bank Government securities portfolios while maintaining stable market rates of interest represented a naive notion of the functioning of the financial system. In 1946, for example, the use of surplus Treasury deposits at commercial banks to retire security issues held principally by commercial banks was an intrusion of administrative control into what would ordinarily be a market process. That is to say, if the central bank had been functioning normally, debt could have been retired without regard to the holders, and the Federal Reserve System could have imposed sufficient pressure upon bank reserves to bring about bank liquidation of financial assets to absorb the funds released by the Treasury into the private money supply. Similarly, the various secondary security proposals were predicated upon the unrealistic assumption that it was possible to regulate commercial bank credit and the money supply by increasing the reserve *ratio* even though the central bank was not in a position to control the total of reserve balances. In brief, the attempt of a central bank to maintain a pegged rate of interest on Government debt must necessarily destroy its ability to exert significant influence on money and credit, and attempts to avoid this outcome through control of the distribution of the debt can be successful only if carried to the point where administrative fiat has been substituted for market processes in the allocation of credit and capital.

C. Debt Management Since the Accord: June, 1 9 5 1–December, 1 9 5 4

The modern period of Treasury debt management began with the "accord" between the Treasury and the Federal Reserve System in March, 1951. Under the accord, the central bank continued to recognize a responsibility to assure that the principal object of debt management would be achieved, *i.e.,* that the Government's cash requirements would be financed. But the accord was recognition of the need for an independent central bank, free to regulate the money supply and over-all economic liquidity in accord with its judgment of the policies required to promote orderly economic growth.

Adjustment to the new setting of freely moving interest rates and independent central bank policy was not an instantaneous process. Old ideas and practices died slowly, both among private market specialists and investors and among official authorities. In part, the gradual transition was a reflection of conscious Treasury and Federal Reserve policy to avoid actions that would make the transition too abrupt and that might result in disorderly attempts to liquidate Government securities. One aspect of this policy was the agreement between the Treasury and System authorities at the time of the accord that Federal Reserve discount rates would not be raised from their 1¾ per cent level during the balance of 1951; another was the practice of the Federal Reserve System, pursued until the last financing in 1952, of giving blanket market support to Treasury financing operations. Also, the Treasury avoided offerings of securities of more than one-year maturity for nearly a year following the accord so as not to interfere with the continuing portfolio adjustments to the new and reduced liquidity of intermediate and longer-term United States Government issues.[2]

The official policy of gradual transition was based not only upon uncertainty as to how firmly the war-created Federal debt had been placed by this time, more than five years after the Victory Loan operation, but upon doubts as to how quickly the public at large and even professional market specialists could be expected to learn to live with a free market. It would appear

2. A major part of this adjustment was effected at the time of the accord through exchanges for the nonmarketable Investment Series B bonds; however, this exchange option was open only to the 2½ per cent bonds of June and December, 1967–72.

that these doubts were well founded. For at least a year after the accord, and probably longer, there was a firmly planted opinion in the Government securities market that there was a minimum price level, in the neighborhood of 96 for the longest-term 2½'s (equivalent to a yield of 2¾ per cent) below which the Federal Reserve System would not allow the market to slide. In fact, the price of the bonds did not break through 96 until the end of 1952, so that this presumed support level was never tested, but the belief that there was a support level—whether or not there actually was one—very probably helped to cushion price and yield movements during the transition period. What was significant in this situation was the refusal to believe that after many years of regulated markets regulation had been swept away and prices and yields were free.

Discussion within the Treasury and the Federal Reserve System also, at times, reflected a basic failure to understand the new milieu and the new role of the Federal Reserve System. In a public address in May, 1952, Secretary Snyder stressed revision in the savings bond program as a means of financing that avoided the commercial banks and minimized pressure upon the market.[3] The Treasury statement to the Patman Subcommittee,[4] in February, 1952, was shot through with references to possible results "when the Treasury raised its interests rates," with comments on the effect the Treasury has on the money supply when it pays off bank-held debt and numerous other statements wholly—or almost wholly—irrelevant when the central bank is independent to regulate total bank credit and the credit markets are free to channel available funds to the highest bidder. Even the emphasis upon funding the debt that had developed by 1952 in the recommendations from many people in the market and from the Federal Reserve System rested, in part, upon a wish to issue

3. Secretary of the Treasury, *Annual Report for 1952,* pp. 469–72.
4. U.S. Congress, *Monetary Policy and the Management of the Public Debt,* Hearings before the Subcommittee on General Credit Control and Debt Management of the Joint Committee on the Economic Report, February–March, 1952. The Treasury statement is reprinted in the *Annual Report for 1951,* pp. 198–403.

securities that would not be purchased by commercial banks or that would not be likely to be resold in the market, thus avoiding some pressure on the market, since they would be purchased by "permanent" investors. In short, the notions persisted in some quarters that the Treasury could control the rates paid in its financing, that it could regulate the ownership of its securities, and that the most desirable result of debt management operations would be to place securities, through some device, in a form that would prevent their being traded in free response to adjustments in competitive rates of interest.

During the first twenty-two months after the March, 1951, "accord" between the Treasury and the Federal Reserve System, the Treasury continued under the administration of Secretary Snyder, and the debt management policies that had been pursued under his direction since the end of the Second World War were continued. Secretary Snyder summarized the objectives of these policies, to be achieved in collaboration with the Federal Reserve System as follows:

Throughout the period since the close of World War II the Treasury and the Federal Reserve System were agreed upon the fundamental objective of maintaining a high level of production, employment, and income with as great price stability as possible under the varying conditions which existed in the economy. The related objectives which were involved as the postwar period proceeded were also a matter of agreement between the two agencies. These included: (1) maintenance of confidence in the credit of the Government; (2) maintenance of a sound market for the securities of the United States Government; (3) restraint, during much of the period, of over-all credit expansion; (4) increase in the ownership of Government securities by nonbank investors and reduction in the holdings of the banking system; (5) adjustment from time to time in the wartime pattern of interest rates, as this became appropriate.[5]

The emphasis upon maintenance of confidence in the credit of the Government and of a sound market for Government securities implied, to Secretary Snyder, a pattern of yields such

5. The quotation is taken from the *Annual Report for 1952*, p. 12, and is a portion of Secretary Snyder's review of the policies of his administration.

that prices of Treasury bonds did not drop very far below par and preferably remained at par or above. Also, the statement continued to reflect a belief that the locus of power in the determination of interest rates paid by the Treasury could and should be with the Treasury. Confronted with a central bank that refused to remain a "handmaiden," achievement of these objectives became most difficult. Attempts to finance outside the short-term area in any size without market support by the Federal Reserve almost certainly would break the pattern of rates that had emerged after the accord, driving bond prices to greater discounts and confronting the Treasury with the need to recognize that it was supply and demand relationships in the market and not Treasury fiat that set the rates the Treasury must pay. Therefore, virtually all Treasury offerings through the end of 1952 were of shorter maturity securities, and the debt management and credit policy problems created by a debt pressing constantly toward the shorter end of the maturity structure became steadily more urgent. Federal Reserve policies over most of this period were directed, in effect, toward rate stability in the short-term market and included direct support of Treasury financing through purchases of rights. The breadth and stability of the short-term Government securities market resulting from this policy made it simpler for the Treasury to conduct the bulk of its financing for nearly a year and a half through the medium of 1⅞ per cent certificates.

At the same time, the policy of financing at short-term was clearly in conflict with the objective of continuing to move Treasury debt from bank to nonbank owners (the central banking function which both Secretary Snyder and Secretary Humphrey claimed for the Treasury). To meet this inconsistency, sales of nonmarketable securities were pressed. A second offering of Investment Series B bonds was made, terms of all savings bond series were revised to make savings bonds more attractive, and a new small denomination current-income bond was developed.

A distinct change in philosophy and objectives of debt manage-

69

ment occurred in January, 1953, when Secretary Humphrey took over administration of the Treasury. The three principles of debt management were to be:

1. Freedom for the Federal Reserve System, with the Treasury financing at "going market rates."
2. Extension of debt maturities.
3. Reduction of bank-held debt.

At approximately the same time, the Federal Open Market Committee abandoned its policy of giving direct support to Treasury financing operations and continued to pursue the policy of monetary and credit restraint it had begun in the last half of 1952.

Initial attempts in the first half of 1953 to act upon the new principles of debt management encountered serious difficulties in the credit and capital market environment resulting from intense private credit demands and restrictive Federal Reserve policies. A small amount of bonds was sold, including the first issue of long-term bonds since the Victory Loan drive in 1945, but it soon became evident that the peak of a boom, when capital markets already were seriously strained, was a most difficult time to sell longer-term Treasury securities.

The leveling off in business activity after the middle of 1953, followed by recession, was accompanied by an aggressive policy of monetary ease by the Federal Reserve System which created a receptive market for Government securities outside the short-term area in the fall of 1953 and through 1954. But a new consideration now arose. To sell long-term bonds in a recession would compete with business demands for capital and, on grounds of general economic policy, would conflict with other Government and Federal Reserve policies aimed at encouraging recovery. For the first time it became apparent that "there is no good time to sell long-term Government bonds," a fact that was to continue to plague Treasury administration of the debt up to the present day.

The problem was resolved by initiating a program of optional exchange offerings, including a short-term security and an inter-

**Table 2—Changes in Marketable Treasury Securities Outstanding
June, 1951—December, 1954 (Changes in billions of dollars)**

Marketable Securities Maturing	June, 1951– December, 1952	January, 1953– December, 1954	Full Period
Within 1 year	14.2	5.9	20.0
1–5 years	— 7.3	— 8.1	—15.4
5–10 years	13.9	10.9	24.8
After 10 years	—10.1	0.6	— 9.5

Source: Board of Governors of the Federal Reserve System, *Federal Reserve Bulletin.*

mediate obligation, that would, presumably, place only as many Government securities outside the short-term market as investors demanded and would, thus, avoid forcing Government securities into the market to pre-empt funds. These split offerings were markedly successful during the last half of calendar 1953 and through 1954. More than one-half of all exchange subscriptions by holders of maturing securities, excluding the Federal Reserve System, were for the longer of the issues offered, and the Treasury, for the first time since the Second World War, made some headway against the steady shortening of the debt structure. Inducing investors, particularly commercial banks, to accept intermediate-term obligations was rather simple at this time, however, because of the extreme liquidity of the banking system both as a result of current Federal Reserve policies and of the debt management policies for the preceding eight years which had loaded their portfolios with liquidity assets. It was not a debt-management performance that could be repeated on quite this scale in an easy credit market without the necessary precondition of very liquid bank portfolios that obtained in late 1953 and 1954.

Reviewing the statistics, we find that the regular marketable coupon securities[6] sold by the Treasury between June, 1951, and December, 1954, included $91 billion of certificates of indebtedness, $34 billion Treasury notes, and $33 billion Treasury bonds. Giving effect to these operations, the maturity structure of the marketable debt was altered as indicated in Table 2.

6. Excludes Treasury bills and tax-anticipation certificates.

The figures in Table 2 suggest how little headway the new Treasury administration after January, 1953, was able to make against the shortening debt structure despite its good intentions, strenuous efforts, and a favorable market in which to finance. Both administrations recognized a desire to reduce commercial bank ownership of Government securities as a valid policy objective. Between June, 1951, and December, 1954, commercial bank holdings increased by $10.8 billion, of which $5 billion occurred under Secretary Snyder's administration and $5.8 billion under Secretary Humphrey's administration.

D. Treasury Financing: 1955–1957

Table 3 summarizes the new marketable securities issued by the Treasury during the three calendar years 1955 to 1957, inclusive.

Table 3—Marketable Securities Issued by Treasury, 1955–1957
(Billions of dollars)

Type of Security	Cash	Refunding	Total
Treasury Bills:			
Regular*	$ 2.6	$ —	$ 2.6
"Special"	5.1	—	5.1
Tax anticipation	7.0	—	7.0
Total	14.7	—	14.7
Certificates of Indebtedness:			
Regular series	3.4	64.6	68.0
Tax-anticipation series	11.6	2.8	14.4
Total	15.0	67.4	82.4
Treasury notes	6.6	45.3†	51.9
Treasury bonds	2.1	1.9	4.0
Total	$38.4	$114.6	$153.0

* Includes only additions to regular series.
† Includes $1.8 billion 1½ per cent Series EA and EO notes issued in exchange for non-marketable Investment Series B bonds.

Of the total $153 billion new marketable securities issued by the Treasury, $126.5 billion were regular issues and $26.5 billion were "special" or tax-anticipation series; 12 per cent of regular series securities were issued on cash subscriptions and 88 per cent were issued in exchange for maturing or called obligations. Regular securities issued consisted of 54 per cent certificates, 41 per cent notes, 3 per cent bonds, and 2 per cent bills.

The interest-bearing public debt was reduced by $2.9 billion during the three years 1955 through 1957 and the total of public issues by $6.1 billion (special issues to Treasury trust funds rose $3.2 billion), so that the sale of nearly $15 billion regular Treasury securities for cash (excludes "special" and tax-anticipation issues employed to finance intra-fiscal year deficits) was principally to finance net redemptions of non-marketable securities ($12 billion) and redemption of marketable securities not exchanged for new issues ($8 billion) rather than to finance operating deficits. Marketable public debt outstanding was increased by $6.4 billion.

Of the $120 billion matured securities for which exchange offerings were made, $55 billion were held by the public (excludes Federal Reserve System and Treasury accounts), and of this total 87 per cent were exchanged for the new securities offered by the Treasury and 13 per cent were presented for cash redemption.

The magnitude of these figures gives an impression of the financing problems the Treasury faced during these three years of generally tight credit availability, and the composition of the securities issued indicates the extent to which the Treasury fell short of its objective to lengthen the maturity structure of the debt. As a result of the financing operations in the three years 1955–1957, marketable debt maturing within one year increased by 18 per cent and marketable debt within five years of maturity grew by more than 30 per cent. As a percentage of total marketable debt, securities maturing within one year increased from 40 to 45 per cent, within five years from 58 to 74 per cent, and marketable debt maturing in more than five years fell from 42 to 26 per cent of the total. Measured in terms of a weighted average maturity, the average length of the marketable debt (excluding Federal Reserve holdings) fell from 5 years 6 months at the end of 1954 to 4 years 7 months at the end of 1957, the shortest average maturity since the war and, presumably, in this century.[7]

The pronounced shortening of the debt in the three years through 1957 occurred because the Treasury was unable to maintain the maturity structure, not to mention lengthening it. Policy objectives did not change; they simply could not be achieved in the market setting within which the Treasury conducted its operations. There were many reasons for this policy failure. It is possible that a more determined approach to the problem and somewhat less soul-searching and indecision would have achieved results more nearly in accord with objectives. It is questionable, however, that a great deal more could have been done than was done to place debt outside the short-term area, given the competing demands for funds and the technical financing methods employed by the Treasury. Most operations in regular debt securities (both cash and refundings) offered investors an option to take an intermediate or longer-term obligation rather than a short maturity, and it may be assumed that through this device the Treasury tapped most of the funds in these maturity areas that were available for investment on the terms offered by the Treasury.

Of course, it could be argued that more attractive terms could have done the job; but on this point we encounter the root problem of Treasury finance. May the Government of the United States consider itself just another borrower in the credit markets? Given the ownership distribution and maturity structure of existing financial assets and the volume and institutional distri-

7. Estimates of average maturity supplied by the Treasury Department. The author has attempted to avoid references to the "average maturity" of the marketable debt since such figures are a statistical abstraction without too much meaning and have, perhaps, been given too much emphasis in official statements. Clearly, the maturity structure of the debt is far more significant than the average maturity. Reduced to its most absurd, the average maturity could be made infinitely long by the sale of a nominal amount ($1) of perpetual bonds. To use a more realistic example, the author is of the opinion that the sale of $4 billion of ten-year bonds is a far more important achievement in its effect on the debt structure than the sale of $1 billion of forty-year bonds, although the effect on average maturity is the same.

74

bution of the flow of new loanable funds, the availability of funds in each maturity sector at any point in time is probably determined with relatively little leeway for marginal shifts between maturity sectors. The years 1955 through 1957 were a period of large and sustained demands for long-term credit to finance residential construction, plant and equipment outlays, and state and local government capital programs. The financing policies followed by the Treasury, in effect, made the Federal Government a net supplier of part of these long-term funds. If policies had been followed that would have prevented the collapse of the Treasury's maturity structure, thus cutting off this source of capital, or that would have lengthened the debt, placing the Treasury in competition for the limited supply of long funds from other sources, what would the result have been? Would the gap between United States Government and high-grade corporate interest rates have closed smoothly, at a higher general level of rates, and market equilibrium have been achieved through the necessary volume of deferrals of other financing that was no longer economically feasible at the new level of rates? Or would the demand for long-term funds have proved to be so inelastic with respect to interest rates that Treasury policies of this sort would simply have created market disequilibrium without significant effect on the ultimate allocation of the supply of capital funds? These questions remain unanswered, presumably because the Treasury felt that the maturity objectives of debt management were not sufficiently important to risk the disruption to the financial markets that might have resulted if more energetic efforts had been made to achieve stated policy objectives.

The process of market rationing of funds of various maturities, outlined in the preceding comments, implies an over-all limitation on the supply of loanable funds applied in such a manner that interest rates serve their allocative function in maintaining market equilibrium between the supply of financial assets and the supply of funds in each maturity sector. Federal Reserve policies imposed effective limitation on the over-all supply of funds and, by so doing, began to bring into focus for the first time since the Second World War (perhaps, for the first time in the history of the Federal Reserve System) the nature of the relationship between central bank policies and Treasury debt management. Later chapters argue that since both policies have their principal economic influence through their effect upon the liquidity of the financial asset structure they are, in fact, parts of a single policy mechanism. At this point it will only be noted that the debt policies of the Treasury and the credit policies of the Federal Reserve System had a profound influence upon each other. On the one hand, Federal Reserve policy influenced the market setting in which the Treasury financed itself, and by increasing the premium on liquidity made it more difficult for the Treasury to finance in other than liquid, short-term securities. On the other hand, the Treasury through its debt management policies affected the working of credit policy in at least two ways. First, the frequency of Treasury financing operations meant that a considerable part of the time the Federal Reserve had to pursue its policies cautiously to avoid direct conflict with Treasury finance. Second, and much more important, Treasury policies tended to increase the over-all liquidity of financial assets and, as a corollary, to supply capital funds that helped to support a volume of investment greater than the current volume of voluntary savings.[8]

Within the framework set by Federal Reserve credit policies and competing demands for funds, debt management might have been more successful in achieving its objectives, and less disruptive of Federal Reserve policy and of the capital markets, if the financing techniques employed had been better adapted to their purpose. Specifically, the frequency with which the Treasury found it necessary to come to market interfered with the

8. The Treasury was a supplier of capital funds through two channels: (1) redemptions of Savings bonds; (2) movement of marketable securities into shorter maturities. Both developments resulted, ultimately, in a net movement of Treasury securities from *investment* portfolios to *liquidity* portfolios. Since commercial banks simultaneously were reducing their portfolios of Governments, the capital funds resulting from this shift originated in an increase in velocity rather than an increase in the money supply.

orderly redistribution of new securities and, at times, kept the market continuously off balance for considerable periods.[9] The size of some of the individual financing operations would have placed a strain on the market apparatus under the best of circumstances, and under the tight market conditions generally prevailing from 1955 through 1957, these huge operations sometimes created almost impossible pressures on the market. And the practice of considering a full range of maturity alternatives as each financing approached created a degree of uncertainty that sometimes seriously complicated the financing itself. These and other technical practices made it more difficult for the Treasury to finance itself and, probably, added to interest costs. The absence of a well-articulated and generally understood set of techniques, developed with a view to making the management of the debt as technically simple as possible, helped to create the impression that each of the many operations was a minor crisis. In short, the management of the public debt would, at best, have been a trying task in these years; but the practices used to manage it appear to have made the task even more trying than it need have been.

Before closing the discussion of Treasury financing operations in the years 1955 through 1957, some mention should be made of the growth during this period of United States agency issues outstanding in the market. Currently, five agencies of the Government issue marketable securities to finance their operations.[10] These securities are not guaranteed either as to interest or principal by the Government, although the legislation authorizing the operation of each agency implies a Government interest and, in fact, the market values agency issues as almost the equivalent of direct Government obligations. For several years prior to 1955, the total marketable debt of these agencies

9. The seasonal imbalance in receipts, making seasonal financing necessary, and the difficulty of financing under an unrealistic debt ceiling were factors which influenced the number of times the Treasury had to come to market and over which the Treasury had little or no control.

10. These are: the Federal Intermediate Credit Banks, the Banks for Cooperatives, the Federal Home Loan Banks, the Federal Land Banks, and the Federal National Mortgage Association.

hovered in the neighborhood of $2 billion, but beginning in 1955 marketable agency debt began to grow rapidly, and by the end of 1957 it totaled $6.2 billion. The largest part of the increase has resulted from the sale, on balance, of $2.7 billion debentures and notes of the Federal National Mortgage Association, an agency that was financed entirely through direct advances from the Treasury before 1955. Of the $2.7 billion borrowed in the market by "Fanny Mae," $1.8 billion was used to repay advances from the Treasury (thus indirectly reducing the Treasury debt by that amount) and the balance to finance an enlarged mortgage portfolio.

At least one agency is in the market nearly every month to refund maturing securities or to sell new securities for cash. Individual agency issues usually are relatively small ($50 to $150 million—although one FNMA note issue totals $800 million), but the coincidence of several in the space of a few weeks may add to several hundreds of millions of dollars. In almost all cases, agency issues are placed directly with an underwriting group which then sells them to customers at a predetermined price that allows a commission to the underwriters. With the growth in agency securities outstanding and the corresponding growth in market activity, the fact that these are somewhat higher-yielding substitutes for Government securities has probably occasioned an upward pull on market rates of interest for direct Treasury issues. However, in view of the much larger volume of direct Treasury issues, the effect of rate changes on Government securities upon the rates the agencies have to pay to finance is clearly more important than the reverse effect of agency rates upon direct Treasury issues.

E. Treasury Financing: 1958–1960

During the three years, 1958 to 1960, the Treasury finally began to develop techniques for managing the public debt appropriate to the conditions of persistently strong credit demand that have characterized most of the postwar period. The techniques employed throughout the earlier postwar years were, by and large, those developed during the 1930's. Security issues were not refunded until they reached maturity or, when it was to the Treasury's advantage, first call date. All refunding operations gave exchange privilege to holders of the maturing securities (rights), and in most cases holders of the "rights" were given an exchange option among two or three issues of different maturities, almost always including a one-year certificate. In a very real sense, the maturity distribution of the debt was left in the hands of the investors. Since other demands for long-term funds were nearly always pressing on the supply and since the Treasury allowed the rate of interest on its long-term debt to get out of touch with rates of interest on competitive investments, there was a persistent tendency for a larger and larger proportion of the debt to move into shorter maturities. Each financing operation seemed to be an independent crisis, requiring new and largely unpredictable decisions as to terms and maturities, rather than one part of a carefully planned debt-management program. Since the Treasury found it necessary to come to market nearly every month, either for cash or to refund, the result was a nearly continuous state of crisis in the Government securities market.

Although the techniques used had been appropriate to the conditions of the 1930's, they were peculiarly inappropriate to the conditions of the 1950s. What was required if the steady shortening of the debt maturity structure was to be halted was the development of new techniques, based upon an awareness of the role of the public debt in the country's financial system, that would make it possible for the Treasury to compete effectively for funds in all maturity sectors. The extent to which the Treasury was successful in recapturing control of the debt is suggested by the changes in maturity distribution during these three years. It will be recalled that in the three preceding years, 1955–1957, marketable debt within one year of maturity had grown from 40 per cent to 45 per cent of total marketable debt, that within five years of maturity from 58 to 74 per cent of the total, and marketable debt more than five years from maturity had fallen from 42 to 26 per cent. In the three years 1958–1960, on the other hand, the percentage of marketable debt maturing within one year was reduced from 45 per cent to 40 per cent, marketable debt maturing within five years grew from 74 to 77 per cent, and debt more than five years from maturity declined only from 26 to 23 per cent. The average maturity of the debt was unchanged from the end of 1957 level at four years and seven months. For all practical purposes, debt management during these three years succeeded in stabilizing the maturity structure of the debt.

This result was achieved in spite of the extremely heavy financing schedule suggested by Table 4. A total of some $200

Table 4—Marketable Securities Issued by Treasury, 1958–1960
(Billions of dollars)

Type of Security	Cash	Refunding	Total
Treasury Bills:			
Regulars*	$ 3.6	$ —	$ 3.6
"Special"	2.7	—	2.7
One-Year	8.0	6.5	14.5
Tax Anticipation	21.0	—	21.0
Total	35.3	6.5	41.8
Certificates of Indebtedness			
Regular Series	—	70.9†	70.9
Tax Anticipation	3.6	—	3.6
Total	5.7	68.8	74.5
Treasury Notes	14.2	45.1‡	59.3
Treasury Bonds	4.6	19.7§	24.3
Total	$59.8	$140.1	$199.9

* Includes only net additions to amount outstanding.
† Includes $2.1 billion sold for cash to refund maturing securities.
‡ Includes $2.8 billion 1½ per cent EA and EO notes issued in exchange for Investment Series B bonds.
§ Includes $1.0 billion sold for cash to refund maturing securities.

billion of new securities was issued from 1958 to 1960, inclusive, nearly one-third more than during the preceding three years. The total public debt grew by $5.3 billion during the three years, and nonmarketable debt was reduced by $10.3 billion (due principally to redemptions of F, G, J, and K bonds and conversions of Investment Series B bonds). Consequently, marketable debt increased by approximately $15.6 billion. The balance of the nearly $60 billion cash financing shown in the table was necessary to cover intra-year needs (the tax-anticipation and "special" securities) and to replace attrition on refunding operations. The $200 billion of new securities issued by the Treasury consisted of 12 per cent of bonds, 30 per cent of notes, 37 per cent of certificates, and 21 per cent of bills.

One of the most important steps taken by Under-Secretary Julian Baird, who was principally responsible for debt management during these three years, was to place a larger part of the short-term debt on a routine roll-over basis. This was accomplished by replacing most of the one-year certificates with two new regular bill series of six-month and one-year maturity. Regular Treasury bills outstanding at the end of 1960, including the six-month and one-year bills, totaled $ 32.4 billion, up from $22.1 billion three years earlier. At the same time, regular certificates outstanding were reduced from $34.6 billion to $19.7 billion. In a sense, the increased use of regular bills reflected recognition of the fact that a large part of the short-term Treasury debt is permanent short-term debt. This being the case, it should be placed in a form that makes its refunding as simple as possible so that it may regularly be rolled over with minimum impact on the market and at minimum interest cost to the Treasury. Regular bills simplify the Treasury's problem since the investors bidding for each new issue determine the rate of interest and since the cash refunding procedure used for bills eliminates attrition. The principal benefit to the market is the elimination of uncertainty as to what maturity and other terms the Treasury will offer; it may be assumed that a maturing bill issue will be replaced by a new bill issue of similar amount and term. The movement to routinize short-term financing contributed significantly to lessening the refunding problem.

Another very important innovation has been the use of

advance refunding to place marketable debt in longer maturities. As discussed elsewhere in the study, an important cause of the Treasury's difficulty in maintaining its maturity structure has been the fact that securities were not refunded until they had reached maturity. By that time they had for some while been short-term investments, regardless of their original maturity, and had in most cases assumed a liquidity function in the portfolios in which they were held. The long-term funds that were originally committed to investment in Governments have been withdrawn to other uses. Consequently, the holders of a maturing bond more often than not are interested only in relatively short-term reinvestment. For the Treasury to refund with a longer obligation would require that *new* long-term funds be tapped out of the market to replace those long-term funds that had been lost to the Treasury some while earlier when the issue now maturing moved from long to short-term classification.

One way to forestall this process is to offer holders of outstanding bonds an option to exchange for a new, longer-term security well before maturity. The first offering of this sort was made in June, 1960, when holders of some $11.2 billion of 2½ per cent bonds scheduled to mature in November, 1961, were offered optional exchange into a 1964 note or a 1968 bond. Later in 1960 holders of four issues of World War II 2½ per cent bonds having maturities from 1967 to 1969 were offered an advance refunding into three bond issues maturing in 1980, 1990, and 1998. The technique has since been used in 1961 by Under Secretary Roosa, and it may be assumed that it will remain an important method for extending Treasury debt.

The Treasury has also experimented in various other ways to improve its management of the debt. One experiment has been to offer securities at prices other than par. Such pricing has the advantage of enabling the Treasury to adjust its effective rate of interest more precisely to the prevailing market than is possible on par offerings. Another has been the employment of cash offerings to refund maturing securities. Cash refunding avoids the problem of redistributing "rights" from holders of the maturing issue not interested in the exchange to investors who are interested. It also has the advantage of retaining with the Treasury control over the size of its issues. On an exchange refunding in which two or more issues are offered, there is no wholly workable way for the Treasury to regulate the amount of exchanges into the various issues. And finally, cash refunding eliminates attrition and thus enables the Treasury to do a better job of scheduling its cash flows.

The largest part of the long-term securities issued by the Treasury during the three years 1958–1960 were sold during the economic recession in late 1957 and the first half of 1958. Interest rates were relatively low at that time, and competing demands for long-term funds were light. The decision to lengthen debt during recession reflected resolution of the uncertainty that had plagued earlier Treasury administrations as to whether it was sound policy to sell long debt during recession. The inflationary consequences of allowing the debt to steadily shorten had become very apparent in the preceding three years, and the Treasury officials concluded that whatever minor restraining effect on economic recovery debt lengthening might have was more than justified by the need to prevent further unplanned additions to the stock of liquid financial assets. A similar policy of lengthening debt in recession was followed in 1960–1961.

Later chapters discuss the relationship of monetary policy and public debt management and point out that conscious synchronization of the two policies is necessary to achieve any given public policy effect upon over-all availabilities of funds at various maturities. So long as there is the necessary compensation through monetary policy, therefore, debt management may move in a direction apparently counter to economic stabilization objectives if this balancing of policies is the optimum mix. However, arriving at the proper balance requires very careful planning if the danger of unplanned and unwanted effects is to be avoided. The results of the Treasury's debt lengthening operations in 1957–58 pointed up the danger and have had significant effect upon subsequent policy planning.

During the last quarter of 1957 and the first half of 1958, the Treasury issued some $12.7 billion of bonds in the 5–10 year maturity area and $1.2 billion of bonds carrying maturities of more than 10 years. Interest rates had declined sharply from their 1957 highs, and a substantial part of the bonds issued by the Treasury went either to commercial banks attempting to maintain income by replacing short-term securities in their portfolios with less-liquid bonds or to speculators who were gambling on a further decline in rates and increase in prices. The net result was a considerable reduction in the liquidity of the economy and, in effect, the attraction of huge amounts of temporary short-term funds into long-term obligations. It should have been apparent to the officials of the Treasury that the bonds they were selling were in excess of the amount that the normal flow of long-term investment funds could absorb, given the relatively large concurrent flow of long-term funds into mortgages and other long-term investments.

By June, 1958, a tremendous supply of United States Government and other longer-term bonds was over-hanging the market either in "underwriting" positions or in speculators' hands. In a refunding operation that month, the Treasury offered holders of $9.6 billion maturing issues a choice between a 1¼ per cent eleven-month certificate or a 2⅝ per cent six-year-eight-month bond; a total of $7.4 billion subscriptions were received for the bond. A considerable part of the new bond issue went either into "street" positions or into unsoundly financed speculative positions. Just at this time it began to become apparent in the economic statistics that the recession had ended and that recovery had begun. In this setting, prices of bonds began to adjust downward, touching off a wave of liquidation from speculative holdings which, by mid-July, had created a wholly disorderly condition in the Government bond market. The rapid upward adjustment of yields and collapse of bond prices added considerably to the Treasury's financing problems for many months afterward. More importantly, the debt management policies of the Treasury during the 1957–1958 recession created a degree of illiquidity in the financial economy which, in combination with the restrictive monetary policy of the Federal Reserve System in 1959, may have contributed importantly to the unsatisfactory character of the 1959–1960 economic expansion.

In spite of the unfortunate results of Treasury debt management in the 1957–1958 recession, the over-all performance in the three years through 1960 was excellent. For the first time since the end of the Second World War, real progress was made toward bringing the debt under control through a soundly-conceived debt management program. Much remains to be done, but the innovations in technique developed by Under-Secretary Baird and his associates at last set the Treasury on the correct road. Perhaps more important than any other development was the growing awareness of the real nature of the relationship between debt management and credit policy and of the role in the public policy mix that debt management can fill. As much as anything else, this growing awareness consisted of jettisoning such irrelevant notions as the idea that the Treasury is able to regulate and should be concerned with the ownership distribution of the public debt. The very absence in recent years of statements that, for anti-inflation reasons, the Treasury attempts to place its debt outside the commercial banks is, by itself, encouraging evidence of real progress toward understanding.

F. Changes in the Composition and Ownership of the Public Debt: February, 1946, to December, 1960

During the nearly fifteen years from February, 1946, through December, 1960, both the composition and ownership distribution of the public debt underwent sweeping changes. These

Table 5—Changes in the Composition and Ownership of the Public Debt, February, 1946—December, 1960*
(Changes in billions of dollars)

Investor Class	Total Change	Marketable Securities					Public Non-marketable	Special Issues	Matured and Non-interest Bearing Debt
		Total	Under 1-year	1-5 years	5-10 years	Over 10 years			
Commercial banks	− 31.2	− 30.4	− 16.1	+ 17.6	− 26.1	− 5.8	− 0.8	—	—
Mutual Savings banks	− 5.2	− 5.4	+ 0.2	+ 1.2	− 0.4	− 6.3	+ 0.2	—	—
Insurance Companies	− 12.5	− 14.9	+ 0.1	+ 1.8	− 1.6	− 15.3	+ 2.4	—	—
United States Government Agencies and Trust Funds	+ 27.1	+ 1.2	− 5.1	+ 12.4	+ 1.5	− 3.2	+ 2.5	+ 23.4	—
Federal Reserve System	+ 4.5	+ 4.5					—	—	—
Nonfinancial Corporations	− 0.2	n.a.†	—	—	—	—	—	—	—
Individuals	+ 2.2	− 0.2	—	—	—	—	+ 2.3	—	—
State and local Governments	+ 10.3	n.a.	—	—	—	—	—	—	—
All other	+ 15.3	n.a.	—	—	—	—	—	—	—
Total change	+ 10.6	− 10.8	+ 5.6	+ 51.8	− 27.7	− 40.3	− 3.7	+ 23.4	+ 1.5

* Based on Treasury Survey data.
† n.a. Not available.

changes are summarized in Table 5. The size of the gross debt did not change substantially, increasing by some $10.6 billion, but there were significant changes in both composition and ownership. February, 1946, was selected as a reference point because the debt reached an immediate post-war peak in that month, following the conclusion of the Victory Loan campaign, and statistics for that date best reflect the structure and ownership of the debt created by war-time financing policies. Treasury deposit balances were at the unusually high level of $26 billion at the time, however, and these balances were used to retire $21 billion of short-term debt by the end of fiscal 1947. On balance, all of this debt retirement represented securities held by commercial banks, whose holdings had been reduced nearly $24 billion by June, 1947. In making comparisons of the affected components, therefore, Table 5 might be adjusted to show an increase in the gross debt of about $31 billion (rather than the $10.6 billion increase), marketable debt maturing within five years would show an increase of almost $78 billion (rather than the $57.4 billion increase), and commercial bank holdings of Government securities would show roughly a $7 billion decline (rather than $31.2 billion).

Several important changes in composition and ownership distribution occurred between February 1946 and the end of 1960:

1. The maturity structure of the marketable debt was significantly shortened.

2. Total public nonmarketable debt would have declined by more than it did had it not been for the issue (in 1951) of Investment Series B bonds for long-term marketable bonds, partially offsetting retirement of Savings notes and several issues of Savings bonds.

3. There was a pronounced shift in the ownership of public marketable debt from investors interested in Government securities as a portfolio investment medium to investors interested in Government securities as a liquidity reserve medium.

4. The almost steady (but diminishing) accrual of net receipts

in the Treasury trust funds resulted in a major shift of Treasury debt from private holders to Treasury accounts.

Turning first to the broad changes in the maturity structure of the marketable debt, the table shows that total marketable debt declined by $10.8 billion; the volume of securities maturing in more than five years was reduced by $68.0 billion, while marketable securities within five years of maturity were increased by $57.4 billion. (If allowance is made for the debt retirement in fiscal 1947, referred to above, the increase in short-term debt has been of the order of $78 billion.) By types of securities, Treasury bills were increased by $22.4 billion, certificates of indebtedness reduced by $23.0 billion, Treasury notes increased by $31.7 billion, and Treasury bonds reduced by $42.8 billion.

The uneven pattern of change among maturity groupings resulted both from the choice of securities sold to finance World War II and the choice of securities to refund debt in the years since the war. Bonds issued by the Treasury during the war tended to be clustered in narrow maturity areas. Specifically, the Treasury's long-term debt in February, 1946, consisted principally of nine issues of 2½ per cent bonds scheduled to mature in the six years 1967 to 1972, inclusive; each of these issues (with the exception of the bank-eligible 2½'s of September 1967–72) had been offered one or more times in the various War Loan and Victory Loan drives.[11] They were outstanding in a total amount of $43.6 billion, of which savings banks and insurance companies owned 48 per cent and individuals and other unclassified investors owned 35 per cent. During the fifteen years through 1960, the largest part of these issues moved into the "5– to 10–year" range from the "over 10–year" range, accounting for a major part of the sharp drop in the latter.[12] An-

11. These were the 2½'s of 1962–67, 1963–68, 1964–69 (two issues), 1965–70, 1966–71, and 1967–72 (three issues, one of which was eligible for bank purchase).

12. Some $13.6 billion of the long-term 2½'s also were exchanged for nonmarketable Investment Series B bonds in 1951, further reducing the marketable debt in the "over 10–year" sector.

other major clustering of war-time bond maturities was in 1958 to 1962; four issues of fully taxable war-time issues were outstanding in this maturity area totaling $14.0 billion.[13] These bonds had either been retired or moved into the 1–5 year range by the end of 1957, helping to explain the large increase in that sector. Finally, six issues of fully taxable war finance bond issues were scheduled to mature from 1952 to 1954, inclusive, in a total amount of $30.4 billion. These bonds have since been refunded, principally into shorter maturities, thus swelling the under-five-year debt sector.

The most important characteristic of post-war debt management has been the difficulty encountered by the Treasury in devising a financing program that would maintain a debt structure with an orderly maturity spacing. It is not suggested that the structure developed by war-time financing policies, with its heavy weighting in longer-term maturities, was necessarily the structure the Treasury should have attempted to maintain. What is suggested is that the critical lack has been the absence of an over-all plan, and the perfection of techniques to effectuate the plan, that would have retained control of the structure of the debt in the Treasury's hands so that the maturity arrangement that emerged would have reflected conscious policy objectives. As described in earlier chapters, the management of debt maturities in every previous period of American financial history since the Civil War has reflected well-defined policy objectives, whereas debt operations since the Second World War have, until quite recently, been characterized by drift and expediency, and individual debt operations have generally been adjusted to "market conditions" (which is another way of saying they were guided by expediency) rather than to long-range policy objectives. A good part of the reason for the Treasury's impotence was the long delay in devising techniques adequate to the management of the debt in the peculiarly difficult circumstances of

13. The 2½'s of 1956–58, the 2¼'s of 1956–59, and the 2¼'s of 1959–62 (two issues).

the past fifteen years, particularly the free-market period since the Treasury-Federal Reserve "accord" in 1951.

The marketable Treasury securities outstanding at the end of the war represented funds irrevocably committed to investment in Government securities until the maturity dates specified on the instruments. There were only three ways the Treasury might have maintained the debt structure, with an equivalent commitment of funds in each maturity range: (1) by inducing holders of maturing or called securities to accept a necessary amount of long bonds in exchange; (2) by offering periodic pre-maturity refunding operations involving debt lengthening; (3) by selling the necessary long bonds for cash, using the proceeds to retire short-term securities. The first and third alternatives would not have been consistent with a stable interest rate pattern, and since either would have involved raising *new* long-term funds, it is unlikely that they could have been successful in placing enough longer debt in the market, in the face of competing demands for capital, to have stabilized the maturity structure. The second alternative has been adopted only recently. It is possible that this technique might have been reasonably successful in earlier years, but it could not have been successful in a setting of pegged interest rates, nor is it likely it could have been fully successful at all times in stabilizing the maturity structure within the framework of an orderly market, in view of the competing demands for capital funds to support the capital expansion of the postwar decade. The apparent conclusion is that it probably would not have been possible to maintain the end-of-the-war maturity structure, even if such an objective could have been defended as an important policy end. At the same time, as following chapters will argue, there apparently was no need for the debt structure to collapse as badly as it has.[14]

The more significant shifts in the ownership of the public debt

14. One action which might have been taken earlier than it was would have been to eliminate the restriction on commercial bank purchases of most bond issues. As late as June, 1951, only $5 billion of the $41 billion bonds more than ten years from maturity were eligible for bank purchase.

have been those related to the role of Treasury securities in investors' portfolios. In general terms, holdings of Government securities may be classified either as investments or as liquidity assets. That is to say, they may be held either for long-term investment, as part of an investment portfolio, or as an income-earning outlet for short-term funds, as an alternative to holding those funds in a cash form. Since the end of the Second World War there has been a pronounced movement of investor holdings of Government securities toward the latter purpose, *i.e.,* the liquidity asset function.

This development has been at least partly a result of the Treasury's lack of success in developing debt-management policies that would preserve an orderly debt structure and that would, therefore, maintain a supply of investment securities outstanding at competitive rates of interest. At the same time, it also appears likely that at least part of the shifting emphasis upon Government securities as liquidity assets has resulted from investor preference rather than Treasury debt policies. Whatever the reasons, the data in the table clearly suggest a movement toward investment in Government securities as liquidity assets. Mutual savings banks and life insurance companies have reduced their holdings of longer-term Government issues sharply, while maintaining liquidity reserve holdings of shorter-term issues. Commercial banks lengthened portfolio maturities for a number of years after World War II, but the lessons learned in the years of credit restraint, 1955–1957 and 1959–1960, have brought a new emphasis upon liquidity in portfolio management. Fire, casualty, and marine insurance companies have added to their holdings of short-term issues in pace with their growing liabilities, but they have reduced their investment in longer-term Governments. State and local governments have been large net buyers of United States Government obligations. Part of this buying undoubtedly has been investment of pension fund money, but an indeterminable—probably larger—part has been the investment of short-term operating balances and construction funds. Foreign and international accounts have been net buyers, but these investments, in most cases, represent dollar reserve balances and must be held in short-term obligations.

On balance, the only significantly large demand for Government securities for long-term investment purposes has been from the Treasury itself. Balances in the Treasury trust funds increased by more than $27 billion between February, 1946, and December, 1960, and investment of these balances is restricted to United States Government direct or guaranteed obligations. Net receipts in the trust accounts have been declining in recent years, and under existing programs it is anticipated that they will continue to dwindle. Thus, net receipts to trust account balances have been negative in fiscal 1959 and 1960 by contrast with an average addition to balances of $2.3 billion in the twelve fiscal years 1947 to 1958, inclusive. The assistance to debt management provided by "cash retirement" of debt via trust fund purchases may be expected to continue to be of less significance in the years ahead than it was in the first twelve postwar years.

I V

The Demand
for Government Securities:
Practices and Policies
of Investing Institutions

In December, 1960, the gross Treasury debt amounted to $290 billion and was expected to increase further during the course of the following year. The net Federal Government debt (excluding trust fund holdings) represented an estimated 28 per cent of all debts, public and private, down substantially from the record 62 per cent of all debts in 1945, but still a very sizable component in the debt structure of the country.[1] The preceding chapter has outlined the management of the public debt between the conclusion of World War II financing and the end of 1960 and the results of debt management upon debt composition and ownership. This chapter will examine the demand for United States Government securities from the point of view of the investment practices of institutions and individuals who own the debt.

1. Estimates prepared by Council of Economic Advisors, *Economic Report of the President,* January, 1961.

The financial assets outstanding that represented the Treasury's $290 billion debt obligation at the end of 1960 involved the commitment by investors of that volume of funds for the maturities included in the debt structure. Part of this investment was nondiscretionary, such as the investment of the Treasury trust funds, which are restricted to United States Government securities, and of the Federal Reserve Banks, the bulk of whose investments are restricted, for all practical purposes, to Governments. Also, some element of nondiscretionary ownership of Government securities is involved in some public pension funds and in the case of financial institutions which hold United States Government securities as part of their legal reserves or as backing for deposits of public monies. The bulk of the debt, however, represents a discretionary and voluntary commitment of funds to this investment form.

In placing its securities with investors, the Treasury competes with all other borrowers, and its ability to sell securities of a type and maturity consistent with its policy objectives depends upon the attractiveness of its offerings, all things considered, relative to the attractiveness of other outlets for funds of the maturity sought by the Treasury. It is true, of course, that the Treasury is a "necessitous borrower" in the sense that inability to borrow money would never be allowed to interfere with the operation of the Government. It is also true that the Government has the power, as demonstrated in World War II, to determine the rates of interest at which it will borrow and to create sufficient money to validate those rates. The power to force its securities on the market at rates and terms determined unilaterally by the Treasury is an emergency power, however, and involves inflationary consequences, discussed in earlier chapters, that are intolerable except when justified by conditions of the utmost urgency. Since the "accord" between the Treasury and the Federal Reserve System in 1951, the Treasury has competed on equal terms with other borrowers for investors' funds, and realistic analysis of Treasury debt management must be in terms of the Treasury as a competitor rather than a favored borrower.

Investment policies vary from one type of investor cassification to another and, within broad classifications, among individual investors or investing institutions. Many, perhaps most purchasers of Treasury Savings bonds invest automatically, through payroll savings plans, without conscious consideration of alternatives; most investments in life insurance and in the liabilities of certain other financial intermediaries are similarly automatic. Tax considerations affect the allocation of funds among alternative investments for broad groups of individual and institutional investors. Some types of financial intermediaries have more or less specific lending functions in the financial mechanism, and investment of funds consistent with these functions has first priority in the allocation of their resources. Other intermediaries are restricted by law or by equally-binding tradition to investments of a particular type or maturity, or to a more or less fixed portfolio distribution among different types and maturities of investments. The pattern is infinitely varied, and shifts in the proportions of investible funds originating with different types of investors will tend to influence the relative availability of funds to different types of borrowers.

By and large, however, the performance of investors in the money and securities markets in recent years suggests that the ultimate allocation of funds among competing investment outlets is guided by rational rather than institutional considerations. That is to say, the volume of investible funds free to shift from one type of investment to another when there are advantages to be derived from such a shift appears to be sufficiently large to assure a pattern of interest rate relationships that is not subject to sudden, random changes. Investments may also be shifted among maturity areas, although the latitude for shifting of this type appears to be more limited and interest rate patterns may alter significantly and for relatively protracted periods; thus, major changes in the availability of commercial bank funds or in the demands for capital funds may radically alter the slope of the rate curve.[2] From the point of view of Treasury debt management, it may be assumed that the allocation of investors' funds as between United States Government securities and other investments at any maturity range, or among maturities, will be determined by the attractiveness of Government securities vis-à-vis alternative investments.

The relative attractiveness of the various types of investments is a function of three factors: (a) rate of return; (b) liquidity (including marketability); (c) risk (both credit and money risk). At any given time, different investors will attach varying weights to these factors in arriving at investment decisions, and the sum of their decisions, after allowing for the influence of institutional practices and time lags in adjusting to changes in demand or supply conditions, will determine the relationship of interest rates on the various securities, the dependent variable, to one another. It follows that interest rates on Government securities may vary for any period of time from rates on competitive investments only to the extent that they differ in risk or liquidity from these other investments or to the extent that institutional investment practices provide some degree of insulation. And it follows from this that the attractiveness of Government securities at this rate differential to individual investors or investor groups will depend upon the importance they attach to the risk and liquidity variation.

The following analysis of changes in the portfolios of various investor groups since 1946 concludes that the differential between market rates on longer-term Government securities and the rates available on alternative investments has generally been greater than could be justified, in the eyes of most major investor groups, on grounds of liquidity or risk differential. The reasons for this situation and its implications will be discussed in the concluding section of this chapter. Before proceeding to a dis-

2. For an excellent discussion of interest rate structure and of the functional relationships among the markets for different types of credit and capital, see: John M. Culbertson, "The Term Structure of Interest Rates," *The Quarterly Journal of Economics*, 71, 4 (November, 1957), 485–517.

cussion of the investment policies of different groups of investors, however, a word should be said about the difficulty of determining what rate spread between long-term United States Government securities and other high-grade investments would be consistent with a broad demand for Governments. In the ten years 1951 through 1960, the rate spread between long-term Governments and the Moody's Aaa corporate bond index ranged from approximately ¼ point in 1951–53 to as low as ⅛ in 1955 (when the 3's of 1995 were sold) and to as high as ½ point in 1957 and again in 1960.

It may be significant that insurance companies and savings banks liquidated Government securities consistently throughout the ten years, despite the shifts in the relative attractiveness of Governments, although rates of net liquidation varied. Actually, comparison with Moody's Aaa corporate index does not accurately depict the rates of interest available on other investments with which United States Government securities were competing. Trading in corporate and municipal bonds in the secondary market is very light relative to the total of such securities outstanding. Major investing institutions confine their purchases of bonds almost exclusively to "direct placements" negotiated with the borrower or to purchases of new issues directly from the underwriting syndicate. There are only sketchy data available on the rates of interest paid on direct placements. An indication of the spread between new issue rates and yields on seasoned issues is provided by the fact that in late 1960, when Moody's index of Aaa corporate bond yields was in the neighborhood of 4.35 per cent, the new issue rate on securities of this quality was in the neighborhood of 4.75 per cent. It is with the latter rates, rather than market yields on seasoned bonds, that a *new* issue of United States Government securities would have to compete.

An attempt to draw conclusions from the interest rate record before 1951 would be unproductive because of the variety of circumstances affecting the relationship. For example, prior to World War I the market rate on Government bonds measured the

9 7

value of their note circulation privilege rather than their investment qualities; the periods of the two world wars could not be considered representative for obvious reasons; and during the 1920's and 1930's, among other influences, the varying importance of the tax exemption feature makes a meaningful analysis almost impossible. Perhaps the only conclusion that can be drawn is that the rate differential between Treasury bonds and other investment media, particularly Aaa corporate bonds, that has generally prevailed in recent years has been too great to induce most institutional investors to become net purchasers of long-term Government securities or to retain in portfolio the Governments they already held.

A. Commercial Bank Investments in Government Securities

Three general principles may be assumed to guide major commercial banks in the management of their asset portfolios. These principles determine commercial bank participation in the Government securities market and dictate the maturity structure of their Government portfolios: (1) Within limits set by the need for liquidity, customer loans have first call upon a bank's resources; within these limits all other investments are of a reserve nature, subject to liquidation to provide for customer credit needs. (2) Every effort is made to remain as fully invested as possible. (3) Portfolio liquidity is important; there should be sufficient secondary reserve assets of relatively short maturity and assured marketability to provide for all foreseeable cash needs.

Two conclusions may be derived from these principles with respect to commercial bank investments in Government securities. In the first place, whether commercial banks as a group are net buyers or net sellers of Government securities at a particular time depends upon the size of customer loan demands and the availability of primary bank reserves. In the second place, the limited availability of other marketable, short-term financial assets will cause commercial banks at all times to maintain relatively large aggregate holdings of shorter-term Government securities (this does not suggest that they may not also be interested in longer maturities).

Table 6 on the distribution of total assets of all commercial banks tends to support these conclusions. After having been reduced rapidly in the years immediately after the war, incident to the Treasury debt retirement at that time, commercial bank investments in Government securities fluctuated seasonally in a narrow range through the middle of 1953. Meanwhile, loan demand was strong, reflected in the rapid expansion of bank loans, and the availability of bank reserves to support credit expansion became steadily more restricted. With the reversal of Federal Reserve policy after the middle of 1953, funds became liberally available to commercial banks; since customer loan demand subsided at the same time, the funds made available by Federal Reserve policy were poured in a steady stream into investments in United States Government securities. Between June, 1953, and December, 1954, commercial bank holdings of Government securities grew by approximately $10 billion. Federal Reserve policy then moved toward restraint on money and credit, and in the following three years of steady and intense customer loan demands and an increasingly limited supply of funds to meet these demands, commercial banks liquidated more than $11 billion of Government securities. A similar pattern was then apparent in the following business cycle as commercial banks added $8.5 billion to their holdings of Governments in 1958, liquidated $12.2 billion during the tight-money episode in 1959 and early 1960 and then added $6.8 billion as money became easier in the last half of 1960. Clearly, net commercial bank participation as buyers or sellers of Government securities is a function of the volume of loan demand and the availability of bank reserves. More narrowly, it is a function of Federal Reserve monetary and credit policy.

99

Table 6—United States Government Securities in Commercial Bank Portfolios

Month Ending		Actuals (Billions of dollars)			U.S. GOVERNMENTS*				Per Cent of Total Loans and Investments		U.S. GOVERNMENTS			
		Total Loans and Investments	Loans	Other Securities	Total	Under 1 Year	Under 5 Years	Over 5 Years	Loans	Other Securities	Total	Under 1 Year	Under 5 Years	Over 5 Years
1951	June	126.0	54.8	12.7	58.5	10.2	39.5	12.0	43	10	47	8	31	10
	December	134.6	57.7	13.3	61.6	14.1	42.1	12.1	44	10	46	11	32	9
1952	June	134.4	59.2	14.0	61.1	12.7	40.6	13.3	44	10	46	9	30	10
	December	141.6	64.2	14.1	63.4	17.0	39.4	16.3	45	10	45	12	28	12
1953	June	138.0	65.0	14.3	58.8	19.6	37.9	13.3	47	10	43	14	28	10
	December	145.7	67.6	14.7	63.4	25.1	41.1	14.6	46	10	44	17	28	10
1954	June	146.4	67.3	15.5	63.6	17.7	32.3	23.7	46	11	43	12	22	16
	December	155.9	70.6	16.3	69.0	15.7	36.6	26.3	45	11	44	10	24	17
1955	June	155.3	75.2	16.8	63.3	7.2	28.9	26.6	48	11	41	5	19	17
	December	160.9	82.6	16.7	61.6	7.7	29.7	24.1	52	11	38	5	18	17
1956	June	160.0	86.9	16.5	56.5	7.4	25.7	23.9	55	10	35	5	16	15
	December	165.1	90.3	16.3	58.6	11.6	36.2	15.2	55	10	35	7	22	15
1957	June	165.6	93.3	16.8	55.5	12.3	35.8	12.8	56	10	34	7	22	9
	December	169.8	94.3	17.7	57.9	13.1	39.6	12.0	56	10	34	8	23	8
1958	June	179.9	95.6	20.1	64.2	13.4	37.9	19.5	53	11	36	7	21	7
	December	185.2	98.2	20.6	66.4	14.4	44.1	14.8	53	11	36	8	24	11
1959	June	185.9	104.5	20.6	60.9	10.0	41.3	12.0	56	11	33	5	22	8
	December	190.3	110.8	20.5	58.9	11.2	40.0	11.9	58	11	31	6	21	6
1960	June	188.9	114.8	19.9	54.2	6.5	39.9	8.1	61	11	29	3	21	4
	December	199.5	117.6	20.9	61.0	14.7	46.3	8.0	59	10	31	7	23	4

* Total holdings of U.S. Government securities are for all commercial banks, while the maturity breakdown covers only banks included in the Treasury Survey, which typically account for about 90 per cent of all commercial bank holdings.

Source: Board of Governors of the Federal Reserve System and United States Treasury Department, Survey of Ownership.

The role of short-term marketable Government securities as secondary reserves in commercial bank portfolios since June, 1951, is indicated in Table 6. Holdings of issues within one year of maturity as a proportion of total loans and investments have fluctuated between a high of 17 per cent in December, 1953, and a low of 3 per cent in June, 1960. These fluctuations have been markedly influenced by the selection of issues by the Treasury for its debt operations and by the more or less random movement of very large issues into the under-one-year range. Data on commercial bank holdings of all marketable Government securities within five years of maturity are somewhat less sensitive to such influences and present a more accurate picture of the relative stability of commercial bank secondary reserve holdings of short-term Government securities.

Changes in commercial bank holdings of specific issues of Government securities provide an interesting insight into the investment policies of commercial banks in handling their Government securities portfolios. War-time debt management resulted in excessively liquid commercial bank portfolios at the end of the Second World War. Bank holdings of Government securities within five years of maturity were equal to 36 per cent of total loans and investments in February, 1946, and as late as June, 1951, more than five years later, such secondary reserve investments equaled no less than 31 per cent of total loans and investments. In the intervening years, however, the Treasury had offered no new marketable securities of more than five-year maturity, and if commercial banks had been passive in their portfolio management, simply rolling over maturing securities for new issues offered by the Treasury, their holdings of securities within five years of maturity would have been some $4.5 billion larger in June, 1951, than they actually were. To prevent a further shortening of their portfolio maturities in excess of any foreseeable need for liquidity, commercial banks actually shifted out of shorter term securities and into maturities beyond five years. Citing some illustrations, commercial banks purchased, net, $0.6 billion 2¼'s of September 1956–59, and

101

$0.5 billion of the 2½'s of March 1956–58. In effect, commercial banks were resisting the effect of Treasury debt management policies upon the liquidity status of their portfolios and, in the process, were providing a steady source of demand to absorb offerings of intermediate and longer-term Government securities from other investors anxious to shift into non-Government investments.

This process of avoiding unnecessary portfolio liquidity through net market purchases of longer maturities continued during the two years from June, 1951, to June, 1953. Total Treasury offerings of new securities other than bills during these two years, both cash and refunding, amounted to $69.2 billion, of which $7.0 billion were bonds bearing maturities of more than five years. In addition to subscriptions for the new bonds, commercial banks were net purchasers of nearly every issue of intermediate and longer-term outstanding securities eligible for commercial bank ownership, although the magnitude of their net market purchases was smaller than in the previous years since the war. Subsequently, during the recession and easy-money period from June, 1953, to December, 1954, the Treasury included $25.7 billion securities of more than five years initial maturity in its $88.3 billion total offerings of coupon securities, and commercial banks owned no less than $19.2 billion of these new longer maturities at the end of 1954. In spite of this assist from the Treasury in maintaining a properly balanced maturity structure in their portfolios, commercial banks also continued to be net purchasers of all issues of outstanding longer-term marketable securities and net sellers of shorter maturities; these operations included net purchases of $1.5 billion of the 2¼'s of June and December, 1959–62. As a consequence of these operations, the table shows that commercial banks successfully offset the movement of securities into shorter maturities with the passage of time; the $10 billion increase in commercial bank holdings of Government securities during this eighteen-month interval was more than accounted for by a $13 billion increase in marketable securities more than five years from maturity.

With the sustained pressure on bank reserves during the three years through 1957, the market-supporting influence of net commercial bank purchases of Government securities in the maturity range beyond five years came to an end. In fact, as the data in the table indicate, the entire $11 billion net liquidation of Government securities by commercial banks occurred in this maturity area, as holdings of shorter maturities actually increased by $3 billion. The problem of commercial bank portfolio management became one of maintaining adequate liquidity in secondary reserve positions rather than the problem of correcting or avoiding undue liquidity that had been reflected in their operations in the postwar period to this point. On balance, commercial bank operations in the market for longer Government securities were neutral; their holdings of outstanding five-year and longer issues were generally unchanged. The shortening of portfolio maturities occurred as a result of the movement of outstanding securities into a shorter maturity range with the passage of time. Actual bank selling thus was in shorter maturities, where the broader market made sales in volume possible and where the shorter term to maturity held capital losses on sales to a minimum. But the significant feature was that banks made no effort to add to longer-term holdings through market purchases to offset the automatic shortening of their portfolios. The pressure of customer loan demands and the absence of reserves to support net new credit forced steady liquidation of short-term Government securities, and the movement of intermediate issues into the short-term area provided necessary new injections of liquidity into bank portfolios.

The fact that the Treasury offered almost no longer-term issues in its cash and refunding operations during this three-year period obviously was not the only reason for the shortening of bank portfolios. In previous years when there was an inadequate supply of longer-term securities available on direct issue from the Treasury to satisfy bank portfolio requirements, commercial banks had maintained a desired portfolio structure by purchasing outstanding securities in the market. The fact that commercial banks did not add to their holdings of outstanding bonds to offset the movement of issues into the short-term area during the years 1955–57 suggests that they were concerned about maintaining adequate portfolio liquidity. It also suggests that the lack of interest on the part of commercial banks in acquiring longer-term issues was an important force preventing the Treasury from selling such issues, rather than the reverse.

A similar investment pattern appeared in the following business cycle. Banks added $6.3 billion to their Government securities portfolios during the recession and easy-money period in the first half of 1958, but the banks covered in the Treasury survey added $7.5 billion to their holdings of bonds more than five years from maturity while reducing their holdings of shorter maturities by $1.7 billion. During the ensuing two years of tight money the banks allowed their portfolios to shorten. Total holdings were reduced by $10.0 billion, while ownership of five-year and longer issues fell by $11.4 billion—nearly 60 per cent. The most liquid portfolio component, securities within one year of maturity, also was reduced by more than one-half, reflecting the pressure upon bank liquidity. It is interesting to note that in the six months of relatively easy money during the last half of 1960 banks turned first to correcting liquidity rather than adding to longer-term holdings; the entire addition to portfolios was in the under-one-year area. The lesson of 1958 had been well learned.

What then may be concluded with respect to commercial bank operations in United States Government securities and the outlook for their operations in the future? In the first place, the record since the war suggests that by 1960 the banks had corrected the unnecessarily liquid portfolios they had held at the end of the war and had by mid-1960 achieved a maturity distribution that was, if anything, a bit less liquid than required in an environment of central bank restraint on primary reserves. It might be assumed that in the future commercial banks will attempt to hold approximately the late 1960 proportion of liquid assets as a secondary reserve against deposit liabilities and to assure liquidity to provide for customer credit needs, and that, unless a volume of alternative money market instruments of equal liquidity is generated, commercial banks will continue in the future to rely upon short-term Governments for liquidity purposes. A second conclusion is that commercial bank ownership of Government securities in excess of the staggered shorter maturities intended to provide liquidity is and will continue to be a function of Federal Reserve policy. When Federal Reserve policies provide member banks with funds in excess of what are needed to meet customer credit demands, and after liquidity needs have been provided for, banks tend to invest excess funds in longer maturities (5– to 15–years) rather than build their short-term portfolios above necessary levels. On the other hand, when available reserves are less than what are needed to provide for customers, banks liquidate secondary reserve assets but, at the same time, attempt to prevent their secondary reserve portfolios falling below conservative levels by allowing intermediate and longer securities to move into the shorter maturity sector without replacement.

On the record of recent years, it would appear that commercial bank holdings of United States Government securities within five years of maturity might be expected to fluctuate in the neighborhood of 20 per cent of total loans and investments. This "normal" secondary reserve demand for short-term Governments should be expected to change gradually over time, as deposit liabilities and total assets increase, as alternative money market assets develop in volume and marketability, and as the working concept of "normal" secondary reserve needs changes. Also, the structure of Treasury debt outstanding within the five-year range—*e.g.,* the movement of large bond issues into the range—will have an effect on the maturity structures of commercial bank portfolios at any given time. Recognizing its limitations, however, a figure of 20 per cent of total loans and investments probably is a reasonably good estimate of commercial bank demand for short-term Government securities.

It is not entirely realistic—although it is analytically convenient—to draw a sharp line at the five-year maturity level between short-term secondary reserve assets and longer-term investments in commercial bank portfolios. Because of the broad and active market for United States Government securities, even bonds in the ten- to fifteen-year maturity range are more liquid, in the sense of marketability, than almost any other assets held by the typical commercial bank.[3] Therefore, the entire Government securities portfolio possesses some elements of liquidity reserve. At the same time, it is significantly easier to buy or sell shorter maturities than intermediate and longer maturities (and, of course, short-term securities provide assured liquidity at maturity), and commercial banks attempt to manage their portfolios so as to have a maturity distribution that is properly weighted at the short end.

Before concluding the analysis of commercial bank investments in Government securities, mention might be made of the alternative investment opportunities open to banks when they have funds to invest in marketable securities. Commercial banks do, of course, invest in corporate and tax-exempt securities; as of the end of 1957, commercial banks held $17.7 billion of investments other than United States Government securities, an amount about 30 per cent as large as their investments in Governments. As shown in the table, investments in securities other than United States Governments have grown somewhat relative to investments in Treasury securities during recent years, although these investments appear to respond to the same influence as do banks' portfolios in United States Government securities. Also, commercial banks hold some volume of commercial paper, bankers' acceptances, and short-term Government agency paper as part of their liquidity reserves. The total of such holdings would necessarily be small relative to short-term Government positions, although probably growing.

It may be anticipated, however, that commercial banks will

3. Commercial banks do not as a general rule invest in truly long-term securities for their own account. The "bank maturity range" extends out perhaps to ten years.

continue to rely principally upon investments in United States Government securities when they have surplus funds to invest and for their liquidity asset requirements. There are many reasons for this conclusion. First, there is no credit risk involved in Governments, and because of the active secondary market there is less money risk if liquidation before maturity should prove to be necessary. Second, most new corporate bonds carry fixed maturities of twenty- to thirty-years or longer, outside the maturity range in which bank investments are usually made; also, the market for outstanding corporate bonds is generally too thin to supply banks with bonds in volume or to absorb selling. Third, while new tax-exempt bond issues usually contain a range of maturities, and commercial banks are the principal buyers of the shorter maturities, yields on high-grade, short-term municipal bonds usually are not too much better than after-tax yields on comparable maturities of United States Government securities; moreover, the thin resale market for these obligations makes them much less liquid than Governments. Fourth, the opportunity to subscribe for new cash issues of Government securities through deposit-account credit provides an income advantage to commercial banks over other investors in the purchase of new Government securities. Fifth, the huge supply of identical or nearly identical securities in each maturity bracket enables commercial banks to work out profitable arbitrages and tax swaps in Government issues much more easily than in any other type of security.[4] In short, the United States Government debt is the largest body of uniform financial assets in existence; these assets

4. Under present tax laws (1961), commercial banks may pay a capital-gains tax on net capital gains during a tax year, but if they incur a net capital loss on securities transactions during the year, the loss may be applied against current income. The difference between the 52 per cent income tax and the 25 per cent capital gains tax makes it profitable for banks to enter into tax swaps when interest rates are high and prices depressed, for the purpose of converting book losses into realized losses that can be used to reduce current income, and then in the other phase of the cycle, when rates are low and prices high, to enter into new swaps, paying a capital gains tax on the price accretion but establishing a new book value against which losses may be taken in the future.

are traded in the most active of all financial markets, and thus they are ideally suited for the continuing money position and investment portfolio adjustments commercial banks are called upon to make. For these reasons, commercial bank investments may be expected to be concentrated in United States Government securities for the foreseeable future.

B. *Mutual Savings Banks*

During the depression decade of the 1930's, mutual savings banks shifted a large proportion of their resources into investment in United States Government securities, both because of the scarce supply of other investments and in order to minimize risk exposure. Consequently, Government securities accounted for approximately one-third of total savings bank assets by June, 1941, even before the impact of war financing was felt. This proportion had been increased to approximately two-thirds of total assets by the end of the Second World War, as shown in Table 7. Mutual savings banks continued to add to their holdings of Government securities during the first two postwar years, reflecting the still limited supply of other investment opportunities to absorb the steadily large flow of new deposit funds. Since late 1947, however, mutual savings banks have gradually but steadily reduced their portfolios of Government securities. The proceeds of this liquidation have supplemented the funds arising from a year-by-year deposit increase and have provided resources for investment in real estate mortgages and other securities, principally the former. By December, 1960, Government securities held by savings banks had been reduced to only 16 per cent of total assets.

Side by side with the reduction in Government securities portfolios, both absolutely and relative to total assets, mutual savings banks have increased their investments in shorter-term marketable Treasury issues. The table shows that these investments

1 0 8

Table 7—Assets of Mutual Savings Banks
(Billions of dollars)

End of Year	Total Loans and Investments	Loans	Other Securities	U.S. GOVERNMENTS			U.S. GOVERNMENTS AS PER CENT OF TOTAL ASSETS	
				Total	Marketable Under 5 Years	Marketable Over 5 Years	Total Governments	Marketable Under 5 Years
1941	10.4	4.9	1.8	3.7	0.6	3.1	36	6
1945	16.2	4.3	1.2	10.7	0.9	9.6	66	6
1950	21.3	8.1	2.3	10.9	0.8	9.3	51	5
1951	22.3	9.9	2.6	9.8	0.6	7.3	44	3
1952	24.0	11.3	3.2	9.4	0.5	6.7	39	2
1953	25.8	12.9	3.7	9.2	0.9	6.4	36	3
1954	27.9	15.0	4.1	8.7	0.7	6.2	31	3
1955	29.9	17.5	4.0	8.5	0.8	5.9	28	3
1956	31.9	19.8	4.2	8.0	1.3	5.0	25	4
1957	33.8	21.2	5.0	7.5	1.7	4.5	22	5
1958	36.3	23.4	5.7	7.3	1.5	4.5	20	4
1959	37.6	25.1	5.6	6.9	1.9	4.2	18	5
1960	39.1	27.1	5.8	6.2	2.0	3.9	16	5

Source: Board of Governors of the Federal Reserve System, Federal Reserve Bulletin; United States Treasury Department, Treasury Bulletin, Survey of Ownership.

have consistently accounted for roughly 3 to 5 per cent of total assets, growing as total assets have increased.

The process that has occurred, therefore, has combined a net liquidation of Government securities to provide funds for other investments and a gradual conversion of remaining holdings into a secondary liquidity reserve. While the less volatile nature of their deposit liabilities makes it unnecessary for mutual savings banks to place as much emphasis upon liquidity as do commercial banks, conservative practice requires that a portfolio of liquid investments be maintained, as a supplement to cash holdings, to provide for anticipated and unanticipated needs for cash. Short- to intermediate-term Government securities are best adapted to this secondary reserve purpose because of their risk-free character and the breadth of the market in which they are traded.

The performance of mutual savings banks in recent years leads to the conclusion, therefore, that the Treasury will continue to find a market among these institutions for short-term marketable liquidity-type securities. Although the record is not sufficiently clear to warrant too great precision in estimating the size of this market, it would appear that savings banks might continue to hold liquid United States Government securities in an amount equal to approximately five per cent of their total assets. Holdings of Treasury bills and certificates, representing the first line of secondary reserve assets, typically have been small and probably will remain at nominal levels, while holdings of notes and bonds within a few years of maturity, with holdings staggered to provide a steady flow of maturities, might be expected to increase as total deposits and assets increase. The Treasury may expect, therefore, to find a small but fairly steady demand for short-intermediate securities among the savings banks.[5]

5. For a further discussion of savings bank investment policies, see Alfred J. Cassaza, *Bank Investment Policy in a Cyclical Economy,* an address before the Savings and Mortgage Conference, the American Bankers Association, New York City, March 11, 1958, reprinted in the *Commercial and Financial Chronicle,* March 20, 1958.

The outlook for savings bank investments in longer-term Government securities is less clear. The steady reduction that has occurred in savings banks' holdings of longer-term Government securities in the fifteen years through December, 1960, has resulted not only from the declining total volume of such securities available to investors but has also reflected conscious portfolio management policy on the part of the savings banks. Mutual savings banks have regularly increased their portfolio liquidity both by the natural movement of outstanding issues toward maturity and by net sales of longer-term Treasury bonds in the market.

By and large, it may be concluded that savings banks are yield-conscious in the management of their portfolios and that they will continue to reduce their holdings of longer-term Treasury issues so long as other high-grade investments are available at significantly more attractive yields. This general conclusion with respect to savings bank investment policies does not, however, preclude the possibility of net purchases of Treasury bonds by these institutions from time to time. For example, savings banks may be willing subscribers to new issues of longer-term Treasury bonds if the yield on these bonds is sufficiently attractive against the current market and in view of expectations on future levels of interest rates to suggest that they may be sold at par, or even at a profit, if the funds should be needed for other investments.[6] Such purchases are influenced not only by investment considerations but also by the marketability of even longer-term Government bonds, so that, in a sense, these investments also are of a liquidity type. Moreover, savings banks are probably influenced by the absolute absence of credit risk on Government securities and would be willing to forego some yield advantage on other investments to hold at least a minimum portfolio of Governments. It is questionable, however, that this

6. Savings banks have purchased moderate amounts of each of the longer bond issues marketed by the Treasury during the past several years. Analysis of this development is contained in Chapter V, which discusses Treasury underwriting.

influence would justify more than a slight yield differential between Governments and high-grade corporate bonds, or that it would result in significant net demand for longer-term Governments except, perhaps, in a period of profound economic uncertainty such as the 1930's.

In one respect, United States Government policy itself undercuts the potential demand savings banks might have for risk-free United States Government bonds. Reference is to the mortgage guarantee and insurance programs of the Veterans Administration and Federal Housing Administration. While there is some risk of loss to the lender in the event of default on a VA or FHA mortgage, savings banks tend to view such mortgages as nearly the equivalent of Government bonds as regards risk. The presence of a body of these mortgages in a savings bank's portfolio unquestionably reduces the volume of Government bonds that would be held to achieve a given risk distribution in the total portfolio. Although less important, the availability of Government agency issues at yields above those on Treasury bonds has the same effect; these issues are not guaranteed by the Treasury but are considered by investors to be virtually riskless. By late 1960, savings banks held nearly 70 per cent of their assets in mortgages, of which almost one-half were Government underwritten. Also at the end of 1960 mutual savings banks owned some $470 million of nonguaranteed Government agency issues, nearly eight times their holdings of such securities six years earlier.

C. Life Insurance Companies

Investments of life insurance companies in United States Government securities have followed much the same pattern as those of the mutual savings banks. Traditionally, life insurance companies have been net purchasers of United States Government securities only when other, higher-yielding investments have not been available in sufficient size to absorb the available supply of funds, or when the yield on Governments was actually competitive with yields on other investments. After reaching 11.5 per cent of total assets in 1919, Government security holdings were steadily reduced during the 1920's, both in absolute size and relative to total assets, and by 1930 amounted to only 1.8 per cent of all life insurance assets. The reduced demand for capital funds from the private sector during the 1930's, the economic uncertainty that gave added attraction to the absence of credit risk on Government issues, and the volume of new Treasury issues to finance budget deficits resulted in a rapid growth in holdings of Government securities, so that such holdings aggregated about 20 per cent of total life insurance investments at the time of United States entry into World War II (see Table 8). During the ensuing war years, Government securities portfolios increased more rapidly than total assets and by the end of 1945 equaled 46 per cent of all life insurance company assets. The steadily large cash flow into insurance companies exceeded the availability of other investment outlets during the two years following World War II, and residual funds continued to be invested in United States Governments. Since the last half of 1947, however, investment holdings of United States Government securities by life insurance companies have been reduced almost without interruption, as total assets increased rapidly, and by the end of 1960 equaled only 5 per cent of total assets.[7]

7. The conclusions with respect to investment policies of life insurance companies and the other investor groups discussed in this chapter refer, of course, to the policies of the companies as a group. In fact, policies of individual companies differ significantly. Willis J. Winn, in *Investment of Life Insurance Funds* (Philadelphia: University of Pennsylvania Press, 1953), estimates that in 1946, when Government securities accounted for nearly one-half of all life insurance assets, some companies had only 15 per cent of total assets in this form while the ratio for other companies ran as high as two-thirds. As of the end of 1960, when the industry figure was five per cent, some life insurance companies held a considerably smaller proportion of total assets in United States Governments.

Table 8—Assets of Life Insurance Companies
(Billions of dollars)

End of Year	Total Assets	Loans, Real Estate, and Other Assets	Securities Other Than U.S. Government	U.S. GOVERNMENT			U.S. GOVERNMENTS AS PER CENT OF TOTAL ASSETS	
				Total	Marketable Under 5 Years	Marketable Over 5 Years	Total Government	Marketable Under 5 Years
1941	32.7	13.1	12.9	6.8	0.7	5.6	21	2
1945	44.8	11.2	13.0	20.6	0.7	19.7	46	2
1950	64.0	22.5	28.0	13.5	1.1	11.7	21	2
1951	68.3	26.4	30.9	11.0	0.8	6.6	16	1
1952	73.4	29.0	34.2	10.3	0.6	5.8	14	1—
1953	78.5	31.6	37.1	9.8	0.6	5.6	12	1
1954	84.5	34.9	40.5	9.1	1.0	4.5	11	1+
1955	90.4	39.1	42.8	8.6	0.6	4.7	10	1—
1956	96.0	43.4	45.1	7.6	0.5	4.0	8	1—
1957	101.3	46.6	47.7	7.0	0.7	3.5	7	1—
1958	107.6	49.2	51.2	7.2	0.7	4.0	7	1—
1959	113.7	52.4	54.4	6.9	0.6	4.1	6	1—
1960	119.7	57.0	56.3	6.4	0.6	4.0	5	1—

Source: Institute of Life Insurance and United States Treasury Department.

Since the end of the war, the maturity distribution of Government securities in life insurance portfolios has been heavily concentrated in longer-term marketable issues and (since 1951) in nonmarketable Investment Series B bonds. Relatively steady but small holdings of Treasury bills and other marketable securities within one year of maturity reflect a characteristic of life insurance companies that has a profound influence on their investment policies. This characteristic is the high degree of predictability of the cash flow. Premium payments by policy holders are, of course, on a contractual basis, as are interest and amortization receipts on existing investments, while policy claims are also highly predictable (barring a major catastrophe). Consequently, the need for liquidity reserves is minimal relative to total assets and liabilities. Cash balances are maintained at a level related to the current flow of payments and receipts, and short-term, liquid investments are held in anticipation of payments on loan commitments falling due in the near future and, to a limited degree, as a contingency reserve. The total of such investments is relatively small, as shown by the fact that the marketable Government securities within five years of maturity totaled only $0.6 billion, or 0.5 per cent of total assets, at the end of 1960. Even if nonmarketable securities are included (principally Investment Series B bonds, which are convertible into 5-year notes), total holdings of liquidity-type Government securities were less than two per cent of total assets at that time. It seems evident that the Treasury cannot rely on the life insurance companies to hold more than nominal amounts of short-term securities.

While life insurance company investments in short-term marketable United States Government securities have been relatively steady, although small in dollar amount, holdings of longer-term marketable issues have been sharply reduced since the end of World War II. Investments in marketable Treasury bonds more than five years from maturity totaled $20.2 billion in February, 1946, but only $4.0 billion in December, 1960.

115

Of the latter amount, only $0.7 billion represented new long-term bonds sold by the Treasury in recent years, while the balance consisted of residual amounts of bonds purchased by the life insurance companies during the Second World War, or bonds for which World War II issues were exchanged in the October, 1960, advance refunding. A major part of the reduction in holdings of marketable bonds occurred in 1951, when life insurance companies exchanged $3.4 billion of long-term 2½ per cent marketable bonds for 2¾ per cent nonmarketable, convertible bonds. In addition, outstanding bonds have been sold in large amounts in the market. Life insurance companies have been net sellers of all issues they had held in portfolio at the end of the war, but the policy generally followed has been to center their selling in shorter maturity bonds. This policy is further evidence of the relative lack of emphasis upon liquidity instruments in life insurance company portfolio policy. As outstanding issues move into the money market range and their prices reflect their value as liquidity investments, life insurance companies sell them.

While life insurance companies have liquidated United States Government securities, on balance, in every year since 1946, except 1958, the pace of liquidation has varied considerably, ranging from $3.3 billion in 1948 to only $0.3 to $0.5 billion in recent years. The most rapid selling occurred between the end of 1947 and April, 1951, as statements by Federal Reserve officials made it increasingly evident that the System would not continue indefinitely its policy of supporting the Government securities market. Over this 3½–year interval, life insurance companies liquidated, on balance, more than $7.0 billion of Government securities; in the nearly ten years since the Treasury-Federal Reserve "accord," through December, 1960, such liquidation totaled $6.5 billion. The more rapid rate of liquidation in the earlier period clearly was made possible by the market-support purchases of the Federal Reserve System and the Treasury and, perhaps, was stimulated by uncertainty as to how long the "pegs" on Government bonds would be maintained.[8] The less rapid liquidation under the free market conditions that have obtained since the "accord" provides one measure of the effectiveness of credit policy during that period or, in a negative sense, the advantage of not having an impotent central bank. Insurance company shifting out of United States Government securities has apparently been slowed by some reluctance to take capital losses on issues selling below par (the lock-in effect), by the more attractive market rates on Government securities, and by the physical limitation on the rate at which longer-term issues can be liquidated.[9]

The record of portfolio management of life insurance companies since the end of the Second World War and the stated policies of these companies lead to the conclusion that life insurance companies will continue to liquidate their positions in United States Government securities so long as there is an income advantage to be derived from shifting into other high-grade investments. As noted earlier in this chapter, two of the influences accounting for the fact that rates of interest on United

8. Holdings of long-term bonds were reduced by more than total holdings of Government securities during the years before the "accord" as life insurance companies sold more long bonds than was required to cover their current need for funds and reinvested the excess cash in short-term Governments as a hedge against the possibility that the pegs would be abandoned. Thus, in April, 1951, at the time the pegs were finally dropped, life insurance companies held more than $800 million of Treasury bills, a much larger amount than they have held before or since.

9. For a further discussion of life insurance company policies, 1951–1955, see: Andrew F. Brimmer, *Some Studies in Monetary Policy, Interest Rates and the Investment Behavior of Life Insurance Companies,* an unpublished doctoral dissertation presented to Harvard University, 1956, pp. 176–186. Mr. Brimmer concluded, on the basis of data through 1955, that insurance company liquidation of Governments is inversely related to interest rate movements, increasing as money becomes easy and interest rates decline (1954) and declining as interest rates rise and outstanding bonds fall to a discount (1953 and 1955). Liquidation subsequently accelerated in 1956 and 1957, however, in spite of steadily rising rates and falling prices, suggesting that insurance companies have become less reluctant to absorb capital losses when a net advantage in yield can be obtained by shifting to other investments, and net purchases were made in 1958 when other investment outlets were limited by recession.

States Government securities are lower than on other high-grade obligations are their liquidity, particularly in the sense of the marketability of short and intermediate-term issues in the active market for those maturities, and their absolute freedom from credit risk. Commercial banks are attracted to Governments principally because of their liquidity. Mutual savings banks also have some interest in Governments because of liquidity considerations, and in addition, although probably to a minor degree, they are influenced by the absence of credit risk in these securities. However, it is unlikely that either of these considerations will be of sufficient importance to life insurance companies under foreseeable circumstances to cause them to become regular net purchasers of Government securities, or to maintain their present portfolios, so long as there is an income advantage to be derived from shifting to other high-grade investments. Life insurance companies require only small holdings of liquid securities in their normal operations, and the broad portfolio diversification they are able to achieve through investments in a range of other obligations provides them with adequate protection against credit risks. One authority has stated the outlook for life insurance investment in Governments as follows:

. . . there is every reason to believe that, given a continued ample supply of private investments, the percentage invested in Governments will continue to decline. With the guaranteed feature of a substantial part of the mortgage account, the large cash flow provided by the relatively recent development of monthly amortization of mortgage loans, and heavy regular sinking fund payments on direct placements, there is less liquidity need to hold Governments than ever before. . . . in prior years of ample investment outlets, investment in U.S. Governments declined almost to the vanishing point.[10]

A major depression or war—or any development that caused private demands for long-term credit to diminish sharply—would probably bring life insurance companies into the market as

10. George T. Conklin, Jr., "A Century of Life Insurance Portfolio Management," in *Investment of Life Insurance Funds*, (Philadelphia: University of Pennsylvania Press, 1953), p. 274.

buyers of United States Governments. It also has been argued that these companies should carry a portfolio of Governments for patriotic reasons or out of concern for public opinion, but this argument is unconvincing. Finally, the Treasury might adopt an aggressive debt-management program aimed at competing with other borrowers for a significant portion of the supply of long-term funds, which would have the effect of eliminating the interest-rate differential between United States Government and other high-grade bonds. In the absence of one of these developments, it may be expected that the Government securities portfolios of life insurance companies will continue to dwindle, approaching a minimum level of one or two billion dollars of short- or intermediate-term liquidity investments.

D. Fire, Casualty, and Marine Insurance Companies

The fire, casualty, and marine insurance companies have added to their investments in United States Government securities during most years since the end of the Second World War, differing in that respect from most other investor groups. Holdings of institutions of this type included in the Treasury's Survey of Ownership nearly doubled between the end of the Second World War and December, 1954, but subsequently were reduced by the end of 1960 to a level about one-half larger than the end of the War figure.

Changes in the maturity composition of the non-life insurance companies' portfolios also tended to move against the current during the several years immediately following the war. Table 9 shows that holdings of marketable bonds more than five years from maturity were enlarged by one-third between 1945 and 1950, and then climbed back to this level in 1952 and 1953 in spite of the exchange of $0.5 billion long-term marketable bonds for nonmarketable obligations in 1951. Holdings of shorter-term

119

securities, within five years of maturity, also were increased from year to year, but between the end of 1945 and December, 1953, the growth in longer-term marketable holdings plus Investment Series B nonmarketable bonds ($1.1 billion) almost equaled the growth in less-than-five-year marketable securities ($1.3 billion). In the face of a steadily shortening Treasury debt structure, this result was achieved by net market purchases in all outstanding issues of longer-term bonds and through subscriptions to Treasury offerings of new bonds. Beginning in 1954, however, the non-life insurance companies have reduced their positions in five-year and longer maturities while maintaining their portfolios of short Government securities. The investment policies followed have included some market sales of longer-term securities, but these have been more than offset by subscriptions to new bond issues, so that the entire reduction has occurred as the result of the movement of securities into shorter maturity ranges with the passage of time.

The pattern of investment behavior indicated by Table 9 has been influenced by two characteristics of the non-life insurance companies: first, their rapid growth since the end of the Second World War; second, the size of their annual loss payments relative to their total assets. The rate of growth through 1954 provided a year-by-year increment of funds for investment in United States Government as well as other securities. However, while total portfolios of Governments increased in each year between 1945 and 1954, the relative size of Government portfolios in total assets had begun to decline by 1950 and has been reduced in each succeeding year. The declining rate of growth since 1954 has apparently caused the non-life insurance companies to sell or redeem securities from their Government holdings in order to continue a program of commitments in higher-yielding loans and securities other than United States Governments, principally the latter. Thus, while the increase in holdings of Government securities by these companies since the end of the war reverses the experience of most other investing institutions, the evidence suggests that in the case of the non-life insurance companies, as

120

Table 9—Assets of Fire, Casualty, and Marine Insurance Companies
(Billions of dollars)

End of Year	Total Assets	Loans and Other Assets	Securities Other Than U.S. Government	U.S. GOVERNMENTS			U.S. GOVERNMENT AS PER CENT OF TOTAL ASSETS	
				Total	Marketable Under 5 Years	Marketable Over 5 Years	Total Government	Marketable Under 5 Years
1945	7.8	1.3	3.1	3.3	0.8	1.9	42	10
1950	13.3	2.5	5.5	5.4	1.4	2.7	41	11
1951	14.5	2.7	6.3	5.5	1.8	2.2	38	12
1952	16.2	3.0	7.4	5.9	1.9	2.5	36	12
1953	17.6	3.2	8.4	6.1	2.1	2.5	35	12
1954	20.2	3.3	10.7	6.2	2.4	2.3	31	12
1955	22.0	3.5	12.5	6.1	2.4	2.1	28	11
1956	22.9	3.6	13.5	5.8	2.7	1.6	25	12
1957	23.3	3.6	14.2	5.5	2.6	1.4	24	11
1958	26.0	4.1	16.4	5.5	2.5	1.7	24	10
1959	28.0	4.3	18.0	5.7	2.7	1.8	22	10
1960	29.6*	4.5*	19.5*	5.6	2.8	1.6	20	10

* Derived from estimates by Bankers Trust Company, The Investment Outlook for 1961.

Source: Best and Company, Aggregates and Averages, and United States Treasury Department.

Note: The Treasury Survey of Ownership does not cover all of the firms included in the Aggregates and Averages series, so that the breakdown of Government securities by maturity (from the Treasury Survey) is not fully comparable with the data for total holdings of U.S. Governments (from Aggregates and Averages). Also, the breakdown by maturity does not include nonmarketable bonds.

in the case of the commercial banks, mutual savings banks and life insurance companies, the portfolio of intermediate and longer-term Government securities is something of a marginal investment, to be drawn upon to supply other demands for credit when there is an income advantage in so doing.

At the same time, the size of the loss claims paid by these insurance companies each year, and the actual and potential variability of these claims, make it mandatory that rather large liquidity reserve portfolios be maintained. The fact that such reserves are maintained is suggested in the table by the remarkably constant relationship that holdings of shorter-term marketable Government securities have borne to total assets over the postwar years. As shown in Table 9, this ratio has been held nearly all of the time in a 10 to 12 per cent range; holdings of marketable Government securities maturing in more than five years, meanwhile, have moved down from 19 per cent of total assets in 1950 to 5 per cent in 1960 (the immediate postwar years, when such holdings were even more than 19 per cent, were omitted in this comparison).

While the individual companies included in the fire, casualty, and marine insurance group vary so significantly in risk coverage and portfolio policies as to make broad generalization decidedly hazardous, the data for the group as a whole strongly suggest a pattern of investment behavior. It appears likely that these companies might add to their holdings of short-term marketable Government securities, over a period of time, in amounts sufficient to maintain liquidity reserves in this form equal to at least 10 per cent of total assets. Their portfolios of longer-term (more than five years to maturity) Governments had been reduced to 5 per cent of total assets by the end of 1960, and there is no evidence to indicate that the process of liquidating these portfolios will be reversed. It should be noted, however, that Treasury bonds of longer maturity than five years are relatively liquid by comparison with most other securities, and a steeply sloped yield curve might induce some movement of funds out of the short-term area and into intermediate bonds on the calculated risk that the assured larger return on such investment would more than compensate for the possible danger that they might have to be liquidated before they had moved into a short-term range where their coupon would enable them to trade close to par on a money basis. Another element of portfolio planning in this regard is the treatment of nonmarketable bonds, not covered in the preceding discussion. These bonds, which are redeemable or convertible into five-year notes on one-month notice, must be judged a second line of liquidity reserve. As they are eliminated from non-life insurance company holdings, it is likely that they will be replaced in large part with short-term marketable securities, but it is possible that properly liquid portfolios will be achieved by moving part of the funds into slightly longer maturity bonds. On balance, however, it appears likely that future demand from these insurance companies for Government securities will be confined largely to shorter-term liquidity instruments.

E. Savings and Loan Associations

Among the major groups of savings-type financial institutions, savings and loan associations have grown most rapidly in the postwar period. Between December, 1945, and December, 1960, their total assets increased from $8.7 billion to $71.5 billion, or by more than seven times (see Table 10). Traditionally, savings and loan associations have specialized in residential mortgage loans, and prior to the Second World War their holdings of United States Government securities had been insignificant. With the virtual disappearance of new private residential mortgages during the war years, however, savings and loan associations invested in Government securities, and by the end of 1945 their holdings totaled $2.4 billion, equal to 28 per cent of total assets. These securities were quickly sold in the immediate postwar years, and by 1948 Government securities portfolios had been reduced to $1.5 billion. From that date to the present, invest-ments in United States Government securities have been in-creased gradually from year to year, approximately in step with the growth in total assets and share capital, and by December, 1960, savings and loan associations held $4.6 billion of Govern-ments. The ratio of Governments to total assets has held in a range of 6 to 7 per cent during the eight years 1953 to 1960, inclusive.

Table 10—Assets of Savings and Loan Associations
(Billions of dollars)

End of Year	Total Assets	Mortgage Loans	U.S. Govt. Securities	Cash and Other Assets	U.S. Government as Per Cent of Total Assets
1941	6.0	4.8	0.1	1.1	2
1945	8.7	5.5	2.4	0.8	28
1950	16.9	13.7	1.5	1.7	9
1951	19.2	15.7	1.6	2.0	8
1952	22.7	18.5	1.8	2.4	8
1953	26.7	22.0	1.9	2.8	7
1954	31.7	26.3	2.0	3.4	6
1955	37.7	31.5	2.3	3.9	6
1956	42.9	35.7	2.8	4.3	7
1957	48.1	40.0	3.2	4.9	7
1958	55.1	45.6	3.8	5.7	7
1959	63.5	53.2	4.5	5.9	7
1960	71.5	60.1	4.6	6.8	6

Source: Federal Savings and Loan Insurance Corporation data.

Federal savings and loan associations affiliated with the Federal Home Loan Bank System are required to maintain a liquidity position in cash and/or United States Government securities equal to 6 per cent of share capital; in recent years this liquidity reserve has averaged between 10 and 11 per cent.[11] Thus, while the motive for holding United States Govern-ment securities is undoubtedly to provide a liquidity offset to the highly illiquid mortgages that constitute much the largest part of the portfolios, the present holdings—in combination with

11. The Home Bank Board may set this liquidity requirement between 4 and 8 per cent.

cash—have averaged well above legal requirements. At the same time, the available data suggest that the maturity distribution of the Government securities portfolio is such as to make it of dubious value as a liquidity reserve. Among the savings and loan associations included in the Treasury's Survey of Ownership (which account for approximately 60 per cent of all holdings of Government securities by savings and loan associations) only 45 per cent of their investments in marketable Governments was within five years of maturity in early 1961.

From the point of view of Treasury debt management, it apparently may be concluded that savings and loan associations will continue to add to their Government securities portfolios by small annual increments, approximately in step with the growth in share capital. While these investments are ostensibly to serve the purpose of a liquidity reserve, it is likely that savings and loan associations will as willingly buy bonds in the intermediate or longer maturity range as short-term securities if a better rate of return may be obtained on the bonds. This emphasis upon yield rather than liquidity raises troublesome questions about the stability of the industry, but for the purposes of this study its only significance is the potential continuing demand for intermediate and longer-term Treasury securities it indicates.[12]

F. Pension Trust Funds

The strong drive toward income security that developed in the late 1930's and that has been so prominent in the postwar years is reflected in the growing importance of pension trust funds in the investment markets. Part of the funds represented by this development are included in the rapid growth of life insurance

12. For an analysis of investment practices of the Savings and Loan Associations see: Robert Van Cleave, *Government Securities in Your Liquidity Position,* an address before the National Savings and Loan League, Cleveland, Ohio, May 23, 1955; available from C. F. Childs and Co., New York.

company assets discussed earlier,[13] and another part will be reviewed in the discussion of Treasury trust funds. Tables 11 and 12 review the postwar portfolio growth of two other pension trust groups, corporate pension trust funds (excluding plans administered by insurance companies), and state and local government pension trust funds. Comprehensive data for these funds are available only for recent years, but the incomplete data for earlier years suggest that they were relatively unimportant prior to World War II. As Tables 11 and 12 show, their combined assets have grown from about $11 billion in 1950 to $48 billion at the end of 1960, or by more than 300 per cent. During these ten years, the combined annual growth in total assets has averaged $3.7 billion and has been at an average annual rate of 19 per cent.[14]

Corporate pension trust funds are usually administered by a commercial bank designated by the employing corporation under by-laws or regulations that specify the types and quality of securities that may be purchased for the investment portfolio. Common stock has grown in relative importance in the total portfolios during recent years, but the administration of the funds is generally conservative and places more emphasis on the soundness and quality of the portfolio than upon achieving maximum return.[15] Liquidity is of relatively minor importance in arranging the composition of corporate pension trust portfolios, and investment decisions ordinarily reflect a balance between credit risk

13. At the close of 1960, private pension plans in force with life insurance companies had total reserves of $19 billion, up 240 per cent from 1950. The growth in these reserves between 1950 and 1960 accounted for 24 per cent of the total growth in assets of life insurance companies. Institute of Life Insurance, *Life Insurance Fact Book, 1961,* p. 37.

14. Goldsmith estimates that between 1929 and 1952 the total assets of noninsured private pension funds grew by 18 times and of state and local government trust funds by nearly 15 times. Raymond W. Goldsmith, *Financial Intermediaries in the American Economy Since 1900,* National Bureau of Economic Research (Princeton, N.J.: Princeton University Press, 1958), pp. 371, 373.

15. *Cf.* Roger F. Murray, "Fresh Look at Pension Funds," *Trusts and Estates,* November, 1955, p. 944.

Table 11—Assets of Corporate Pension Trust Funds*
(Billions of dollars)

End of Year	Total Assets	Corporate Securities	Other Assets	UNITED STATES GOVERNMENT SECURITIES				Governments as Per Cent of Total Assets
				Total	Marketable Bonds	Others Marketable	Non-marketable	
1939	1.0	0.4	0.2	0.4	n.a.†	n.a.	n.a.	40
1945	2.7	0.9	0.2	1.5	n.a.	n.a.	n.a.	55
1950	5.4	2.9	0.4	2.1	1.0	0.1	0.6	39
1951	6.9	4.2	0.5	2.2	0.7	0.1	1.0	32
1952	8.5	5.8	0.5	2.2	0.6	0.2	1.0	26
1953	10.2	7.2	0.7	2.3	0.8	0.2	1.0	22
1954	12.2	9.1	0.8	2.3	0.8	0.2	1.1	19
1955	14.2	10.7	1.0	2.5	1.0	0.2	1.1	18
1956	16.6	13.1	1.3	2.3	1.0	0.3	0.7	14
1957	19.3	15.7	1.6	2.0	1.0	0.5	0.5	11
1958	22.1	18.3	1.8	2.0	1.0	0.5	0.4	10
1959	25.3	20.9	2.3	2.1	1.0	0.8	0.2	9
1960	28.7	24.1	2.6	2.0	0.9	0.8	0.2	8

* Excludes pension plans placed with insurance companies.
† n.a. Not available.
Source: Securities and Exchange Commission, *Uninsured Pension Plans, 1952–1957*. Data for earlier years compiled and estimated by Wesley C. Lindow, Irving Trust Company, New York, from various sources. Breakdown of Government securities by types from United States Treasury Department, *Survey of Ownership* for years covered; Treasurey Survey includes somewhat smaller sample, so components do not necessarily add to totals.

Table 12—Assets of State and Local Government Retirement Funds
(Billions of dollars)

End of Year	Total Assets	U.S. Government Bonds	State and Local Government Securities	Other Investments	U.S. Governments as Per Cent of Total Assets
1949	4.9	2.4	1.5	0.5	49
1950	5.6	2.7	1.7	0.7	48
1951	6.4	3.2	1.8	1.0	50
1952	7.3	3.6	1.9	1.4	49
1953	8.2	4.0	2.1	1.8	49
1954	9.3	4.3	2.4	2.4	46
1955	10.5	4.6	2.7	3.1	44
1956	11.8	4.9	3.1	3.7	41
1957	13.3	5.3	3.5	4.4	40
1958	15.0	5.5	4.0	5.4	36
1959	16.9	6.0	4.4	6.4	36
1960	18.5	6.0	4.3	8.0	32

Source: Governmental Finances, Bureau of the Census; Finances of Employee-Retirement Systems of State and Local Governments, Bureau of the Census.

and yield considerations. As a general rule, the fund management is not required to hold United States Government securities, although such obligations may be included in the portfolio either to provide a marginal element of liquidity or to achieve a balanced risk structure.[16]

Government securities represented an estimated 55 per cent of total corporate pension trust fund assets at the end of the Second World War, but this ratio has declined steadily since the war and by December, 1960, such investments were only 7 per cent of total assets. The relative reduction in the importance of United States Government securities resulted from the diversion of new funds into other types of investments rather than from net liquidation of Government securities. Thus, between 1950 and 1960 the investment of corporate pension funds in Government securities remained almost unchanged, as shown in the

16. State and national banks in New York State were trustees for 1,024 pension trust funds in 1955. Of these funds, 627 were subject to no general restrictions as to investments and only 19 were restricted to U.S. Government issues (the remainder had various limitations). Source: New York State Banking Department, *Pension and Other Employee Welfare Plans*, 1955, Table 27.

128

table, while investments in corporate securities and other assets were increased from $3.3 billion to $26.7 billion. Within the Government securities portfolio, there was a pronounced shift out of nonmarketable F and G bonds and Investment Series B bonds into marketable securities from 1955 to the present. This shift was fostered by the relatively low rates of interest on Savings bonds relative to market rates and by profitable swap opportunities out of investment series bonds. Part of the funds derived from this switch went into Treasury bills and other short-term securities, suggesting that the Savings bonds had in some cases been a liquidity reserve, and some went into long-term marketable Treasury bonds. The detailed statistics of holdings by issue suggest that the corporate pension funds in managing their Government bond portfolios have subscribed to new Treasury bond issues but have made room in their portfolios for these subscriptions by selling other longer-term Treasury bonds.

In summary, the evidence suggests that corporate pension trust funds feel some attraction to United States Government securities, partly for liquidity purposes, but principally for the purpose of maintaining a risk-free component in the investment portfolio. While the statistics support the conclusion that longer-term Government securities will continue to have a place in corporate pension fund portfolios, they do not suggest however, that these funds will be net purchasers of Government securities in the future if recent interest-rate relationships are maintained. In fact, if the pattern of recent years continues, the evidence suggests that a relatively steady position in Government securities might come increasingly to be considered a liquidity reserve against the growing body of other assets rather than as a part of the longer-term investment portfolio.

The investment practices of the state and local government pension funds are controlled by the laws or regulations of the governmental unit that has established the pension system. Until recent years, the majority of these pension funds were restricted in their investments to United States Government securities and the securities of state or local governments (frequently of the state and/or municipality maintaining the fund).[17] It is estimated that these public pension funds had only ten per cent of their total assets in the form of corporate securities at the end of 1950, while United States Government securities accounted for nearly 50 per cent and state and local government securities 30 per cent. Subsequently, however, the regulations controlling the investments of many of these pension funds have been amended to permit the purchase of high-grade corporate bonds and, in some cases, equities and mortgages, and an increasing proportion of net new funds has been channelled into these investments. By December, 1960, the relative share of United States Government securities in total state and local pension fund assets had been reduced to about one-third and of other government securities to one-fourth, while corporate security holdings had increased to about two-fifths. Between 1949 and 1960, 55 per cent of the net increase in assets went into corporate securities, 27 per cent into United States Governments, and 21 per cent into other governments.

In appraising the investment practices of the state and local pension funds with a view to determining the prospective demand for Government securities, the most important fact to keep in mind is that the regulations governing investments of these funds have been in a transitional phase for some years. The direction of change is toward broadening the range of securities eligible for investment so as to increase the income potential. In almost all cases, the liberalizing provisions have had the effect of reducing the demand for United States Government securities. This movement has been somewhat more rapid at the state level than at the city level, although the effect on investment portfolios has been in the same direction in both cases. It is interesting to note that among the ten most populous states, only one (Indiana) was

17. As late as 1956, nearly one-half of all state-administered retirement systems were thus restricted. By 1960, only one-fifth of all state retirement funds had similar restrictions.

included in the fifteen states in 1960 holding more than 60 per cent of employee pension fund investments in United States Government securities. Similarly, among the five largest cities only Philadelphia held more than 60 per cent in United States Governments. It may be concluded that needlessly restrictive limitations on public pension fund investments have died most slowly in the smaller states and municipalities, where a lower degree of investment sophistication might be expected.[18]

The rapid rate of growth in the total assets of state and local government pension funds has made it possible to channel an increasing proportion of new funds into corporate securities while continuing to purchase, net, about $0.4 billion of United States Government securities nearly every year. That is to say, although United States Government securities have declined steadily in relative importance in the investment portfolios of the state and local pension funds, the absolute net volume of purchases of Government securities has held relatively steady. If the recent movement toward broadening the investment authorization of these pension funds should continue, however, as it probably will, it might be anticipated that net purchases of United States Government securities will tend to decline and purchases of corporate bonds to accelerate further (this conclusion assumes the continuation of an income advantage of corporate bonds over Treasury bonds).

On the available evidence it may be concluded that state and local government pension funds will continue to be net buyers of United States Government securities, although perhaps at a dwindling rate. Since the bulk of this investment very probably will be in longer-term maturities,[19] the Treasury may conclude that, for at least the next few years, there will be an annual demand from these institutions for $400 million or so of Treas-

18. This conclusion is generally accurate, but the diversity of behavior among states and communities of all sizes is so pronounced that the differences between units of various sizes are not as significant as might be expected.

19. A maturity breakdown of these holdings is not available.

ury bonds. The demand reflects a "captive market," however, based on institutional arrangements rather than objective investment considerations, and it is thus an essentially unstable source of demand for Treasury securities.

G. Nonfinancial Corporations

Investments by nonfinancial corporations in United States Government securities represent, principally, the temporary employment of funds scheduled for specific expenditures in the near future. Cash reserves accumulated for the payment of Federal income taxes, for dividend payments, and for other near-term cash needs, along with seasonal excess funds that will be needed in the business at the season of peak operations, account for the bulk of corporate investments in United States Government obligations. Consequently, almost all corporate holdings of Government securities are Treasury bills, certificates of indebtedness, or other marketable issues within one or two years of maturity. At the end of 1960, the 497 large corporations in the Treasury's *Survey of Ownership* owned $10.7 billion marketable Governments, of which $8.3 billion were within one year of maturity and only $1.2 billion had more than two years to run to maturity. Nonbank corporations do not customarily hold nonmarketable Government securities, except that during and following the Second World War they owned the greater part of the Savings notes which the Treasury had designed explicitly for corporate investment; the last of these notes was retired in 1955.

Table 13 traces the course of corporate investments in United States Government securities and of other, related components of corporate balance sheets since 1946. Semi-annual data were used for the years since 1950 because of the wide seasonal swings in Government securities holdings and Federal tax liabil-

Table 13—Current Assets and Liabilities of United States Corporations*
(Billions of dollars)

End of Period	CURRENT ASSETS			CURRENT LIABILITIES		RATIOS (Per Cent)		
	Total	Cash	U.S. Governments	Total	Federal Tax	U.S. Governments to Total Current Assets	Cash and Governments to Total Current Assets	U.S. Governments to Federal Tax Liability
	(1)	(2)	(3)	(4)	(5)	(6)	(7)	(8)
1946 March	96.4	21.6	19.8	44.6	9.3	21	43	213
December	108.1	22.8	15.3	51.9	8.5	14	35	180
1947 December	123.6	25.0	14.1	61.5	10.7	11	32	132
1948 December	133.0	25.3	14.8	64.4	11.5	11	30	129
1949 December	133.1	26.5	16.8	60.7	9.3	13	32	181
1950 June	141.7	26.8	18.4	64.0	10.8	13	32	170
December	161.5	28.1	19.7	79.8	16.7	12	29	118
1951 June	171.1	28.4	20.1	85.1	18.4	12	28	109
December	179.1	30.0	20.7	92.6	21.3	12	28	97
1952 June	176.7	30.0	18.8	87.9	17.3	11	28	109
December	186.2	30.8	19.9	96.1	18.1	11	27	110
1953 June	186.8	30.0	18.7	94.3	15.8	10	26	118
December	190.6	31.1	21.5	98.9	18.7	11	28	115
1954 June	180.7	29.4	16.9	87.1	11.7	9	26	144
December	194.6	33.4	19.2	102.8	15.5	10	27	124
1955 June	197.5	32.5	18.7	101.1	12.0	9	26	156
December	214.6	34.0	23.3	115.7	18.4	11	27	127
1956 June	214.7	32.1	17.4	112.1	12.3	8	23	141
December	225.7	34.7	18.6	121.3	16.8	8	24	111
1957 June	224.5	32.5	15.7	117.6	12.2	7	21	129
December	228.9	34.1	16.9	120.6	15.0	7	22	113
1958 June	232.9	34.2	13.9	117.9	9.8	6	21	142
December	255.3	37.4	18.8	136.6	12.9	7	22	146
1959 June	254.8	35.6	20.0	129.3	13.7	8	22	146
December	278.7	37.2	22.6	151.2	15.3	8	21	148
1960 June	283.0	34.6	20.7	152.9	12.9	7	20	160
December	287.4	37.0	19.7	154.9	13.8	7	20	144

*All United States corporations except banks and insurance companies.
Source: Securities and Exchange Commission.

ities over this period. Beginning in 1950, under the so-called "Mills plan" for corporate tax payment, tax payments have been accelerated, with the result that more than 50 per cent of all corporate taxes have been payable in the first half of each calendar year. A pattern of 25 per cent payments in each quarter had been re-established by calendar 1960, but the law permits underestimation of tax liabilities in the September and December payments, so that payments are still concentrated in March and June.

The third and fifth columns of Table 13 indicate the effect that this transitional process has had upon corporate holdings of Government securities and tax liabilities at half-year dates. The most important aspect of the transition, however, in terms of the effects it will have upon the demand for Government securities, is the fact that beginning in 1960 corporate tax liabilities will at no time equal more than three-fourths of the annual tax liability, whereas prior to 1951 corporate tax liabilities at all times ranged between four and five quarters total.[20] Column eight shows that in the last several years there has generally been a close correlation between tax liabilities and Government securities owned, so that the reduction in average tax liabilities might be expected to be reflected in a commensurate reduction in Government security holdings. Corporate profits may be expected to grow secularly, offsetting the influence of the change in the corporate tax payment schedule, but it would be necessary for profits to exceed $60 billion under the new schedule to generate the same demand for Government securi-

20. For example, under the new, accelerated program a corporation just before a quarterly tax date will owe taxes for the three previous quarters, and just after the tax date it will still owe taxes on its profits for the two preceding quarters. Under the old—pre–1950—schedule, a corporation just before a quarterly tax date owed taxes on profits for the five preceding quarters and just after the tax date still owed taxes on profits earned in the four preceding quarters. Therefore, average corporate tax liabilities will have been reduced by 40 to 50 per cent under the accelerated corporate tax payment arrangement, and the need to carry Government securities as reserve for these liabilities will have been reduced proportionately.

ties.[21] Of course, the growth over time in dividend reserves and similar appropriations of cash for specific purposes will also create a demand for Government securities.

In spite of the effects of the shifting tax payment schedule and of other influences, such as the competition from short-term agency issues, the weight of the evidence suggests that non-financial corporations will tend to add to their holdings of short-term Government securities over time. It is to be expected that corporate profits (and thus tax liabilities), dividends, and other cash accruals available for short-term investment will increase secularly, and that the growth of other money-market instruments will not be sufficiently rapid to prevent the channeling of at least some of these liquid resources into the Government securities market. The outlook, therefore, appears to be for a gradual increase in corporate demand for short-term Government securities over the years ahead.

H. State and Local Governments and Foreign Accounts

The investment positions summarized in the following table consist largely of governmental or official funds. In the case of state and local governments, the data have been adjusted to exclude estimated investments of pension and retirement trust funds and represent principally, therefore, temporary investments of working balances, funds already allocated for construction or other specific projects, and similar short-term cash balances in excess of immediate expenditures. In the case of the

21. The approach taken here views the matter wholly from the point of view of debt management. Logically, the acceleration of corporate tax payments that reduced outstanding tax liabilities should, all else equal, have provided the funds for a corresponding reduction in the debt. The logic of this case, however, provides cold comfort to the debt manager who nonetheless has a deficit to finance.

foreign and international accounts, much the largest part of the holdings of United States Government securities represents investments by official institutions and central banks of foreign dollar reserve balances. The bulk of the investments in both categories, therefore, is very likely in shorter-term securities; the logic of the case suggests that even the bonds and notes owned by foreign accounts, shown in Table 14, are largely shorter-maturity obligations.

Table 14—Ownership of United States Government Securities by State and Local Governments, Foreign Accounts, and International Agencies*
(Billions of dollars)

End of Year	Grand Total	State and Local Governments	FOREIGN AND INTERNATIONAL ACCOUNTS		
			Total	Bills and Certificates	Notes and Bonds
1945	n.a.†	n.a.	n.a.	1.8	n.a.
1950	9.2	6.1	3.1	1.5	1.6
1951	9.4	6.4	3.0	2.1	0.9
1952	11.6	7.6	4.0	2.8	1.2
1953	13.5	8.8	4.7	3.6	1.1
1954	15.2	10.2	5.0	3.9	1.1
1955	16.6	10.6	6.1	4.5	1.6
1956	17.9	11.3	6.6	5.1	1.5
1957	18.7	11.8	6.9	5.5	1.4
1958	18.2	11.2	7.0	5.5	1.5
1959	21.5	11.8	9.7	7.5	2.2
1960	20.6	10.7	9.9	7.6	2.3

* Excludes specal non-interest-bearing notes held by the International Monetary Fund and the International Development Association. Also, state and local holdings adjusted to exclude estimated investments by state and local government pension funds.
† n.a. Not available.
Source: Board of Governors of the Federal Reserve System for foreign and international accounts and U.S. Treasury Department, Survey of Ownership for state and local governments.

Between 1950 and 1960, state and local government holdings of United States Government securities increased by $5.6 billion, or 90 per cent. Over the same time span, expenditures for goods and services by these governmental units grew by about 140 per cent, construction expenditures of state and local governments expanded by roughly 115 per cent, and annual sales of new tax-exempt securities were increased by nearly 100 per cent.[22] The funds that state and local governments have for investment in United States Government securities, at any given time, are in large part their combined temporary surpluses of tax and other regular receipts over current expenditure needs, which results from the uneven spacing of tax receipts over the year, and the proceeds of bond issues for construction or other purposes that have not yet been spent. The level of holdings of United States Government securities by state and local governments, therefore, might be considered a function of the gross level of receipts and expenditures and the level of state and local construction activity. If both factors should tend to increase secularly, it should follow that state and local investments in Treasury securities also will continue to grow, though not necessarily at the rate of recent years. Such holdings would be concentrated in securities of less than five years maturity.

The growth in foreign and international account investments in United States Government securities since 1950 is a direct reflection of the general improvement in the international reserves of most foreign countries. So long as dollars continue to be the principal international currency and dollar balances, or their equivalent, are considered identical with gold in foreign reserves, the leading Western nations probably will continue to carry a sizable portion of their reserves in the form of investments in United States Government securities. There are no acceptable grounds for prediction of future changes in the size of these holdings, however, since they are a by-product of a range of possible developments and policy decisions that could at any time move them in either direction. It is likely, however, that foreign investments in United States Government securities are potentially more volatile on the "down" side than the "up" side. Deterioration in the balance of payments of the rest of the world vis-à-vis the United States, fear of a devaluation of the dollar in terms of gold, war jitters, or a range of other possible developments could, in a relatively brief time, lead to a sizable

22. Board of Governors of the Federal Reserve System, Flow of Funds Accounts.

1 3 7

shift from dollar securities into gold. In short, it would be difficult for the Treasury to include these accounts as either a plus or minus factor in estimating potential demand for United States Government securities in the next few years.

I. Individuals

Participation by individual citizens in the ownership of the public debt received strong impetus from the financing policies pursued by the Treasury during the Second World War. As shown in Table 15, the emphasis upon sales of Savings bonds and other securities to individual investors as a means of closing the "inflationary gap" resulted in a 500 per cent increase in such holdings, from about $10 billion to more than $60 billion. Combined cash sales of Savings bonds of all types continued to exceed cash redemptions through calendar 1950, but beginning with 1951 cash sales have fallen short of cash redemptions. The redemption value of all Savings bonds outstanding held reasonably steady through 1955, however, as accrued discounts offset the excess of cash redemptions over cash sales. Since 1955, the more attractive rates of interest on competing forms of saving and investment and the Treasury's abandonment of all but the E and H series have caused sales of United States Government Savings bonds to decline and redemptions to rise, and by the end of 1960 the total redemption value of all Savings bonds outstanding had fallen roughly $10.8 billion from the $58 billion peak maintained from 1950 through 1955.

Investments of individuals in United States Government Savings bonds are concentrated in the Series E and H bonds. The redemption value of these bonds held by individuals has continued to grow, albeit at a very slow pace, through 1960. Cash sales of Series E bonds have consistently been below cash redemptions, but the accrued interest on E bonds and small net sales of Series H bonds have been sufficient to lift the redemp-

138

Table 15—Liquid Assets of Individuals in the United States
(Billions of dollars)

End of Year	LIQUID ASSETS			U.S. Governments as Per Cent of Total	CLASSIFICATION OF GOVERNMENT SECURITIES		
	Total	U.S. Government Securities	Other*		A-E and H Savings Bonds	F, G, J, K Savings Bonds	Other, Mostly Marketable
1940	62	10	52	16	3	—	8
1945	188	63	125	34	34	9	21
1950	212	67	145	32	34	15	17
1951	219	66	153	30	35	14	16
1952	229	66	163	29	35	14	16
1953	238	66	171	28	37	13	15
1954	246	65	181	27	38	12	13
1955	257	67	190	26	40	10	15
1956	268	68	200	25	41	9	16
1957	280	69	211	25	42	7	15
1958	292	67	225	23	43	5	15
1959	310	74	236	24	42	4	23
1960	322	74	248	23	43	3	21

*Includes currency, deposits, and savings and loan shares.
Source: Liquid assets from Securities and Exchange Commission data. Breakdown of Government securities holdings from U.S. Treasury Department, Survey of Ownership.
Note: Data on liquid asset holdings and classification of Governmnt securities are estimated independently and employ different definitions. Therefore, totals of Government securities held by individuals are not equal in the two estimates.

tion value of outstanding bonds by $3.1 billion between the end of 1955 and the end of 1960. This performance of the Government Savings bonds designed for individuals, in the face of the sharp run-up in rates of interest on competing outlets for savings, is impressive evidence of the extent to which the Savings bond program has become, in a sense, a part of the savings habits of smaller savers. The record of the past ten years of freely moving market rates of interest shows that net sales of E and H Savings bonds have responded to movements in the rate of return on competitive investments, but this response has tended to be marginal, and the great body of Savings bonds outstanding has not been disturbed.[23] The apparent conclusion for Treasury debt management is that the automaticity of the Payroll Savings Plan and such other attractions as the privilege of deferring the declaration of interest income until maturity should, on average over the years, provide at least enough new cash sales of E and H bonds to hold the total outstanding constant and, probably, provide for a slow secular increase. The deferral of income reporting could, in fact, become an important incentive for larger sales if the savings institutions should be required to withhold taxes on interest income.

Individual investors have also held large amounts of F, G, J, and K Savings bonds since the Second World War, typically accounting for about 60 per cent of all such bonds outstanding. These bonds have been held by larger investors who are more

23. Rates of interest to maturity on E and H bonds have been changed from time to time in response to movements of market rates—from 2.90 to 3 per cent in 1952, from 3 to 3¼ per cent in April, 1957, and from 3¼ to 3¾ per cent in 1959. It is interesting to note, however, that net cash redemptions during the two quarters preceding the rate change in April, 1957, totaled only $52 million and $220 million, respectively, while net cash redemptions in the two quarters following the change totaled $247 million and $288 million. Moreover, much of the fall-off in sales during the quarter just preceding the change could be attributed to the publicity given the proposed change. This evidence seems to suggest that buyers of E and H savings bonds are not sensitive to small rate differentials and that it might have been better in 1957 not to have "rocked the boat" by calling their attention to the existence of the differential.

sensitive to rate differentials and, as a result, redemptions began to exceed sales at about the time of the Treasury-Federal Reserve "accord" in 1951, as market rates of interest rose. The rate of net redemptions snowballed during 1955 and 1956, when big war-time issues of F and G bonds matured and sales of J and K bonds fell far short of replacing these maturities. Consequently, the Treasury withdrew the Series J and K bonds from sale in early 1957, and the total outstanding will continue to decline as bonds mature or are redeemed. By the end of 1960, estimated holdings of individual investors had been reduced to $2.7 billion from the peak of $15.1 billion in December, 1950. As the remaining F, G, J, and K bonds held by individuals mature or are redeemed, it is unlikely that a significant portion of the proceeds will be reinvested in Series E and H bonds, both because of the likelihood of more attractive rates of interest on other investments and because of the size limitation on investments in E and H bonds. The run-off of these bonds will, in all probability, continue to result in a net decline in individual holdings of Treasury Savings bonds during the next few years unless net sales of E and H bonds expand more rapidly than the record of the past several years would suggest.

Only fragmentary data are available on the distribution of marketable Treasury securities among individual investors. As Table 15 shows, it is estimated that such investments reached a peak in the neighborhood of $21 billion at the end of World War II, fell to about $13 billion by 1954, and since have climbed back to about $21 billion by the end of 1960. The fact that individual holdings of marketable Treasury securities have grown substantially since 1954, while holdings of F, G, J, and K bonds have been reduced, suggests that a large part of the funds withdrawn from Savings bonds went into other Treasury issues. To the extent that this has occurred, it is indicated that the investors involved were primarily guided by credit risk considerations rather than yield in making their investment decisions. However, yield considerations clearly were behind the large increase in 1959, when rates of interest on marketable Governments—particularly an issue of 5 per cent notes—exerted a strong pull on individual investors.

On balance, it would appear likely that growth in individual holdings of marketable United States Government securities will continue to absorb part of the run-off of F, G, J, and K bonds. This conclusion rests partly on the conservative investment practices of personal trust accounts, which loom so large in total individual holdings of Government securities. It also rests on the attractiveness of longer-term marketable Government bonds, when they are selling at a discount from par, for estate purposes. All of the long-term 2½ per cent bonds sold during the Second World War Loan drives, as well as the long-term issues marketed in recent years, contain a provision that they shall be optionally redeemable at par and accrued interest for payment of estate taxes upon death of the owner if they are included in his estate. The importance of this provision is apparent when it is considered that most of the 2½'s and the 3's traded at discounts of 10 to 15 points during much of the third quarter of 1961. In planning the estate of an elderly or critically ill person, these United States Government bonds promised a more attractive yield than any alternative investment. Part of the increase in individuals' holdings of marketable Government securities in recent years, as prices of long bonds have fallen far below par, undoubtedly has been due to this provision, and a similar response may confidently be expected in the future when prices decline.

J. Federal Reserve System and Treasury Trust Accounts

The Federal Reserve System's holdings of United States Government securities increased by only $3 billion between the end of 1945 and December, 1960. Reserves to support the increase in the money supply during those fifteen years were provided principally by other influences on the level of bank reserves and by reductions in reserve requirements.

There have been, however, marked changes in the composition of the Federal Reserve System's Open Market Account from one year to the next since the end of the war. The System Account at the end of 1945 was heavily concentrated in Treasury bills and certificates of indebtedness, the logical outcome of a pegged rate curve that induced other investors to dispose of the lowest-yielding securities to the agency supporting the curve, and the Account held only a handful of securities maturing in more than five years (see Table 16). As the Treasury and the Federal Reserve System gradually freed themselves from the war-time rate curve in the years following the war, longer-maturity obligations were purchased in sizable volume and short-term securities sold. In part, this shift in the composition of the System Account resulted from improved demand for short-term money market securities as the market yields on these instruments were first allowed to break away from the curve, but a more important influence, in all probability, was uncertainty as to the permanence of the Federal Reserve System's pegs on long-term rates. Thus, the heaviest buying by the System Account in support of the pegs occurred in the months following the reduction in support prices on Christmas Eve, 1947, and in the months of open Treasury-Federal Reserve dispute leading up to the "accord" in March, 1951, both periods of great uncertainty as to future policy.

System Open Market Account holdings of Treasury bonds more than five years from maturity had increased to $4.5 billion by March, 1951, and investment in shorter-term securities had been reduced by nearly $6 billion from the total at the end of 1945. The System exchanged $2.4 billion of long-term 2½ per cent marketable bonds for the 2¾ per cent convertible Investment Series B bonds in April, 1951, and by the end of 1952 all of these bonds had been converted into five-year, marketable

143

Table 16—United States Government Securities Owned by Federal Reserve System and Treasury Trust Accounts
(Billions of dollars)

End of Year	Total	Less than 5 Years	More than 5 Years	TREASURY TRUST ACCOUNTS Total	Marketable Under 5 Years	Marketable Over 5 Years	Public Non-marketable	Special Issues
1940	2.2			7.1				
1945	24.3	24.0	0.3	27.0		5.1	—	20.0
1950	20.8	17.3	3.5	39.2	0.3	3.2	—	33.7
1951	23.8	21.3 *	2.5	42.3	0.2	3.0	2.9	36.1
1952	24.7	21.9	2.8	45.9	0.2	3.2	3.4	39.2
1953	25.9	23.1	2.8	48.3	0.4	3.3	3.4	41.2
1954	24.9	22.5	2.4	49.6	0.2	3.4	3.4	42.6
1955	24.8	22.4	2.4	51.7	0.8	3.4	3.4	43.9
1956	24.9	22.5	2.4	54.0	1.6	3.4	3.2	45.6
1957	24.2	22.8	1.4	55.2	3.0	3.3	2.9	45.8
1958	26.3	24.9	1.5	54.4	2.4	4.2	3.0	44.8
1959	26.6	25.2	1.5	53.7	2.9	4.5	2.7	43.5
1960	27.4	25.9	1.5	55.1	3.9	4.2	2.6	44.3

* Includes $1.2 billion Investment Series B convertible bonds. These bonds were converted into five-year notes during the course of 1952.
Source: Board of Governors, Federal Reserve System; United States Treasury Department.

1½ per cent notes. Subsequently, the Federal Reserve System has confined its open-market operations largely to short-term securities, and, since 1953, almost exclusively to Treasury bills. The maturity structure of the System Account has steadily shortened under this open-market policy, and by December, 1960, the System Account held only $1.5 billion of Government securities maturing in more than five years.

What conclusions may be drawn as to future Federal Reserve participation in the Government securities market? First, it is more than likely that System open-market operations will continue to be confined largely to short-term Government securities, principally bills. Even though the so-called "bills only" policy was abandoned by the System in early 1961, it is probably appropriate that Treasury debt managers should not consider the central bank a potential net buyer of significant amounts of its long-term obligations. Second, it is to be expected that reserves will be supplied to the commercial banking system over time to support secular growth in money and credit, and part of these reserves probably will be supplied through System purchases of Government securities. Gold movements, changes in reserve requirements, and other factors will, of course, continue to influence the need to supply reserves through open market operations; as noted earlier, these influences have been of sufficient magnitude to support the entire growth in bank credit and the money supply since the end of the war. Barring unforeseeable developments, however, it is unlikely that international settlements will generate a flow of gold to the United States comparable to that in the immediate postwar years, and there are limits on the extent to which reserve requirements can be reduced, so that it is probable that open-market operations will, in the future, be called upon to supply a major part of the reserves needed for monetary growth. The conclusion, therefore, is that the Federal Reserve System should be a net buyer of short-term Government securities and, on balance, of a small amount of intermediate or longer-term obligations.

The data in Table 16 show that the Treasury has been its own best customer for United States Government securities. Most of the trust accounts whose funds the Treasury invests were established during the 1930's. At the end of 1929, total assets of United States Government investment accounts amounted to less than $1 billion. By 1940, these investment accounts had climbed to more than $7 billion, and by the end of the Second World War to $27 billion. Between December, 1945, and December, 1957, total assets in the Treasury investment accounts more than doubled, increasing by $28.2 billion to a record $55.2 billion. Of the total increase, $25.8 billion was invested in special, non-marketable securities issued by the Treasury directly to the investment accounts, and $2.4 billion was invested in public Treasury issues. Holdings of public marketable obligations actually declined by $0.7 billion between 1945 and 1957, while the investment accounts acquired $2.9 billion of nonmarketable Investment Series bonds. The total of investments for the trust accounts declined slightly between 1957 and 1960, but holdings of marketable securities were increased. Net purchases of marketable issues amounted to $1.8 billion over these three years, partly as the result of operations in 1958 to stabilize the Government securities market.

Of the more than fifty Treasury trust funds whose assets are included in the data in the table, five accounted for almost 90 per cent of total assets at the end of 1960. These are the Old Age and Survivors Insurance fund ($19.0 billion), the Unemployment Insurance Trust fund ($6.8 billion), the Veterans Life Insurance funds (three funds totaling $6.9 billion), the Civil Service Retirement and Disability fund ($11.9 billion), and the Railroad Retirement account ($3.8 billion). The Veterans Life Insurance funds hold special issues exclusively (3 and 3½ per cent notes and certificates of indebtedness), but each of the other major trust funds holds both special issues and public issues, although in all cases special issues predominate in their portfolios. The rules governing the investments of the

146

Treasury trust funds vary, but, in general, they specify that the funds shall be invested in direct or guaranteed obligations of the United States Government, without reference to whether these obligations should be special issues or public issues. However, in each case the investment of trust fund money must realize some minimum rate of return in order to satisfy the actuarial requirements on which the fund is based. The fact that market rates of interest have generally been below the income requirements of the trust funds during the past twenty years has made it necessary for the Treasury to issue special securities carrying rates of interest in line with the funds' income requirements.

In the six years 1955 to 1960, inclusive, market rates of interest rose to a range that would satisfy the income requirements of the major funds, and net purchases of marketable public issues totaling $4.6 billion were made. These purchases represented about four-fifths of the total increase in trust fund assets during the six years. Purchases of marketable securities included $1.8 billion acquired through special allotments to the trust funds of new Treasury issues sold for cash; the remaining $2.8 billion were purchased in the market. The primary consideration in determining whether trust account funds should be invested in special issues or in marketable obligations is the Treasury's trust responsibility to maximize the income of the various accounts rather than consideration of the Treasury's own cash requirements. Thus, net market purchases were made for the trust accounts in 1955 to 1960, when market rates of interest usually were higher than rates on special issues available to most of the trust funds, although the Treasury found it necessary to go to the market frequently during these three years to raise new money for cash, and the market purchases for the trust accounts, in effect, added to this need for cash. At the same time, the Treasury finds it necessary to proceed cautiously in its market operations for the trust accounts so as not to dominate the market and create artificial interest rate patterns on Government securities (artificial in the sense that rates do not accurately reflect private supply and demand influences).

Under present legislation, the total of Treasury trust fund assets might be expected to be approximately steady to slightly higher in the years ahead. The rate of growth has been trending generally downward since the end of World War II, and in the past few years assets actually have been reduced. A cyclical pattern should be expected in the next several years, with small net accretions to total assets or net outlays in periods of recession, when unemployment and social security payments tend to rise, and larger net additions to assets in periods of recovery and business prosperity. Abstracting from these cyclical movements, however, the Treasury trust accounts should be small net buyers of United States Government securities—either special issues or marketable obligations—for some years to come.

K. Summary and Conclusions

Assuming that the interest rate relationships of recent years between United States Government securities and alternative investments are maintained in the future, the foregoing discussion of the investment practices of various investing groups would suggest that Treasury efforts to lengthen the maturity structure of the marketable debt by increasing the proportions of intermediate and long-term obligations in the total marketable debt will be unsuccessful. The superior liquidity (marketability) and risk characteristic of longer-term Government securities relative to other types of investment are not sufficiently important to the major groups of institutional investors to induce them to forego the higher rate of return available on other high-grade investments. There are exceptions, of course. Individuals who are planning their estates find long-term Government issues attractive, particularly when these bonds are selling at a discount. Some state and municipal pension trust funds provide a "captive market" since they are limited in their investments to United States Governments or even less attractive (to an investor that does not pay taxes) tax-exempt securities. Some Federal savings and loan associations apparently purchase longer-term Governments to satisfy the "liquidity" requirement that they maintain a certain percentage of their share capital in Governments and/or cash. Also, commercial banks reach out toward the ten-year maturity range in their investment operations at times when the Federal Reserve System supplies them with more reserves than are necessary to provide for customer credit needs and adequate primary and secondary reserves. And, of course, the Treasury trust accounts should provide a small demand for longer-term United States Government securities.

By and large, however, the movement of the Treasury debt throughout the fifteen years since the end of the Second World War, including the nearly ten years of unsupported markets from early 1951 through 1960, has been into the hands of investors who hold Government securities as short-term liquidity, or secondary reserve investments. This conclusion applies not only to the nature and purpose of the investors who have added to their investments in Government securities (e.g., state and local governments, foreign and international accounts, etc.) but also to the recasting of Government portfolios to fill liquidity functions in the asset structure of investors whose principal interest is in longer-term investments. This movement in investment portfolios has been reflected in the structure of the Treasury debt, where, since December, 1950, publicly-held marketable debt within five years of maturity has grown by more than $45 billion while longer marketable debt held by the public has declined by $12 billion. Over the same years, public holdings of nonmarketable Savings bonds and notes have been reduced by $17 billion.

There are several reasons for the transformation of United States Government debt from an investment role to a liquidity role in the portfolios of most investors. In the first place, the huge supply of securities and the active market in which they are traded have made Government securities the principal instrument for short-term financial adjustments, and this has led to a demand for shorter-term Government securities that has grown in step with the growth in the economy. In the second place, the leading financial intermediaries tend to specialize in their lending-investing operations in instruments that involve a personal relationship—such as business operating credit, mortgages, bonds bought on direct placement, etc.—and acquire "impersonal" investments only as they are needed to balance the risk structure of their portfolios or to provide a necessary liquidity reserve. In the third place, the United States Government's mortgage insurance and guarantee programs have tended to weaken the appeal of longer-term Government bonds on their strongest point, the fact that they are riskless. The guarantee or insurance provided by the Federal Government on VA and FHA mortgage loans has made these loans virtually the equivalent of Government bonds in the eyes of many investors, thus reducing their need for direct-obligation Treasury securities to achieve a given risk structure in their portfolios.

The foregoing discussion, in a sense, begs the question. United States Government securities have largely moved out of the category of portfolio investments in the hands of most holders and into the category of liquidity instruments because the Treasury has chosen to finance at short-term and to allow longer-term debt to move into shorter-maturity brackets without replacement. In short, there are not more longer-term Government securities in investor portfolios because the Treasury has not issued them. There are many facets to the question of whether the Treasury could or should have issued more longer-term securities. To have pre-empted capital funds would have reduced the supply of capital funds available to support the private and public investment outlays of the postwar years. Would such a result have been desirable at any time? Or would the attempt simply have caused interest rates to spiral higher without significant success for the Treasury in raising long-term funds? How elastic is the demand for capital in response to interest rate changes? Did the increase in the supply of liquid instruments hamper the efforts of the Federal Reserve System to regulate liquidity? How important is it that the Treasury struggle to sell more longer-term debt, when the market demand for short and intermediate maturities enables the Treasury to finance at lower interest cost in those maturities?

Discussion of the matters raised by these questions will be deferred to later chapters. Without prejudging the questions related to whether the Treasury *should* have sought to tap more longer-term funds in its financing of the past several years, the conclusion of the discussion in this chapter is that it *could* have done so only by an aggressive policy that would have narrowed the gap between market rates of interest on long-term Governments and high-grade corporate bonds. The prevailing rate spread has represented an equilibrium condition sustained by the failure of the Treasury to maintain its maturity structure and by the existence of sufficient demand from "captive buyers" to absorb the net selling of Governments at that rate spread by other investors. It follows that absorption of a larger supply of longer-term Government securities would require narrowing this spread to the point where the necessary number of investors would voluntarily forego selling Governments for the purpose of transferring funds to other investments and, depending upon the amount of bonds the Treasury wished to place in the long-term area, where some investors would redirect funds from other investments to Governments. There probably is no "normal" spread between Governments and other high-grade taxable bonds. The spreads prevailing in recent years have reflected a "normal" condition in which long-term Government bonds were gradually disappearing from investment portfolios. If the Treasury should choose to reverse this process, the behavior of the major investors with whom the Treasury would have to place its bonds suggests that the "normal" long-term Government rate would have to be close to or equal to the market rate on high-grade corporate bonds of equivalent maturities.[24]

24. This discussion does not mention the difference between market rates on outstanding bonds and on new issues. Rates on new issues of corporate bonds are higher, by varying amounts, than effective rates on outstanding issues of like quality, the spread depending upon the availability of funds and the pressure of new demands for capital. In order to place new long-term Treasury debt securely with investors in a continuing program of Treasury funding that competed effectively with other demands for funds, the "new issue" Government rate presumably would have to approach the new issue rate for Aaa corporates, which might place it above the rate for seasoned Aaa corporate bonds.

V

Current Techniques
of Treasury Finance
and Role of Investor Groups
as Underwriters

Treasury debt management since the end of the Second World War has, by and large, employed the financing techniques developed during the depression decade of the 1930's. As the earlier discussion of the history of debt management has pointed out, techniques of Treasury finance have evolved from period to period in adjustment to the particular financing problems, market conditions, and policy objectives at the time. Thus, the techniques developed in the 1930's were effective in selling intermediate and longer-term obligations, both for cash and in exchange for maturing securities. Policy objectives at the time stressed funding the debt, since the time when repayment would be economically feasible was so uncertain. The market setting was one wherein longer-term obligations could be sold with minimum disturbance to the capital markets; investment demand for United States Government bonds was strong because of the absence of competing demands for long-term funds. These techniques, which were novel in many respects at the time they were developed, have since acquired the status of "traditional practices," and until the last few years there has tended to be resistance to innovation both from Treasury officials and from market professionals. It is not at all certain that the techniques the Treasury has taken over from the 1930's have been most efficiently adapted to the problems, policies, and market circumstances of the post-World War II period.

The Second Liberty Bond Act, as amended, is the principal source of authority for the Secretary of the Treasury in the selection of issues, terms, and techniques for the management of the public debt of the United States.[1] In general, it authorizes the Secretary of the Treasury to issue, at his discretion, such amounts of marketable Treasury bills, certificates of indebtedness, notes, and bonds, and of nonmarketable savings bonds, as are required to finance the Government. The Secretary is authorized to determine the type or types of securities, within these general designations, to be issued for cash or in refunding of existing debt. Congress has retained control over the total amount of direct and guaranteed United States debt by establishing a limit on the total of such debt that may be outstanding at any one time,[2] but there are no limits on the amount of debt in any one form (*i.e.*, bills, notes, bonds, etc.). The Secretary may determine the coupon rate of interest to be attached to the securities issued, with the proviso that the rate may not exceed 4¼ per cent in the case of public marketable bonds or 3¾ per cent in the case of public nonmarketable securities, and he also is authorized to determine the price at which securities are to be sold, whether par or a price above or below par.[3]

1. The Second Liberty Bond Act was originally adopted on September 24, 1917, and has been amended from time to time in subsequent years; 55 Stat. 7, 31 USC.

2. Second Liberty Bond Act, as amended; 31 USC, Sec. 21. For a history of the debt limit see H. J. Cooke and M. Katzen, "The Public Debt Limit," *The Journal of Finance*, September, 1954, p. 298.

3. While the legislation is clear in stating that marketable Treasury bonds may be sold at a price to be determined by the Secretary and that the

Operating under the broad authority granted by the Second Liberty Bond Act, postwar Treasury debt management techniques were remarkably uniform until the past three years. Before turning to a more detailed discussion, the general outline of these techniques might be indicated. The important elements are:

1. Holders of maturing or called securities, other than bills, are offered an opportunity to exchange for one or more new issues; thus, maturing coupon securities have a potential "rights" value. "Cash" refunding was used for the first time in 1960.

2. Exchange subscriptions are allotted in full. Unexchanged securities are redeemed at maturity, and the resulting cash drain on the Treasury becomes a part of the Treasury's general cash requirements. The "cash" refunding in 1960 (and in 1961) eliminated attrition.

3. Refunding offerings, whether on exchange or for cash, customarily include one or more intermediate or longer-term obligations, in addition to a short-term security; this procedure reflects the attempt by the Treasury to resist, insofar as possible, an increase in short-term debt outstanding.

4. In its new cash financing, the Treasury permits depositary commercial banks to pay for their own and their customers' allotments through credit to Treasury tax and loan account.

5. Coupon-bearing securities, whether issued for cash or refunding, are usually sold at par, with a coupon rate of interest judged by the Treasury to be sufficiently attractive against current market rates to assure a successful offering. The first break with this tradition was in June, 1958, when a long-term bond was sold at a small premium, but most offerings of coupon securities have continued to be at par.

Secretary may determine the coupon rate of interest, up to 4¼ per cent, there has been some uncertainty as to whether the Secretary could issue such securities below par at an effective rate above 4¼ per cent. In early 1961, the Attorney General in a letter to the Secretary of the Treasury said that in his opinion the limit applied only to the coupon rate, not to the effective rate.

A. Techniques for Issuing Bonds, Notes, and Certificates

A. SETTING TERMS

Perhaps the most striking aspect of recent Treasury debt management is the fact that every major financing, with the exception of the regular Treasury bill auctions, involves a separate set of policy decisions with respect to the types and maturities of securities to be offered, the potential impact of various offerings upon the economy and what impact is desired, their effect upon the market for outstanding obligations, whether a refunding should be cash or exchange, etc. As noted earlier, techniques have been relatively constant until quite recently, but in the process of adhering to "traditional" techniques—and perhaps partly because of this adherence—the Treasury has failed to develop a debt-management program consistent with a clearly enunciated debt-management policy. The closest thing to a firm policy objective that has been visible has been the desire to "lengthen the average maturity of the debt" by selling as many securities at as long a term as possible. But there has been no fully articulated program toward this or any other policy objective.

Initial investigation of possible offerings begins at least six weeks or two months before maturity of an issue that is to be refunded or before the anticipated need for funds in the case of a cash offering. Discussions at this time are held within the Treasury and between senior officials of the Treasury and the Federal Reserve System,[4] as well as with other officials in an economic advisory capacity in the Administration. Meanwhile, the Government finance committees of the American Bankers Association and the Investment Bankers Association meet in-

4. The Treasury officials directly responsible for debt management are the Under Secretary for Monetary Affairs and the Assistant to the Secretary for debt-management matters; at the end of 1960, these positions were held, respectively, by Julian B. Baird and J. Dewey Daane. The final decision in any operation, of course, rests with the Secretary of the Treasury.

1 5 6

dependently to review the Treasury's requirements, market conditions, and the apparent demand for securities of various types, preparatory to consideration of the recommendations they might offer the Treasury. If there is a possibility that a long-term bond might be included in the offering, committees representing institutional investor groups such as the life insurance companies and mutual savings banks might also be asked to give preliminary consideration to what the Treasury might offer. As the round of discussions continues, the scope of the immediate financing problem and the feasibility of the various alternatives that might be employed come into clearer focus. Final discussions are held approximately two and one-half weeks before the date on which the new securities are to be issued for cash or exchange. The responsible Treasury officials meet at that time with the Government finance committees of the ABA and IBA (usually on a Tuesday and Wednesday), and with committees of other investor groups if they are involved, receive their final recommendations, and then receive the recommendations of the Federal Reserve officials. On the basis of these recommendations and of their own interpretation of Treasury requirements and of the market situation, the Treasury then arrives at its decision, which typically is announced to the press on Thursday afternoon for offering to the public on the following Monday.

It is almost literally true that in any given financing operation, cash or refunding, the securities that the Treasury might offer range from short-term certificates of indebtedness to long-term bonds, or any combination of these securities. Other decisions also are frequently involved. For example, should a refunding include only the currently maturing issue or should it be extended to cover all coupon issues maturing in the next few months? In the case of a refunding, should the maturing issue be given exchange rights? If two or more issues of different types (*i.e.*, certificates, notes, bonds) are to be refunded simultaneously, should all issues be given equal right to exchange into any issues the Treasury offers or should the exchange privilege be limited in some fashion? In the case of an offering for new cash, should

157

all subscriptions be treated equally or should preferential allotments be given certain groups of subscribers? And what cash payment should be required with subscription in order to limit speculative interest in a cash offering?

The smallest Treasury financing probably will represent the placement of at least $1 billion of new securities, and a typical operation runs to several billions of dollars. Movements of investment funds in this size unavoidably have a pronounced impact upon all financial markets, and the impact can be particularly sharp if the financing includes securities outside the short-term maturity sector. Consequently, as the date of the expected Treasury announcement of financing approaches, the financial markets tend to become progressively more uneasy and more subject to the influence of rumors as to the issues and interest rates the Treasury will offer. It would be an exaggeration to say that trading comes to a stop at such times, but the uncertainties in the outlook frequently cause dealers and underwriters in corporate and tax-exempt bonds, as well as Government securities dealers, to take a cautious approach and avoid commitments until there has been an opportunity to assess the effect of the Treasury's offering on prices and yields of fixed-income securities of all types. Of course, the extent of the uncertainty and its effect upon trading volume and securities prices, as the market discounts the terms it expects the Treasury to offer, depends in part upon the current objective of Federal Reserve credit policy. If the money and securities markets have an abundant supply of funds, the uncertainty occasioned by the imminence of a Treasury financing may be minimized, although even at such times the possibility that a long-term bond might be included in the offering can have a paralyzing effect upon the market. And in periods of severe restraint on the availability of funds, the approach of a major Treasury debt operation, and the uncertainties engendered by such operations, can have a temporarily demoralizing influence on all securities markets.

It should be stressed that the disturbing influence of a Treasury refunding operation is felt not only when the securities being

158

refunded were originally intermediate or long-term obligations, but in every operation involving fixed rate securities, including the frequent refundings of certificates of indebtedness and short-term notes. This circumstance results from the fact noted earlier, that the Treasury in almost every financing operation, without regard to the nature of the securities being refunded, has made a separate set of decisions with respect to securities to be offered; there has been no predictable pattern or program of certificates being exchanged for certificates, bonds for bonds, etc. Thus, investors and market professionals are subjected to almost absolute uncertainty several times each year as refunding dates approach. The only known constant is the Treasury's desire to "lengthen the debt" whenever circumstances permit. This constant, of course, tends to compound the disturbing influence upon the market. The Treasury follows a similar technique in its cash financing, except in the financing of intra-fiscal year deficits, when tax anticipation securities are usually employed.

It would be appropriate at this point to comment upon the practice of asking the ABA and IBA committees for their recommendations. The members of these committees approach their responsibilities conscientiously, and their recommendations reflect their best judgment of what investors want or will take rather than any personal preferences they might have as to what they, as individual businessmen, would most like to see offered. At the same time, the approach taken is that of the market technician, and the recommendations usually are for issues which the Treasury could sell most easily or with least disturbance to the market. The service performed by these committees clearly is valuable in informing the Treasury of investor sentiment and preferences. At the same time, the fact that the Treasury gives some weight to these recommendations tends to give validity to the spate of rumors, growing out of opinions, that dominate the market in the weeks leading up to a financing announcement. Thus, market attitudes harden around a limited set of Treasury alternatives—whether these attitudes were based originally on actual investor preferences or on nothing more than often-repeated judgments of what "can" be done—and the Treasury steps outside these limited alternatives only at the risk of "rocking the boat" with an offering that the market has already been conditioned to believe is "unwanted." The disturbing aspect of this situation is that a debt-management policy of encouraging investors to believe that the Treasury will offer "what the market wants" is no policy at all. It has often been said that Treasury debt-management decisions, because of the size of the debt, dominate the financial markets. Just the reverse often appears to be the case, in fact, as the Treasury, perhaps fearful of its own power, has allowed market opinions to dominate its decisions.

B.   OFFERING SECURITIES ON EXCHANGE

During the eight calendar years 1953 to 1960, inclusive, the Treasury undertook 31 separate refunding operations in which new securities were offered in exchange for maturing securities. A total of 56 new issues were offered to investors in exchange for 68 maturing issues. Total maturities amounted to $330 billion and subscriptions for securities offered in exchange totaled $310 billion. All of these exchange operations entailed 100 per cent allotment for maturing securities tendered in exchange.

The Treasury's financing announcement brings to an end the period of market uncertainty as to the terms the Treasury will offer, and opens a new period of uncertainty as to the reception the offering will have. As mentioned earlier, the Treasury customarily announces its offering after the market has closed on a Thursday afternoon, with subscription books scheduled to open the following Monday.[5] The market has one trading day, Friday, to react to the terms before the books open. This reaction is not confined to "rights"—the issues being refunded—but

5. Occasionally in its cash operations the Treasury has released a preliminary announcement some days earlier stating that it intends to offer an approximate amount of securities in a specified maturity range. The market's adjustment to this announcement assists the Treasury in setting a rate of interest on the offering.

extends to all issues in the same maturity areas as those the Treasury is offering and also to securities in maturity areas where the market had thought the Treasury might place a new issue. Typically, if the rate of interest offered on any particular issue appears attractive relative to effective yields at current prices on outstanding issues of roughly similar maturity, presaging a sizable exchange into the new issue, competitive outstanding issues will adjust down in price after the announcement. Similarly, if the Treasury does not include in its offering a maturity that the market had anticipated, issues in that maturity area, whose prices would probably have declined in anticipation of the offering, will tend to advance.

The principal influence upon market reaction to the Treasury announcement is the current state of money and credit availability. Even if money is plentifully available and commercial banks are actively purchasing Government securities, the pervasive uncertainty prior to the actual Treasury announcement might have caused a period of hesitation. Once the air has been cleared by the actual announcement, however, prices of all outstanding issues may tend to resume their advance, carrying the "rights" to even more attractive premiums than they might have achieved before the announcement.[6] On the other hand, when money is tight and interest rates are tending to rise, the market reaction to the announcement may be highly uncertain. Under such circumstances it is likely that the maturing issue (or issues) will have traded prior to the announcement on a "money basis," *i.e.*, at a price equivalent to its yield value as a short-term invest-

6. In a period of easy money and declining interest rates, "rights" will frequently go to a negative yield, reflecting the anticipated premium on the securities the Treasury will offer (or has offered) in exchange. For example, assume that the current market rate for two-week money is one per cent and an issue of 2½ per cent certificates two weeks from maturity is quoted "on a rights basis" at a premium of %₄, to yield approximately —one per cent; the price of the "rights" would indicate an expected premium of at least ⁵%₄ on one or more of the issues in the Treasury offering. It is seen from this illustration that in an offering consisting of more than one issue, the issue expected to go to the largest premium will tend to control the price of the "rights."

ment, rather than on a "rights basis." If the new securities offered by the Treasury are clearly attractive against the current market, the maturing issue will acquire a rights value, which it may hold through the refunding. The upward pull exerted by the new issue on market rates of interest may, however, destroy this "rights" premium before the refunding is completed and return the maturing issue to a "money basis."

Treasury subscription books customarily remain open for three business days on an exchange offering, usually Monday through Wednesday of the week following the Treasury's preliminary announcement. During this period, the maturing issue (or issues) continues to trade as rights to the exchange option offered by the Treasury, and the new securities begin trading on a "when-issued" basis (*i.e.*, for delivery when issued by the Treasury).[7] Obviously, the rights and the when-issued securities must remain in a determinable relationship to each other so long as the maturing issue retains a rights premium; its premium is simply a reflection of the value of the new issue. In periods of severe strain on the money and securities markets, however, when rights fail to hold a premium, or at any time that the coupon placed on the new issue is not attractive against current market rates, the maturing issue will fall to a price equivalent to its value as a short-term investment (which may still be a premium if the coupon on the maturing issue is greater than current market rates for a comparable maturity) and the price of when-issued securities will fall to the neighborhood of par. When-issued prices may even fall to a discount on the dealers' bid side of the market, but offered prices cannot go to a discount while the books are open since the holder of the rights has an option to take cash rather than exchange, and he obviously would not consciously

7. Customarily, the Treasury asks the dealers not to quote or trade the new securities "when issued" until subscription books open. An exception was made in the case of the February, 1958, refunding, however, when dealers were permitted to commence when-issued trading immediately after the announcement so as to allow a better opportunity for the market to place proper relative values on the five issues of "rights" and three new issues in this very complicated refunding.

162

exchange for the new issue and simultaneously sell his subscription below par.

It is an interesting feature of Treasury finance that the Treasury, alone among the major borrowers in the market, does not have the assistance of an underwriting syndicate with a vested interest in the success of the operation. The nearest thing to an underwriting syndicate assisting the Treasury is the group of private Government securities dealers who attempt to make broad and continuous markets in all issues of Government securities. Dealers will have traded the "rights" actively in the period leading up to the Treasury exchange announcement and, depending upon the pressure of offerings and their own guessing on what the Treasury will offer, will have a more or less sizable inventory in rights by the time terms are announced. After the terms of the Treasury offering are known, the dealers swing into full operation as the channel through which rights held by investors not interested in the exchange can be made available to other investors interested in acquiring the new securities offered by the Treasury.

If it is possible to do so, dealers attempt to maintain at least a small premium on the rights, since in the absence of a rights premium holders of rights have no inducement to sell and the redistribution of rights necessary to a successful refunding cannot take place. The ability to hold a premium on rights, however, depends upon the general availability of money and credit and the relative attractiveness of the when-issued securities, as remarked earlier. If the money market has been under strain and a significant portion of the maturing issue had been held by investors to cover cash needs, or if the terms of the new issue are not attractive, demand for when-issued securities may fall short of offerings of rights so long as rights are at a premium. In this case, in order to protect themselves, dealers will be forced to lower their quotes on rights to par or a price above or below par where their effective yield is in line with yields on short-term Treasury bills.

Dealers may be subject to still another pressure during periods of severe restraint on the money market. Principally because of the brief time that subscription books are open and the mechanical difficulties that would be encountered in exchanging physical possession of rights to the dealers and then to other investors, dealers typically buy rights during an exchange operation and sell when-issued securities against these purchases of rights (usually their purchases of rights exceed when-issued sales, so that they are net purchasers for their own positions). This operation involves acquiring securities (rights) that have to be carried and financed until they can be exchanged for the new securities (usually about ten days), and if, as is frequently the case in a tight market, the coupon rate on the rights is less than the current cost of dealer financing, the net cost might absorb a good part of the profit the dealer had hoped to make on the operation and be a serious deterrent to his participation in the refunding.[8]

The net result of the behavior of the rights and when-issued securities while exchange subscription books are open is the amount of attrition, or cash turn-in. There will be a certain number of holders of any maturing issue who have a need for the cash represented by the investment on or around maturity date, and these investors will not ordinarily be interested in exchanging for the new issue (unless they wish to speculate that it will go to a profitable premium before issue). Therefore, as mentioned above, the measure of a successful exchange refunding is the extent to which these holdings, which will not be ex-

8. Still another problem sometimes arises when the coupon rate on the rights is well below current market rates of interest. Rights with, let us say, two weeks to run to maturity might provide an inducement for holders to sell even if the price is at a slight discount from par so long as the yield to maturity at this price is less than the yield on an alternative two-week investment (e.g., in Treasury bills). However, if the investor had bought the securities originally at a discount, and thus was taking part of his income as capital gains, the difference between the capital gains tax rate and the corporate income tax rate might destroy the profitability of the swap. This problem has been particularly important in attempts to refund the 1½ per cent notes issued on conversion for the 2¾ per cent Investment Series B bond.

changed, are transferred to investors interested in the new securities.

C. CASH FINANCING IN REGULAR COUPON SECURITIES

The first cash financing in regular, interest-bearing marketable securities after the Second World War occurred in June, 1952, when the Treasury sold for cash $4.2 billion of six-year bonds. Beginning in 1953, the need for cash financing in permanent debt obligations has brought the Treasury to market at least once in every year except 1956. Exclusive of offerings of tax-anticipation securities and the cash refunding in 1960, the Treasury in the eight years 1953–1960, inclusive, sold twenty-eight issues of marketable securities in twenty-three separate cash financing operations (including four issues of one-year bills). Total cash financing in regular marketable obligations (other than weekly bills) in these eight years amounted to $50 billion, of which $3.4 billion was raised through two issues of certificates, $27.2 billion through twelve issues of Treasury notes, $12.1 billion through ten issues of bonds, and $7.5 billion through four issues of one-year bills.

The procedure followed in setting terms and announcing the offering of new securities for cash is very similar to that used in refunding operations. Treasury officials consult committees of the ABA and IBA, discuss their problems with Federal Reserve officials and other Government officers, and finally select the issue (or issues), and rates of interest, that promise to be most attractive to the market and as consistent as possible with the Treasury's continuing objective of avoiding further additions to the short-term debt. In the event that consideration is given to a long-term bond, representatives of the insurance companies and savings banks are invited to participate in the discussions and to advise the Treasury as to the probable availability of funds in their industries for investment in long-term Governments.

The terms of the offering, once decided upon, are usually

165

released to the press after the market closes on Thursday, and subscription books are open the following Monday for one day only. Dealers do not quote the new issue while subscription books are open, and their function at this time is to advise customers on whether or not to subscribe, and to decide how large an allotment of the new issue they should attempt to get for their own positions. Meanwhile, outstanding securities competitive with the new issue adjust in price to the terms offered by the Treasury, and the extent of this adjustment is influential in determining investor interest in the new securities. When-issued trading begins on the following day, and from that point until payment is made on delivery of the issue (usually about ten days), trading is characterized by investors buying to round out their allotments, selling by investors allotted more than they wanted or by speculative subscribers, and selling of outstanding issues by investors raising funds to pay for their allotments of the new securities. The price and interest-rate adjustments at this time, as the market absorbs the new issue, measure the Treasury's success in judging the market for the securities and in placing them with investors willing to hold them.

While techniques in handling cash operations in regular coupon securities are similar to the techniques used in exchange refunding insofar as the procedure followed in setting terms and announcing offerings is concerned, they differ in other important respects. Perhaps the most important difference relates to the payment procedure. In its exchange refunding operations, the Treasury simply offers holders of maturing obligations the opportunity to exchange their holdings for new securities; payment for the new issue is made by surrender of the maturing obligations.[9] In a cash financing, however, an actual transfer of funds

9. Occasionally a cash payment is required for interest adjustment. For example, holders of the 2 per cent bonds due June 15, 1954, who presented them in exchange for the new 2½ per cent bonds of 1961 on February 15, 1954, were required to pay the Treasury the interest differential (½ per cent) for four months (February 15 to June 15). Such interest adjustments are customary when the date on which the new securities are issued is not the date on which the old issue matures.

166

to the account of the Treasury is necessary. The problem of transferring large amounts of funds to the Treasury in settlement for its new loans without serious disturbance to the private economy was finally solved during the First World War, when the procedure was established of allowing payment to be made to deposit balances maintained by the Treasury at a large number of depositary banks. Since that time, Treasury cash financing in marketable securities other than Treasury bills has almost always provided that depositary commercial banks might pay for their own and their customers' subscriptions through deposit credits on their books to account of the Treasury.

An interesting situation has grown up around the provision for payment through "tax and loan account" that has virtually made the commercial banking system the underwriter of Treasury cash issues of short-term securities at times of pressure on the money and capital markets. At such times, most commercial banks do not have funds available for net new investment in United States Government securities and, in fact, they probably are being forced to liquidate short-term Governments. However, since payment for a new Treasury cash issue means an immediate loss of funds equal only to the reserve requirements against the deposit created for the Treasury, it is possible for a commercial bank to subscribe for the new issue, sell that part of its allotment in the market that would be required to cover the increase in required reserves, and then continue to earn income on the balance of its allotment, with no actual outlay of cash involved, until it becomes necessary to sell as the Treasury withdraws its deposit balance. Alternatively, the bank might sell its entire allotment immediately and use the funds thus acquired to repay an advance at the Reserve Bank or for other purposes; in this case, the bank has used its subscription to the Treasury cash offering as a means of acquiring reserves. The significant aspect of this arrangement is that commercial banks are enabled to sell the securities allotted to them at a discount from purchase price and still make a profit on the transaction. Consequently, when commercial banks are under severe reserve pressure, other in-

167

vestors tend to withhold their subscriptions during a Treasury cash offering of short-term securities, planning to buy the securities at a discount as banks unload them on the market. The extent to which this occurs is illustrated by the Treasury's cash sale of $2,437 million certificates in March, 1957, of which commercial banks were awarded all but $76 million. Within three months, commercial bank holdings of this issue (the banks included in the Treasury *Survey of Ownership*) had been reduced by $1.7 billion from their combined cash allotment and earlier exchange allotment of the same issue.[10]

In one respect, it might be argued that this practice of commercial banks is detrimental to Treasury financing since it tends to drive new cash issues to an immediate discount. But the more important consideration is that in a tight money market, such as that which prevailed throughout 1957, there simply are not large reservoirs of idle, nonbank funds available at any one time to absorb a major cash offering, and the process of commercial bank underwriting enables the Treasury to finance in reasonably large amounts as it needs cash, and in a manner consistent with Federal Reserve policy objectives. One way to

10. An arithmetic example might help to illustrate one of the methods of calculating a bank's break-even point in this operation. Assume that reserve requirements are 20 per cent and that the rate of interest on the security offered by the Treasury is 3 per cent. Also assume that the estimated average life of the Treasury deposit created by the subscription is thirty days. In this case, a bank receiving a $1 million allotment could sell $200 thousand of the securities immediately to acquire reserves to cover the increase in reserve requirements, and expect to earn 3 per cent for thirty days on the remaining $800 thousand. The income at 3 per cent on this average investment for thirty days would amount to roughly $2 thousand. With the value of $\frac{1}{32}$ in price equal to $312 per million of securities owned, the bank could sell all of its allotment, as necessary to cover Treasury withdrawals, at an average price of $99\frac{26}{32}$ and still more than break even. This price would be equivalent to a yield on a 3 per cent one-year certificate of 3.20 per cent; however, on a five-year note, for example, the yield change associated with a $\frac{6}{32}$ price movement would be only 4 basis points. Because of the increasing amplitude of potential price movement as maturity lengthens, the significance of the "bonus" to commercial banks lessens the longer the maturity, and is of true significance in Treasury financing only on short-term obligations.

view the operation is to consider the commercial banks as under-writers who hold the new securities in custody until the Treasury actually draws against its account, at which time the securities are sold to nonbank investors to absorb the new money released by the net Treasury outlays. To the extent that this is done, the Treasury cash financing does not occasion an increase in the money supply.[11] Of course, in periods when money is easy and bank reserves abundantly available, there is no presumption that commercial banks will immediately sell their allotments of new cash issues, driving the price to a discount, and nonbank investors subscribe at the time of the Treasury offering for the securities they wish. Thus, of the $6.4 billion shorter-term securi-ties (other than tax instruments) sold by the Treasury in 1954, commercial banks were awarded only 59 per cent, by contrast with commercial bank allotments amounting to 95 per cent of the $4.1 billion of such shorter-term securities sold by the Treasury in 1957.

Another area in which Treasury cash financing techniques differ from the techniques employed in exchange refunding is in the process of allotting new securities to subscribers. In an ex-change refunding, the upper limit on subscriptions is set by the total of the maturing issue (or issues) outstanding that might be tendered for exchange, and in each exchange refunding during the eight years 1953–1960, inclusive, subscriptions have been allotted in full. A problem arises in the case of cash offerings, however, in that there is no way of determining in advance, with any degree of accuracy, what the total subscription for a given offering will be at the terms offered by the Treasury. Therefore, since the Treasury has definite cash requirements, and since the

11. In the three years of credit restraint, 1955–1957, the public marketable debt increased by $5.4 billion, and the Treasury sold $10.5 billion marketable interest-bearing securities for cash, other than tax-anticipation issues, of which commercial banks were awarded $7.8 billion. Over the same three years, commercial bank holdings of Government securities were reduced, on balance, by $3.7 billion. In 1957 alone, when the Treasury sold $8.2 billion of interest-bearing marketable cash issues to the public, including $6.5 billion to com-mercial banks, bank holdings of Governments were reduced by $1.0 billion.

proximity of the debt ceiling in recent years has usually set a very close limit on the amount the Treasury is legally able to borrow, it is necessary for the Treasury to reserve the right to limit allotments of new cash issues. The procedure followed by the Treasury is to announce a cash offering of a specified amount of securities of a given maturity and rate of interest, at par, with the right reserved to the Treasury to allot securities on a formula it shall develop.[12] In response to this procedure of partial and unknown allotments, investors are uncertain as to the size of subscription it is necessary to submit in order to receive the allotment they wish. Prior to and during the time subscription books are open, the principal topic of discussion in the Government securities market is speculation on what the allotment percentage will be and, thus, on the amount by which subscriptions should be padded.

The procedure has at least two disadvantages. First, it forces investors to subscribe without any sure knowledge of the actual amount of securities they will receive. If the allotment is smaller than expected, investors with funds apportioned for purchase of the issue have to "round out" their allotments through market purchases, driving the price to a premium and, perhaps, creating windfall profits for speculators; if the allotment is larger than expected, the reverse happens as investors attempt to sell

12. The offering of 3 per cent bonds of 1995 on July 11, 1955, in an amount of $750 million, or thereabouts, is typical. Treasury Department *Circular No. 962,* announcing this offering, reads in part:

> Subscriptions from commercial banks for their own account . . . will be restricted . . . to an amount not exceeding 25 per cent of the combined capital, surplus and undivided profits, or 10 per cent of the combined amount of time certificates of deposit . . . and of savings deposits, of the subscribing bank. . . .
>
> The Secretary of the Treasury reserves the right to reject or reduce any subscription, to allot less than the amount of bonds applied for, and to make different percentage allotments to various classes of subscribers. . . .

In this operation, subscriptions from "savings-type investors" were allotted 65 per cent and subscriptions from all other investors were allotted 30 per cent, with minimum allotments of $25,000 on subscriptions larger than that amount. Source, United States Treasury Department, *Annual Report for 1956* and *Treasury Bulletin.*

their larger-than-anticipated allotments, driving the new issue to a discount and creating the impression that the issue was a failure. Second, some investors with a legitimate investment demand for the new securities are prevented by restrictions of one sort or another upon the investment officer from padding their subscriptions to the extent that would be necessary to secure the allotment they are able to pay for. They are, there-fore, driven into the secondary market to round out their allot-ments through when-issued purchases, perhaps at a premium. Some investors have become disgruntled over this situation, which they consider an unbusinesslike method of financing, and have tended to withdraw from participation in Treasury cash financing.

One technique the Treasury has used in its cash financing has contributed directly to speculation in Treasury cash offerings and, upon occasion, to serious after-market problems. This is the practice of requiring a relatively small cash payment with subscriptions.[13] In the case of shorter-term offerings of certificates or notes, the possible price appreciation on the new securities is relatively small, and a small cash payment on subscription is not an important inducement to speculation. In the case of longer-term obligations, however, where price movements may be substantial,[14] the possibility of a small cash outlay at the time of subscription, together with the small margins (usually 5 per cent or less) required by banks on loans against Governments, provides a very real inducement to speculation.[15] The sale of the 3¼'s of 1978–83 in April 1953 provides the best illustra-

13. The discussion here refers to nonbank investors since commercial banks are not required to submit a cash payment with their subscriptions.

14. For example, the 3⅞ per cent bonds of 1974, issued at par on December 2, 1957, were trading at 107¾ by December 31, 1957.

15. One reason for the low cash payment requirement is a strange notion, which has died very slowly among officials and some market professionals, that the success of a cash offering is somehow related to the amount of over-subscription, whether that over-subscription reflects speculative fever, obvious padding, or real investment demand. This odd shibboleth has, at times, undoubtedly been an influence on the selection of terms, and to this day some market people still tend to think of an issue as less than successful if the allotment ratio is higher than they had anticipated.

tion of the effects of speculation on a Treasury bond offering for cash. The 3¼ per cent coupon on the new bonds appeared to be more than ample, and it was generally conceded that the 3¼'s would rise to a healthy premium as soon as when-issued trading began. Consequently, a great number of smaller investors, principally individuals, were drawn in for a "free ride" to a quick profit.[16] The combination of a coupon well above what the market had anticipated, the low cash payment requirement, and the Treasury's publicity program ballooned subscriptions to more than $5 billion. Among total allotments to private investors of $1,070 million, however, $261 million were to individuals, $248 million to "all other," and $158 million to dealers and brokers. In these categories alone, more than two-thirds of the issue was placed with investors many of whom, in all probability, were interested in profitable resale rather than permanent investment (in addition, allotments to commercial banks, who function in an underwriting capacity, totalled $131 million). As pressures on the capital markets increased in April and May, 1953, the sometimes panicky unloading of 3¼'s by speculators and other weak holders was an important influence in the congested, almost disorderly market that developed. By contrast, the second *tranche* of 3's of 1995, offered for cash in an amount of $750 million in July, 1955, also a time of increasing tightness in the credit markets, was an orderly operation with a good after-market (although total subscriptions were much smaller than in the other operation). Speculative subscriptions were minimal in view of the slight profit prospects on an issue priced close to the market, and combined allotments to individuals, dealers and brokers, corporations and "all others" were only $167 million. Low cash payment requirements also ballooned speculative interest in the 4's of 1969, offered for payment October 1, 1957, but in this operation there was no discrimination against commercial banks in the allotment ratio (they received $296

16. The market advisory services stressed the profit possibilities; *cf.* Sylvia Porter, *Reporting on Governments*, April 11, 1953.

million, of total allotments to private investors amounting to $557 million), so that allotments to unstable subscribers were held to levels below what they would have been if banks had been discriminated against.

Before leaving the discussion of current cash financing techniques, a few concluding comments would be in order. If seasonal tax anticipation financing is excluded, the principal drain of funds necessitating Treasury cash financing in marketable securities in recent years has resulted from attrition on marketable or nonmarketable debt already outstanding. To the extent that the cash refunding technique developed by the Treasury in late 1960 successfully reduces attrition on refinancing the marketable debt, the need for cash operations other than in tax-anticipation issues should be reduced substantially. Occasional cash financing to cover deficits could then be scheduled to have the impact upon credit markets and liquidity dictated by current economic policy objectives. With respect to techniques for handling cash operations, two conclusions stand out. First, Treasury cash requirements in recent years, when they have arisen, customarily have been so large that it was not to be expected there would be available at that specific time a volume of nonbank investment funds sufficient to take down the entire offering; this statement has been generally true regardless of the maturity of the securities offered. It is indicated, therefore, that if the Treasury wishes to minimize the amount of underwriting required and to place a maximum proportion of its new securities directly with nonbank investors holding the funds to purchase them, it should attempt to limit the size of its offerings and should develop techniques that would enable these investors to subscribe in confidence that they would get the allotment they wished. Second, so long as the offering is in excess of the current availability of investible funds in its maturity range, the overage probably will be underwritten with commercial bank credit. The only question is whether the underwriting should be by individuals and others encouraged by the terms of the offering to speculate on a quick profit, with allotments financed on a bank loan, or by commercial banks directly. In recent years the technique frequently followed has been to discriminate against commercial bank subscriptions, but the performance of new issues when banks have underwritten the offering, as against market performance when "others" have done the underwriting, raises serious questions as to the wisdom of this policy.

D. CASH REFUNDING

The problems created by exchange refunding finally led the Treasury in August, 1960, to experiment with cash refunding (maturing securities were subsequently refunded through cash offerings in 1961, under the new Treasury administration of Secretary Dillon and Under Secretary Roosa). Cash refunding involves the sale of a new issue for cash in an amount approximately equal to an issue(s) that is maturing and for settlement on the date that the old issue matures. The maturing securities are then retired with the proceeds of the new cash issue. Payment for the new securities may be made by tendering the maturing securities, but holders of the maturing issue do not have "rights" to full or preferred allotment as they do in the case of exchange refunding.

Two problems of exchange refunding, in particular, had plagued the Treasury. First, the uncertain size of turn-ins or "attrition" seriously complicated the scheduling of cash flows and of cash financing. Second, the loss of control over the maturity structure of the debt when holders of maturing issues were offered an option among securities of different maturity (necessary to resist the steady shortening of the debt) had become increasingly serious. The lesson was driven home with particular force in the June, 1958, refunding, when holders of $7.4 billion out of total maturities of $9.6 billion elected the intermediate bond rather than the one-year certificate and the over-issue of bonds helped precipitate a disorderly market collapse. A wish

174

to forestall a similar episode in the future when speculative currents might be running strongly was an important reason for the decision to experiment with cash refunding of maturing securities.

In technical detail, cash refunding differs little from cash offerings to raise new money. The same procedure is followed in deciding upon issues to be offered and the terms on which they should be offered. Terms are announced on a Thursday about two weeks from maturity of the issue(s) to be refunded, and subscription books are open the following Monday (for one day only, rather than the three days usually allowed on exchange offerings). Typically, two or more issues are offered to investors, including a one-year maturity and at least one of longer term, in a total amount approximately equal to the amount maturing. The amount to be awarded in each issue is specified, however, rather than being left to decision of investors. Also, the total amount may be either greater or less than the amount maturing if the Treasury wishes to use the financing to borrow money, net, or to retire debt. Payment is in cash, although maturing securities may be used to make payment in lieu of cash; tax and loan account payment by commercial banks is not permitted.

While cash refunding is clearly superior to exchange refunding in many respects, particularly as it gives the Treasury closer control over the debt, the technique has its weaknesses. In particular, it may prove to be a "fair weather" technique, not safely usable for large refunding operations at times when competing demands for a limited supply of funds create pressures in the capital markets—precisely those times when it would be most useful to forestall large attrition. Also, the technique should be used with discretion so as not to place an unreasonable redistribution process on the market when the refunding is very large or when the technical circumstances surrounding the operation suggest an exchange rather than cash refunding. For example, if the ownership distribution of the maturing securities is such as to suggest a good exchange interest for the new securities the Treasury intends to offer, a better result might be obtained on exchange than through a cash refunding. Perhaps most important, cash refunding does not correct the basic weakness of refunding procedures followed by the Treasury before 1960—*i.e.*, the failure to offer a refunding option *before* maturity so as to avoid losing the longer-term funds committed to the investment.

E. FINANCING IN REGULAR TREASURY BILLS

The portion of its debt operations in which the Treasury has encountered the fewest problems is the handling of discount Treasury bills. Regular bills outstanding reached a peak of $17.0 billion at the end of 1945 and subsequently were reduced in amount to $11.5 billion by mid–1949. Additions to Treasury bills in following years had brought the total outstanding to an all-time high of $32.4 billion by December, 1960, of which $19.6 billion were in the three-month series, $6.3 billion in the six-month series, and $6.5 billion in the one-year series.

Techniques of Treasury financing in regular bills are quite uncomplicated. At the end of 1960 there were thirty issues of regular discount Treasury bills outstanding, twenty-six maturing each Thursday in the following six months and four maturing at the middle of January, April, July, and October. Each Monday the Treasury sells at auction two new bill issues for payment the following Thursday, one bearing a twenty-six-week maturity and the other a thirteen-week maturity. Actually, the thirteen-week bill issue is an additional amount of the twenty-six week bills that had been sold thirteen weeks earlier. Holders of the maturing bills which the new bills replace may tender them in payment for the new bills if they choose, but they do not have an exchange right to allotment of new bills. Each issue of bills is sold at auction, on a discount basis, with allotments made to highest bidders down to the price at which sufficient subscriptions have been received to cover the amount of bills offered by the Treasury.[17] Investors are allowed to tender for up to $200 thousand of thirteen-week bills and $100 thousand of twenty-six-week bills in each auction on a noncompetitive basis, and these small tenders are allotted in full at the average price determined by the competitive bids; otherwise, allotments are made wholly on a competitive basis.[18]

Treasury bills are beyond question the most widely held and most popular income-earning liquidity instrument in the United States money market. Bills are held for the investment of short-term funds by financial institutions of all types, incorporated and unincorporated business concerns, state and local governments, foreign private and official investors, trust and pension funds, and by a good many individuals. All of these investors may, and many do, tender directly for awards of new bills. Small, noncompetitive tenders are received at all Federal Reserve Banks (the Reserve Banks are agents for the Treasury in all debt operations) in approximate ratio to the economic importance of the District, but the bulk of the competitive tenders are made in New York. In a typical auction, all but about $300–400 million of total competitive awards are in New York City.

17. For example, on Monday, February 6, 1960, the Treasury offered $1.1 billion Treasury bills at auction to be dated Thursday, February 9, and to mature Thursday, May 11, 1960. Bids were received totaling $1.9 billion, of which $1.1 billion were accepted. The highest price on the competitive bids was 99.413, equivalent to a rate of discount of 2.322 per cent, and the lowest price accepted was 99.394, equivalent to a rate of discount of 2.397 per cent. Average price for the $1.1 billion was 99.400 and average rate 2.374 per cent. In addition, on the same day the Treasury auctioned $500 million of twenty-six-week bills at an average price of 98.703 and average rate of 2.566 per cent.

18. This includes allotments on tenders for the Federal Reserve System Open Market Account. The Open Market Account submits a tender whenever it holds maturing bills, sometimes intending to roll-over its holdings, sometimes intending to run them off. It does not receive preferential treatment, however, and if a tender intended to be in the range of accepted prices should miss, the System would not get an allotment. Incidentally, the Federal Reserve System does not purchase bills, or any other regular securities, directly from the Treasury for cash. Its allotments of bills are always paid for through exchange of the maturing issue, and the System Account never tenders for more of the new bills than it holds of the maturing issue.

Thus, in an auction of two bill issues totaling $1.6 billion, approximately $300–400 million might be awarded on noncompetitive tenders, $300 million or so might be awarded on competitive tenders outside New York, and the remaining $1.0–1.1 billion of competitive awards would be in New York. The clustering of competitive tenders in the money market center is a normal outgrowth of the auction process, in which it is important to be close to the center of the market so as to be able to judge the minimum price that is likely to be necessary to get an allotment. In the case of most out-of-town investors it is simpler to have a New York bank submit the tender on the basis of the latest report in the market as to where the bidding will stop than it is to attempt to arrive at an independent evaluation.

The dealers in United States Government securities play an important role in the bill auction and in making markets for the constantly heavy volume of trading in new and outstanding bills by investors making money-market adjustments. Each Monday, during the course of the auction, the dealers are in touch with all of their bank and nonbank customers, and from these contacts form a picture of the emerging demand for the new bills. Typically, the average rate on the new bills will be about five basis points (.05 of one per cent) above the quoted market rate on the longest outstanding bills, but the plans of investors as they become known to the dealers may suggest a larger or smaller spread. Usually a clear consensus of the "to be sure" price and the "stop out" price has formed by a few minutes before subscriptions close at 1:30 P.M. (New York time) and this consensus, as relayed by the dealers, is the basis on which investors tender. Dealers themselves, as a group, usually bid to get allotments of about $300 million thirteen-week bills, and about $150 million twenty-six-week bills, although this amount may vary considerably from one auction to the next, depending upon the outlook for secondary market demand for the bills. The new bills then begin trading when-issued on Tuesday, and dealers ordinarily attempt to dispose of their allotments before it is necessary to pay for the bills on Thursday.

As noted earlier, the Treasury has had very few problems in its weekly financing through regular Treasury bills. In the auction held on June 1, 1953, at the time of the near-crisis in the Government securities market, there was some uncertainty for a time as to whether bids would be adequate to cover the auction, and in fact the coverage was slim. Similar, through less dramatic, uncertainties have arisen in a few other bill auctions in recent years, but by and large the Treasury rolls over its weekly bill maturity with a minimum of disturbance to the market and of agony to itself.

Moreover, the regular weekly bills have been the medium through which the Treasury has accomplished a considerable amount of cash financing. By periodic additions of $100 or $200 million to bills offered in the weekly auctions, and through the inauguration of the six-month series in December, 1958, weekly maturities have been increased from $900–1,000 million in 1949 to $1.6 billion by the end of 1960. In total over the eleven years, some $14.6 billion of new money was raised through weekly bills. At the same time, it should not be concluded from the smooth functioning of the weekly auction that there is an extensive potential demand at any one time for additional amounts of discount bills. In early 1951, when weekly bill issues were $1.0–1.1 billion, total tenders averaged $1.8–1.9 billion, or a coverage of unsatisfied bids in the neighborhood of $800 million each week. By the last quarter of 1960, the average weekly issue (three-month and six-month combined) had been increased to $1.6 billion, while average tenders had grown to about $3.1 billion, nearly doubling the margin and suggesting that investor demand for bills has grown secularly. However, typically, three-fourths, or more, of the margin of tenders over the amount of the issue represents bids by dealers and New York banks that are intentionally entered well below the expected minimum price in the auction, as underwriting bids. The increase in the margin is due principally to the fact that there are now two weekly issues to be underwritten. Therefore, the potential margin of actual unsatisfied customer demand for bills in a typical weekly auction is relatively small, and efforts to raise new cash through adding to bill maturities, all else equal, probably should be gradual rather than in large amounts.

Beginning in 1959, the Treasury has had outstanding four issues of one-year bills in addition to the regular weekly maturities. The one-year bills mature in the middle of January, April, July, and October each year, and at the end of 1960 were outstanding in the amount of $1.5 billion for each except the April, 1961, issue, which was $2.0 billion. In technical detail, the method of selling one-year bills is identical to that used in selling three-month and six-month bills. The Treasury offers at auction an amount equal to the maturing issue (or more or less if money is to be borrowed or repaid) and awards bills in this amount to the highest bidders. The maturing bills then are repaid with the proceeds of the new issue.

As described earlier, the principal purpose in inaugurating the one-year bill series was to simplify and rationalize the permanent short-term debt. After an initial period of seasoning, the one-year bills have become a well-accepted component of Treasury debt. The Treasury's debt-management problems in the short-term area have been reduced and the impact upon the market of such financing lessened by the partial substitution of auction bills for certificates of indebtedness.

F.   TAX-ANTICIPATION FINANCING

Since 1950, Treasury revenues have reflected the process of first shifting corporate income tax payments from a schedule of four equal payments in the quarterly months (March, June, September, December) of the calendar year following the year in which the tax liability was incurred to two equal payments in the first two quarters of that year, and next, to four equal payments at quarterly dates with the first two payments due in the last half of the calendar year for which the tax is being levied. Corporate income tax liabilities again returned to an even quarterly basis in 1960, when the transition process was completed. Even though liabilities are now on an even quarterly basis, however, the law permits corporations to underestimate in their September and December payments, so that tax receipts are still heavier in March and June. The Treasury has, in the eight years 1953 through 1960, adjusted to this irregularity through the sale of tax-anticipation securities for cash in the July-December period to finance the cash deficit at that time, and has then retired these securities out of surplus revenues in the January-June half year.

In total, the Treasury has sold $62.2 billion tax-anticipation obligations in the eight years 1953 to 1960, inclusive, of which $27.6 billion were certificates of indebtedness, sold at a fixed rate of interest, and $34.7 billion were Treasury bills sold at discount.[19] All tax-anticipation bills were, of course, sold for cash payment, but $2.8 billion of the tax certificates were issued in exchange for maturing regular series obligations. Because of the seasonal pattern of tax receipts, the largest part of all tax obligations have been sold in the first half of the fiscal year to mature at the March or June tax dates, but some $13 billion matured in the calendar year in which they were sold. These included $7.7 billion sold to finance the Treasury between the March and June tax dates, to mature in June (1954, 1955, and 1960), $3.8 billion also sold to finance the interval between March and June, to mature in September (1953, 1957, and 1959), and $1.5 sold in May, 1959, to mature in December of that year.

Financing techniques employed in the sale of tax-anticipation certificates and bills are nearly identical to those used in the sale of regular Treasury obligations for cash, but one minor variation might be noted. Tax issues generally bear a maturity date that falls a week or so after a quarterly tax date (*e.g.,* March 22)

19. The data for 1956 include $3.4 billion of "special" bills which were replaced with June tax bills at maturity in January and February, 1957; on the other hand, the data for 1957 do not include $1.75 billion "special" bills since these were refunded with permanent debt instruments in February, 1958.

and bear interest to that date, but they are acceptable at par, with interest to maturity, in payment of taxes on the tax date. The only purpose of this added bonus is to encourage their purchase by investors who plan to use them to pay taxes. Another minor difference is that the decision-making process in settling on terms is simplified since the amount of cash needed and the length of time it will be needed are known, so that the only decisions to make are whether the offering should be bills or certificates and, if the latter, the coupon rate of interest that should be placed on the offering. Otherwise, the procedure is the same as that described for regular cash offerings.

Tax-anticipation securities are designed primarily for corporate investors, being tailored to provide for investment of tax funds to the date taxes are due. Therefore, while commercial banks are the principal underwriters of the Treasury, as they are in cash offerings of regular short-term securities, corporate subscriptions for tax issues tend to reduce the proportion of the total allotted to commercial banks. Of the $27.6 billion of tax certificates sold by the Treasury in the calendar years 1953–1960, commercial banks were awarded $17.2 billion, or about 60 per cent. The commercial bank subscriptions are principally for underwriting purposes (to get the Treasury deposit) and banks sell their allotments as corporate tax reserves build up. By the end of the calendar year in which these tax certificates were sold, commercial banks had sold or redeemed $9.2 billion of their original allotments, while other investors (principally nonfinancial corporations in this instance) had added $6.3 billion to their original purchases on direct issue from the Treasury. The breakdown of tax bill allotments by investor grouping is not published in detail, but the data do indicate the extent of reliance upon commercial banks as underwriters. Commercial banks bought more than $30 billion of the total $34.6 billion, or some seven-eighths of the total. In a competitive auction, the value of the Treasury deposit is reflected directly in the prices that banks bid for tax-anticipation bills (which provide for payment through credit to tax and loan account, whereas regular bills are sold for cash payment). The equivalent rates of discount at which banks bid, therefore, are usually several basis points below the current market rate of interest for obligations of similar term. Other investors are discouraged from bidding or, if they do, they usually are outbid by the banks. In the three most recent years, 1958–1960, virtually all of the tax-anticipation bills sold by the Treasury have gone to banks.

In principle, tax-anticipation securities should be resorted to only when the forecasts of receipts and expenditures suggest that the funds will be available within the fiscal year to redeem the obligations, *i.e.,* only if the best information shows that the current cash deficit is purely seasonal. At times during recent years, the Treasury has resorted to tax-anticipation securities or "special" bill issues for reasons of expediency, when it was reasonably clear that the current need for cash was more than seasonal and called for permanent financing. For example, at the time the two issues of "special" three-month bills were sold in October and November, 1956, and the issue of June, 1957, tax-anticipation bills was sold in December of that year, it appeared unlikely that the Treasury would have the necessary surplus cash even to retire the already outstanding March, 1957, tax issue. In fact, the Treasury found it necessary to refund the two special bills at maturity into June, 1957, tax bills, sell $3.4 billion of regular certificates and notes for cash in late March, 1957, sell $1.5 billion of September, 1957, tax bills in late May, and $3.0 billion of March, 1958, tax bills at the beginning of July. As difficult as the market condition might have appeared in late 1956, the extremely complex financing program and more difficult market conditions the Treasury confronted in the first half of 1957 provided a valuable object lesson in the danger of attempting to avoid a necessary financing job by using a temporizing device that simply deferred the day of reckoning.

G. FIXING COUPON RATES ON NEW TREASURY ISSUES

The discussion earlier in this chapter of the process followed in determining the issues to be offered in a Treasury cash or ex-

183

change financing made only passing reference to the selection of coupon rates of interest to be attached to the new securities. Since the process of setting the rate of interest involves considerations and problems that are independent of the type of security to be offered, it will be treated separately here.

The controlling consideration is that the rate of interest offered on the new issue should be sufficiently attractive against current market rates on similar maturities to induce investors to subscribe for the securities. It follows that the rate of interest selected should be somewhat above current market rates (new issue rates on securities of all types—corporate, tax-exempt, and United States Government—are always higher than market rates on seasoned issues). Working from a yield curve based on the latest market price quotations on outstanding securities, the Treasury selects a rate of interest lying somewhat above the plotted yield curve at the maturity sector already determined upon. Typically, the rate on the new securities has been about ⅛ per cent above market rates, but there has been considerable variation.[20] On certificate offerings, for example, the indicated spread between new issue and market rates has ranged from a low of five basis points in the November, 1954, refunding to a high of 35 basis points in the November, 1957, refunding. There has been no evidence of consistent variation in the rate spread as between different maturities offered, in spite of the fact that a given rate premium is equivalent to a larger price premium the longer the maturities of the instrument.[21]

The record of the relationship between new issues rates and the yield curve helps to illustrate the most important difficulty

20. The practice of offering all securities at par (a practice that was finally abandoned in the June, 1958, cash financing) has complicated the process of rate selection. The Treasury has not used fractions smaller than ⅛ per cent in its coupon rates of interest, and frequently this has meant either selecting a rate too close to the curve or a rate that was unnecessarily attractive against the current market.

21. That is to say, a 10 basis point premium on a one-year certificate is equivalent to roughly $\frac{3}{32}$ in price, whereas a similar rate premium on a 10-year bond is equivalent to nearly a full point price premium.

faced by the Treasury in assigning rates of interest to its new securities. This is the fact that the spread between the yield curve and rates on new securities offered in refundings averaged larger between mid–1953 and mid–1954 and late 1957 and mid–1958, periods when interest rates were declining and generally low, than during the years 1955–1957 (through July) and 1959–1960 (through March), when interest rates were rising. For example, when price premiums are compared for new issues with maturities of fifteen months or less, the average for the mid–1953 to mid–1954 refundings was $0.18, compared to $0.065 for 1955 and 1956 and $0.08 for the first seven months of 1957.[22] This finding is rather startling in view of the fact that the greater difficulty of financing in periods of credit restraint and rising interest rates would lead to the expectation that the Treasury would, if anything, be more generous in its pricing at such times. The record indicates either that the Treasury debt managers have consciously overpriced their securities at times when market conditions have been most difficult for a successful financing, thus adding to their attrition problem, or that the rate relationship indicated by the foregoing figures suggests the existence of influences beyond the Treasury's control. It is unlikely that it is the former.[23]

The more likely explanation is that the Treasury intended to price its securities as attractively at one time as another, but that market rate developments created the appearance of less generous pricing in periods of tight money. Specifically, when restraint on money and credit has created a condition of pressure on the securities markets, causing interest rates to rise more or less steadily, there is a tendency for the market to discount the anticipated influence of a Treasury financing by moving interest

22. In arriving at these figures, the coupon yield was plotted against the yield curve describing closing market prices the day before the Treasury's announcement of terms.

23. This assertion needs some qualification. It is possible that political opposition to ever-higher rates of interest may have influenced the Treasury to over-price its securities in the 1955–1957 and 1959–1960 periods, but in the writer's judgment this influence was not significant.

rates higher in the maturity areas expected to be affected, causing something of a temporary bulge in the yield curve. At times of easy money, on the other hand, when interest rates are declining, the market ordinarily expects the financing to have little, if any, effect, particularly in the short-term area.[24] Consequently, if the Treasury were to set its new issue rates with the same spread from the yield curve at all times it would be ignoring the fact that, when money is tight, the curve has already discounted part of the yield premium expected.

Why, then, should not the Treasury do precisely this, consciously being more liberal in its pricing when money is tight? This question is at the center of the most difficult aspect of the pricing problem. In the case of cash financing in a period of tight money it is assumed that the commercial banks, attracted by the opportunity to pay through book credit, will provide temporary underwriting in a way that does not increase the money supply, as described earlier in this chapter. In a refunding operation, however, there is no incentive for the banks, dealers, or others to underwrite unless there is a clear prospect of a profit from the new issue rising to a premium. Dealer awards of new securities issued on exchange in the five years 1956–1960 did, in fact, average nearly $400 million per operation, indicating some underwriting assistance to the Treasury, but it is likely that the largest part of these awards had already been offset by when-issued sales of the new securities, particularly in times of tight money and rising interest rates. Essentially, the problem faced by the Treasury in refunding at a time of pressure on money and credit is the fact that some proportion of the maturing issue is held by investors who need the cash on or about the maturity date and have no interest in the new issue, while at the same time the pool of idle funds among other investors available for net investment in the new securities falls short of the

24. In fact, the Treasury in recent years has usually attempted to reduce the short-term debt when money has been easy, and the anticipated reduction in the supply of short-term securities has tended to drive rates in this sector of the market lower in advance of refunding operations.

planned cash turn-in of the first group of investors. This type of basic illiquidity is to be expected at times when Federal Reserve efforts to limit money and credit are truly effective. If the Treasury should attempt to minimize attrition under these circumstances by attaching an extremely attractive coupon to its new issue, the primary effect probably would be simply to move market rates of interest higher. The available supply of funds to purchase rights or when-issued securities from holders needing cash would not be enlarged, and the additional funds attracted into the rights would tend to come from the sale of other securities of similar maturity to the new issue. These sales could be effected only at higher rates for outstanding obligations, so that the net effect probably would be to move market rates a notch higher and eliminate the rate spread in favor of the new issue that the Treasury had tried to achieve.[25]

Before closing the discussion on Treasury techniques for setting coupon rates on new securities, one final point might be made. Contrary to beliefs held in some political circles—and apparently among some economists—the rate of interest on new Treasury securities is determined by the level of market rates; the Treasury does not control the rate of interest it pays to borrow or refund, and could not if it wished to. Its rate-setting function is limited to determining the rate it must pay in the current market if its offering is to be successful.

H.   ALLOTMENTS TO INVESTOR GROUPS

Data are available for the eight years 1953 through 1960 on the allocation of new securities among investor groups. It was noted earlier that allotments of tax-anticipation certificates to commercial banks during these eight years accounted for about three-fifths of all tax certificates sold, and that commercial bank

25. It might be argued that the higher rates would quickly draw more idle funds into investment. While a rising level of interest rates does appear to encourage economizing on money balances, this process evidently occurs slowly and probably could not be counted upon to supply a large volume of new funds in a brief period.

allotments of tax-anticipation bills accounted for an even larger part of the total of such bills sold. Allotments to nonfinancial corporations accounted for most of the balance of tax issues. These data suggest the important role of commercial banks as underwriters of Treasury cash financing through tax issues.

The data in Table 17, showing allotments of regular issues of Treasury certificates, notes, and bonds over the past eight years, offer further evidence of the extent to which Treasury cash offerings are initially underwritten by the commercial banking system. Commercial banks were awarded 59 per cent of all regular coupon securities sold by the Treasury for cash between 1953 and 1960, with their proportion of total allotments ranging from 84 per cent on issues of certificates to 65 per cent of note issues, and 36 per cent of bond issues. The very high percentage of certificate allotments to commercial banks is accounted for by the technical advantage given to commercial banks, particularly when the market is tight and interest rates rising, by the privilege of making payment through tax and loan account credit. Allotments to dealers and brokers should also be considered as underwriting purchases; their allotments represented 6 per cent of total regular cash issues, consisting of nominal amounts of regular certificates, 6 per cent of notes, and 9 per cent of bonds. Allotments of cash issues to other groups of investors have generally been relatively small. Savings-type investors (including insurance companies, mutual savings banks, private pension funds, and state and local government pension funds) accounted for 11 per cent of all cash awards. Participation of this group of investors was concentrated in bond offerings, where they accounted for 26 per cent of all bonds sold for cash (partly as a result of Treasury techniques that discriminate in favor of these investors, as described below). Nonfinancial corporations received 7 per cent of all cash allotments, principally accounted for by awards of Treasury notes. Individuals and "others" accounted for 8 per cent and 4 per cent, respectively, of all cash awards. United States Government and Federal Reserve accounts were relatively unimportant as purchasers of new Treasury

Table 17—Allotments by Investor Class on Subscriptions for Marketable Issues of Treasury Bonds, Notes, and Regular Certificates of Indebtedness 1953–1960 (Billions of dollars)

	CERTIFICATES OF INDEBTEDNESS		TREASURY NOTES		TREASURY BONDS	
	Cash	Exchange	Cash	Exchange	Cash	Exchange
Q 200						
United States Government Investment Accounts and Federal Reserve System	0.3	103.4	0.8	45.9	0.8	1.2
Commercial Banks	3.1	33.4	17.5	27.8	3.7	29.2
Individuals	*	2.8	1.8	1.6	0.9	1.6
Insurance Companies	*	1.5	0.8	1.6	1.0	2.7
Mutual Savings Banks	*	0.8	0.7	0.9	0.8	1.7
Corporations†	0.1	18.3	2.1	9.0	0.5	2.5
Private Pension Funds†	*	0.7	0.3	0.4	0.4	0.4
State and Local Pension Funds	*	0.1	0.1	0.3	0.5	0.4
Other funds	*	8.4	0.2	4.0	0.1	1.6
Dealers and Brokers	*	3.8	1.6	3.7	0.9	3.6
All others†	*	7.5	1.1	3.8	0.7	1.9
Totals	3.7	180.7	27.0	99.0	10.3	46.8

Source: United States Treasury Department, Treasury Bulletin.

* Less than $50 million.

† Prior to July, 1953, allotments to corporations and private pension and retirement plans are reported by the Treasury in the "all others" classification. The data in this table have been adjusted to prorate allotments on issues in the first half of 1953 among corporate and pension accounts and "all other" accounts in accord with their performance in subsequent financings.

securities sold for cash. In all cases, the allotments under the heading United States Government and Federal Reserve System were to Treasury investment accounts and represented special allotments over and above the amount of securities advertised for sale to the public.

In gross dollar amount, refunding operations were far greater than cash operations in the eight years 1953 to 1960, inclusive, amounting to something more than $320 billion against $41 billion securities sold for cash. The data are swollen, of course, by the inclusion each year of the regular certificate roll-overs. Concentration of Federal Reserve open-market account holdings in short maturities is reflected in the fact that United States Government and Federal Reserve subscriptions accounted for 47 per cent of all securities issued in exchange for matured or called obligations; such official subscriptions represented 58 per cent of all exchange subscriptions for certificates and 46 per cent of all exchange subscriptions for notes. Next in importance were the commercial banks, representing 28 per cent of all exchange subscriptions. While commercial bank exchange subscriptions for certificates and notes were very large in absolute amount, the preponderant importance of the Federal Reserve System in shorter-term coupon securities caused commercial bank subscriptions for certificates and notes to represent, respectively, only 19 per cent and 28 per cent of the total. On the other hand, commercial bank exchange subscriptions for new bonds represented 62 per cent of all bonds issued, with subscriptions tending to concentrate in intermediate obligations. Nonfinancial corporations subscribed for 9 per cent of all securities issued in exchange operations, 1953 through 1960, receiving 10 per cent of all certificates issued, 8 per cent of all notes, and 5 per cent of bonds.

Other groups of investors have been relatively unimportant in the total of exchange subscriptions, although their participation in bonds issued on exchange has been of some importance. Individuals accounted for only 3 per cent of exchange subscriptions for bonds, and dealers and brokers took 8 per cent.

One interesting fact brought out in Table 17 is that the "savings-type" investors took only small amounts of the long bonds issued on refunding operations; their combined subscriptions were only eleven per cent of total allotments. In part, this poor showing of the savings institutions reflects the fact that they held relatively small amounts of the securities being refunded. It also reflects the lack of interest of most institutions of this type in United States Government bonds at the rates of interest that generally prevail relative to competitive rates. Their relatively larger participation in cash subscriptions was a result, in substantial part, of a feeling of obligation to assist the Treasury by subscribing for the cash issue, often planning to offset the subscription by sales of outstanding securities.

By and large, the distribution of securities issued in refunding operations has followed the ownership pattern of the maturing securities that has evolved from the shifting about of the issues during their life. Some redistribution of "rights" always occurs in the weeks prior to the announcement of terms, and this redistribution may be accelerated if there is speculation that the Treasury may offer an issue on which a speculative profit may be made. Treasury ownership statistics suggest, however, that the volume of trading in anticipation of an imminent exchange offering typically involves only marginal amounts of the rights. The data in the table on exchange awards to dealers and brokers suggest that shifts of ownership while exchange subscription books are open also are marginal. Dealers, as a general practice, exchange the rights they hold at the conclusion of the exchange operation and, as discussed earlier, they typically sell when-issued securities rather than rights during the exchange. Thus, their exchange subscriptions give a reasonably good indication of the volume of ownership redistribution incident to a refunding; as Table 17 shows, these subscriptions accounted for only about 3 per cent of all exchange subscriptions.

The conclusion that only marginal ownership shifts occur incident to a Treasury refunding suggests that exchange offerings should be designed to appeal to the holders of the maturing issue (or issues), and since these outstanding issues are, without exception, short-term instruments as they approach maturity (whatever they might have been originally), the bulk of them will be held by commercial banks and other investors whose principal interest in Governments is their liquidity. It might seem to follow from this that only shorter obligations can be offered successfully to refund maturing issues that are so held, and as a general proposition this conclusion is accurate. However, commercial banks—either as underwriters or in subscriptions for their own portfolios—have readily taken large blocks of both intermediate and longer-term bonds at times of easy money and low or declining interest rates. Between mid–1953 and the end of 1954, approximately four-fifths of banks' exchange subscriptions in operations where an option was offered were for the longer maturity. During 1955, when money was still relatively easy but interest rates had started to rise, commercial banks entered only about three-fifths of their subscriptions for the longer maturity when an option was offered. In 1956–57, with interest rates rising almost steadily and with growing strain on money and credit, banks entered almost three-fifths of their subscriptions on optional offerings for the shorter maturity. Then, in the last quarter of 1957 and the first half of 1958, with money again easy, banks exchanged 80 per cent for longer maturities when an option was given; but from mid–1958 through 1960 they took only 40 per cent in the longer option.

In short, the Treasury has found that it is possible to place longer-term notes and bonds of various maturities through its exchange operations, in spite of the fact that maturing issues are held principally by "short-term" investors, but such placements may be made in substantial size only when the Federal Reserve System is maintaining an easy money market. At such times, the commercial banking system absorbs longer-term offerings, both for portfolio investment and as an underwriting investment for subsequent resale. Thus, Table 17 shows that commercial banks accounted for more than 60 per cent of exchange subscriptions for bonds in the eight years 1953 to 1960. The paradox pointed up by the foregoing analysis, however, is that the Treasury has been able to place substantial amounts of securities outside the short-term area only at times when the Federal Reserve System has been attempting to improve credit availability and liquidity. In its effects upon the availability of longer-term funds to other borrowers and upon the liquidity of financial assets, debt management has consistently moved in a direction opposite to that being followed by credit policy.

Discussion of Treasury financing techniques in recent years and of investor subscriptions underwriting Treasury operations would not be complete without reference to the procedures the Treasury has adopted from time to time in its cash operations to control the placement of the new securities. Altogether, eleven issues of Treasury bonds were offered for cash subscription between the completion of the Victory Loan drive in 1946 and the end of 1960. The first bond offering for cash was in June, 1952, and the last was in April, 1960. In each of these operations the Treasury resorted to one device or another in an effort to place as many securities as possible with "savings-type" investors and to limit allotments to commercial banks and "speculative" investors. In nearly all of the operations, commercial bank subscriptions were limited to a percentage of capital, surplus, and undivided profits or of time and savings deposits, or both. Also, in nearly all of the operations, "savings-type" investors received preferential allotments and commercial banks and others received smaller allotments. The net effect of these two types of restrictions is apparent in Table 17, where it can be seen that whereas commercial banks were allotted more than 60 per cent of all bonds issued in exchange for maturing securities between 1953 and 1960, they were allotted only 36 per cent of bonds sold on cash subscriptions.

The wish of the debt managers to place their new bonds firmly with long-term investors is understandable, in view of the unfortunate market performance that has sometimes characterized new issues in which speculative subscriptions have been heavy. At the same time, there is considerable reason for ques-

193

tioning whether the procedures that have been followed have been best adapted to achieve that end or have been proper debt-management techniques. In the first place, the record of operations by life insurance companies and mutual savings banks, as well as other "savings-type" investors, suggests that they have subscribed to new cash issues of Treasury bonds out of a feeling of patriotism or because their industry spokesmen have "committed" them for a certain volume of subscriptions, but that they have not intended to add to their holdings of Governments. Thus, the new issue is taken into portfolio and other securities (frequently of equivalent term) are sold to make room for it. To the extent that this happens, the Treasury obviously has not "placed its debt firmly."

The more important criticism of the techniques the Treasury has used to limit subscriptions or to make preferential allotments, however, is that they appear to be an intrusion of administrative decision into an area that might best be left to market determination. Obviously, the ownership distribution of any given issue will depend upon its investment characteristics, upon the portfolio requirements of investors, and upon the availability and characteristics of alternative investments. The Treasury cannot guide its securities to their final resting place through restrictive conditions on their original issue; in a free market, this results from the interplay of investor demand and investment supply. At the same time, by discriminating against commercial banks, the Treasury has acted against its own best interests by weakening the competitive position of the institutions that are in the best position to provide the underwriting required in a cash offering of Treasury bonds. Some underwriting is, of course, necessary since there probably will not be, at any one time, a sufficient supply of capital seeking investment to absorb the entire Treasury offering immediately. During the period the new bonds are held by underwriters, until they are gradually placed in investment portfolios, short-term credit must be employed to finance them, and this credit ultimately is supplied by commercial banks. To the extent that the underwriting is by individuals or other relatively small speculators in the issue, financed

194

by bank loans, it is likely that the bonds will overhang the market after issue and that "panic" selling may develop if the floating supply of bonds depresses the price to par or below. Because of their relatively limited capital resources, dealers also may find it necessary to unload their allotments if an unfavorable after-market develops; it should be noted, however, that dealers tend to avoid overcommitting their resources in a new Treasury issue, particularly if there are significant uncertainties as to its after-issue price. Commercial banks, on the other hand, have the resources to underwrite a Treasury cash offering of bonds without strain, and they have the "staying power" to hold the new securities until the market is in a position to absorb them without difficulty.

The Treasury's policy of discriminating against commercial banks on cash offerings of bonds apparently reflects a desire to avoid adding to the money supply by financing through the banks, an attitude that can be traced to the techniques employed to finance the Second World War.[26] At a time when a principal objective of financing techniques was to minimize inflationary

26. In his *National Debt in War and Transition,* Henry C. Murphy notes (pp. 88–89) that the criteria of real success in war financing were too complex to be understood by a large sales organization, and that a quantitatively measurable proximate goal was necessary. "This goal was found in the objective of selling Government securities to nonbank investors. . . . This goal . . . [was] so easy to grasp and to measure and so agreeable to traditional patterns of thought that, it must be confessed, [it] became the ultimate—and not merely the proximate—objective of the war borrowing program to the vast majority of officials connected with it from top to bottom" (p. 88).

Statements of Treasury officials referred constantly to the objective of limiting or reducing commercial banks' holdings of Government securities during the war and immediate postwar years, and the durability of this wartime catchphrase as an operating policy is suggested by the following quotation from a speech by the Secretary of the Treasury in 1953. "This administration is doing two things to make our nearly $275 billion debt less inflationary and less dangerous to the value of money and our economy. We are extending the maturity of the debt by placing longer-term issues whenever conditions permit, and as rapidly as possible we are moving more of the debt away from the banks and into the hands of long-term investors." From address by Secretary of the Treasury Humphrey before the Investment Bankers Association of America, Hollywood, Florida, December 1, 1953; contained in *Annual Report* of the Secretary for 1953, pp. 250–255.

pressures by tying up as much as possible of the funds represented by the "forced saving" engendered by defense requirements, and when effective central bank control of bank credit and the money supply was impossible, the attempt to minimize the volume of residual sales to commercial banks made good sense. With independent and effective Federal Reserve policies, however, net changes in commercial bank portfolios over any significant time interval are the result of the central bank's policies, and Treasury attempts to avoid sales of securities to the banks are outmoded and irrelevant.

VI

The Dealer Market
for United States
Government Securities

A principal inducement to many, perhaps most, investors in Government securities is the broad and active secondary market in which Government obligations may be liquidated when needs for cash arise. To the extent that there is a justification for the rate differentials which have prevailed in recent years between United States Government securities and other high-grade, taxable obligations of similar maturity, this justification probably rests more upon the liquidity characteristics of Government securities arising from their marketability than upon their credit risk characteristics.

A great many brokerage firms participate in the Government securities market on an agency basis for customers, and most leading commercial banks throughout the country stand ready to buy or sell Government issues as a service for smaller correspondent banks or other customers. The heart of the Government securities market, however, is a small group of dealer firms, located principally in New York City, which specialize in these obligations. In a sense, these firms provide a wholesale market to which large banks, other financial institutions, nonfinancial corporations, and official accounts may turn to execute transactions which typically run to several millions of dollars. The great bulk of all secondary trading in Government securities is handled by the specialized dealer firms, and their aggregate dollar volume probably exceeds by a considerable margin the combined volume of trading in this country in all other marketable securities.[1] The scope and characteristics of the dealer market in Government securities are important determinants of Treasury debt policy and of the financing alternatives available to the Treasury.

A. History of the Government Securities Market

Prior to the Civil War, only a rudimentary market for United States Government securities existed, due principally to the small volume of Treasury debt at that time. During the years following the War of 1812, as the volume of private and other government securities expanded and as an active financial market developed, Treasury debt was reduced almost steadily; at no time between 1828 and 1860 did the total of United States Government securities outstanding exceed $70 million. Apparently most trading in Government obligations that did take place was handled "over-

---

1. Only sketchy data are available on trading in the "over-the-counter" securities market, of which the Government securities market is a part. Irwin Friend, *et al.*, in *The Over the Counter Securities Markets* (New York: McGraw-Hill, 1958) estimate that sales of United States Government securities by brokers and dealers in the three months September–November, 1949, totaled $26.2 billion and that over-the-counter sales of all other securities in the same three months amounted to $9.0 billion (p. 116; data include distribution of new issues as well as resales). Average quarterly trading volume on the New York Stock Exchange in 1949 was $2.2 billion (New York Stock Exchange, *Fact Book,* 1958). It is likely that total market trading on the American Stock Exchange, in bankers acceptances, in commercial paper, and in all other marketable paper might be added, if they were available, and the sum total of trading in all securities other than Governments would equal little more than one-half the dollar volume of trading in United States Government securities, based on Friend's estimates.

the-counter" in private banking houses which engaged in buying and selling bonds of all types, as dealers, for their own accounts. Indicative of the narrow market for United States Government securities just before the Civil War was the difficulty encountered by Secretary Thomas in December, 1860, when he attempted to raise funds to pay past-due Government salaries and bills. The Secretary offered $5 million of notes to the lowest bidders (in terms of interest rate), but only $1.8 million bids were received at rates of 12 per cent or less. After negotiation, a syndicate of New York banks took the balance of the issue at 12 per cent.

As described in earlier chapters, the first private concern to develop a specialized interest in United States Government securities was the Philadelphia banking house of Jay Cooke and Company. Acting as agent for the Treasury, on a commission basis, Cooke was responsible for the largest and most successful United States Government financing operations during the Civil War. In addition to his activities as a salesman of Government securities, Jay Cooke played an important part in the secondary market, employing both his own and Treasury funds to maintain breadth and stability in the market.

In the years following the Civil War, the most important influences on the market for United States Government securities were the note circulation privilege carried by Government bonds and, particularly after 1880, the sharp reduction in the Treasury debt. As a consequence of these two influences, the rate of interest on Government bonds fell away from competitive rates—to the point that in 1900 the Treasury was able to refund and consolidate the remnants of the Civil War debt at 2 per cent, while high-grade railroad bonds yielded 4 per cent—and nearly all Government securities moved into the portfolios of national banks. Meanwhile, the specialized dealer operation that Jay Cooke and the firms associated with him[2] had developed during the war became of relatively less importance during the era of railroad and industrial financing, and the largest part of the

2. Principally Fisk and Hatch, and Vermilye and Company.

trading in Government issues was taken over by brokerage houses operating through the stock exchange.

The technical problems created by the exercise of the circulation privilege on United States Government bonds against a market background of fluctuating interest rate relationships between Governments and other investments soon created a need for specialists, however, and by 1900 the pendulum had swung back toward a specialized, over-the-counter dealer market. One of the pioneers in the modern Government securities market describes this transition as follows:

Under the Act of 1900, qualifying banks were authorized to issue currency against Government bonds deposited by them up to 100 per cent of the par value of the bonds so long as they were quoted at par, or above par. . . .

Banks which were designated a "Government depositary" of Treasury funds also were required to pledge acceptable securities to secure those Public Deposits, and Government bonds were specified for a notable part of the collateral. Such use of Government bonds—to obtain a national bank charter and to secure Public Deposits and circulation—created the business motive for private banking houses to perform as dealers and supply the bonds needed by banks. Because of their scientific presentation of the subject, demonstrating with calculation tables figured at various prices the profit to be derived, dealers were rewarded by banks with their bond business. . . .

A circulation account was easily put into effect by the dealer, who financed the par value cost of the bonds and received the currency from the Comptroller of the Currency against deposit of the bonds in Washington, assigned to the Treasurer of the United States in trust for a bank's account. The dealer requested the Treasury to prepare plates and currency for a specified bank, which currency the dealer arranged to complete with facsimile signatures of the bank's officers. The dealer accepted the currency in payment for the par value of the bonds, and put it into circulation. The bank only paid the dealer the premium price of the bonds. The operation was automatic, as the circulation account was established without disturbing the bank's balances to pay for the par value of the bonds. . . .

For specialized service, the transactions in Government bonds which previously had been executed on the Stock Exchange gradually went to a few dealers who maintained over-the-counter market at net prices, with no commission charge. That business flourished from the profit in the price spread differences of ⅛ to ¼ between the dealers' bid and asked quotations. In effect, a circulation account converted one form of currency into another form. Around that business the dealers' profession developed.[3]

This, then, was the principal function of the dealer market in United States Government securities in the first fifteen years of the twentieth century, when the total Treasury debt held steadily at a level slightly above $1 billion. The participation of the United States in the First World War, and the rapid increase in the debt to $26 billion by 1919, required a much broader market than had existed earlier. The modern market in Government securities had its origin at this time. Not only did the total of securities outstanding increase by more than twenty times, but the ownership of these securities, which formerly had been concentrated with commercial banks, now was widely spread among individuals and other nonbank investors. Partly as a result of the Treasury's financing policies, partly as an unavoidable consequence of the unprecedented size of the financing operations, a considerable part of the new securities was not firmly placed on original issue, and the task of redistributing these securities created the need for a broader market. The War Finance Corporation, created in 1918, attempted to provide some stability to the market through its program of purchases, but its operations were limited, and the policy of the Treasury was to encourage the development of a broad private market for Government securities.

As a first move toward developing such a market, the Treasury in May, 1920, withdrew its prohibition upon dealer trading in outstanding issues of certificates of indebtedness at prices below par; dealers were already maintaining active markets in Liberty Bonds and Victory Notes at prices—determined by market forces—below par. At the same time, the Federal Reserve Bank of New York began extending sales contract (repurchase) agreements to dealers as a means of assisting them in carrying

---

3. Childs, C. F., *Concerning United States Government Securities* (Chicago: R. B. Donnelley and Sons Co., 1947), pp. 361–62.

certificates at times of tight money and high financing costs. By the end of 1920, nearly all certificate issues were quoted at premiums and dealers reported an active demand for these money market instruments. When, in 1921, the Treasury began its program of issuing three- to five-year notes, the Federal Reserve Bank of New York, at the request of the Secretary of the Treasury, again assisted in the development of the market by extending repurchase agreements to dealers.

It is interesting to note that during this period the Treasury lent its support to the development of trading in Government securities on the Stock Exchange. Although the Federal Reserve Bank assisted the dealer market through repurchase agreements, all of its outright transactions for account of the Treasury were handled on the Stock Exchange, through commercial bank intermediaries, on instructions from the Treasury. By 1925, however, the volume of trading in Government securities in the dealer market had reached a level several times that on the Stock Exchange, and it became obvious that the large orders for the Treasury could be handled more advantageously through the over-the-counter dealer market. Trading in Government securities on the Stock Exchange has since remained small and currently is an infinitesimal fraction of trading in the over-the-counter market.

When a market develops along the line of competitive force, with a minimum of Governmental intervention—or, as in the case of the over-the-counter Government securities market, with some Government opposition—it may be assumed that the practices and institutions of that market are best adapted to the function the market performs. What were the logical reasons, then, for the development of the market for United States Government securities, the largest financial market in the world (in trading volume), as an over-the-counter dealer market, with negotiated prices, rather than as a brokers' market, with prices on each transaction determined at auction?

The first and most compelling reason is the dollar size of individual transactions in Government securities. During the

1920's, the ownership of the war-created Government debt became concentrated in the hands of commercial banks, large non-bank financial institutions, and other large investors; this ownership pattern has continued to the present day. When these institutions employ Government securities for money-market or portfolio adjustments, a single investing or liquidating program frequently runs to tens of millions of dollars and may exceed $100 million.[4] Orders of this size, if placed in an auction market, could move the price of the security substantially, to the disadvantage of the institution placing the order. Dealers, who are in constant touch with all potential sources of supply or demand throughout the country, are in a position to negotiate a price on such large orders that is in line with the current market, buying or selling for their own account. They then can reverse the operation, either by locating customers on the opposite side of the market for the particular issue involved, or by arranging a series of swaps, perhaps involving several customers and several issues, that will have the net effect of unwinding the long (or short) position the dealer assumed when he bought (or sold) the original issue. The flexibility of the distribution process in handling large orders in the over-the-counter market, by contrast with the inflexibility of the auction procedure, led naturally to a shift of trading toward the dealer market as the economy absorbed the debt of World War I, of the 1930's, and of the Second World War.

Another important reason for the development of the Government securities market in the formative years of the 1920's as an over-the-counter dealer market was the fact that dealers competed aggressively for new business and, free of the restrictive trading rules of the Stock Exchange, were able to develop new services and techniques for serving their customers. It was at

4. Friend, *et al., op. cit.,* p. 198, estimate that more than 90 per cent of all trades in Government securities are in excess of $100,000, while only 4 per cent of all trades in common stock run to this size. The same source (p. 178) estimates that only one per cent of market transactions in United States Government securities, by value, are for individuals.

this period that the telephone became the dealer's principal instrument. Dealers remained in continuous telephone contact with their more important customers all over the country, keeping them informed of market developments and of attractive investment opportunities. Moreover, they stood ready to quote bid and offered prices over the telephone and to execute large transactions "over the wire." In this way, the customer was able to buy or sell at a predetermined price, with a minimum of cost and inconvenience, and with immediate execution of his order. In short, the dealers in the over-the-counter market for Government securities offered a superior service at a lower cost; the virtual disappearance of trading in United States Government securities on the Stock Exchange and its transfer to the dealer market was the completely logical result.

The over-the-counter market structure and procedures developed during the 1920's have been continued, with only minor modifications, down to the present. As the Treasury retired debt during the 1920's, some dealer firms left the business, but the growth of the debt during the 1930's and 1940's, and the broader market made possible by the large debt, brought in new firms. At no time, however, has there been more than a handful of dealer firms engaged in making broad markets in United States Government securities. Perhaps the most important force for change in the Government securities market has been the growth in the volume of securities outstanding, making them the largest single outlet for investment funds and, more important, making short-term Government issues the dominant instruments in the money market. This change has moved the short-term Government securities market to the heart of the money market and has created new problems for dealers in financing their positions and in adjusting techniques to the vast daily volume of trading that has resulted from their money-market function. Central to this change has been the development, beginning in 1929, of Treasury bills as an instrument of Treasury finance. The fixed rate curve during World War II and the management of the market by Federal Reserve authorities during the period of debt absorption after the war caused temporary deviations from the course of free market development, but since 1951 the market has been free to adapt itself to the constantly changing forces impinging upon it. The following section describes the organization and functioning of the dealer market for United States Government securities as of the end of 1960.

B. Market Organization

In discussing the organization of the Government securities market, it is useful to draw a clear distinction between the great number of brokers, commercial banks and other intermediaries throughout the country who may, from time to time or fairly regularly, execute orders in Government securities for a customer, and the dealers who specialize in making broad, continuous markets for Government securities. Most of the more than 3,000 brokers and dealers registered with the Securities and Exchange Commission will execute orders in Government securities, and there are more than 80 commercial banks which maintain trading facilities with whom Government securities might be bought or sold.[5] However, the total trading in United States Government securities by all of these concerns probably amounts to only a very small fraction of the volume handled by the dealer firms specializing in this market. The trades outside the primary dealer market would, in nearly all cases, be reflected in the dealer market in any event, since the intermediary presumably would be acting in the capacity of agent and would turn to a dealer to execute the order.

Number of dealers. Currently (end of 1961), there are thirteen nonbank dealer firms specializing in making markets for United States Government securities, and six large commercial banks (four in New York and two in Chicago) maintain separate

5. Friend, *et al., op. cit.,* p. 113; estimate of banks maintaining trading departments is for 1949.

dealer departments specializing in Government issues. Among the nonbank firms, six are substantially more important in the market than the remainder; three of these six are corporations, the other three are partnerships. All of the nonbank dealers maintain their trading offices in the financial district in New York City, although the home office of one of the firms is in Chicago and the nonbank dealers, as a group, maintain a total of 34 branch offices in 14 separate cities. These nineteen firms during the first six months of 1961 handled a daily average of $1.5 billion in transactions, representing an annual volume rate of some $375 billion.[6] Most dealers during this period complained that the market was inactive, so it may be assumed that this figure does not overestimate the typical volume of trading.

Pricing. Many of the dealers (both bank and nonbank) publish daily quotation sheets, showing bid and offer prices and yields on all outstanding marketable United States Government and Government agency issues as of the close of business on the previous day. These quotation sheets, however, are not effective bids or offers at which the dealer will transact business as of the opening of business the next day. Prices and yields change constantly, in response to developing supply and demand conditions and the myriad of influences—some real, some "psychological" —that affect the market outlook. Virtually all trading in the Government securities market is conducted over the telephone, and dealers stand ready at all times to quote their current prices on any securities in which a customer (or another dealer) might be interested. Dealers employ salesmen who visit customers throughout the country, as well as call them by telephone, but these salesmen do not take the initiative in quoting bid or offered prices. Because of the constantly changing influences in the market, responsibility for quoting prices rests with the senior traders, who are continuously in touch with the flow of orders through the market and thus are able to judge the technical strength or weakness of individual issues.

6. The Federal Reserve System began publishing statistics for dealer positions and trading volume on a consistent and continuous basis in 1961.

The bid and offer prices quoted over the telephone by a dealer are usually the "outside" prices at which the dealer will buy or sell; they are not necessarily the actual prices at which a trade will be effected. If the customer actually has an order to execute and is not just checking prices, the dealer usually will shade his prices in order to compete for the business; the "inside" market on which large transactions are executed usually reflects a smaller price spread between bid and offer quotations than the dealer quotes on a routine request. In other words, each large transaction is a negotiated deal and will not necessarily be at either the bid or offer price currently quoted by most dealers in the market.

Treasury bonds, notes, and certificates are currently quoted on a price basis, with fractions in $\frac{1}{32}$ of a point (although prices on the "inside" market frequently are refined to $\frac{1}{64}$, and occasionally to $\frac{1}{128}$), and Treasury bills are quoted on a yield basis, with quotations reading to two decimal points. Dealers' quotations usually contain a spread of $\frac{4}{32}$ to $\frac{8}{32}$ between bid and offer prices on longer-term securities, $\frac{2}{32}$ to $\frac{4}{32}$ on intermediate obligations, and $\frac{1}{32}$ to $\frac{2}{32}$ on certificates or short-term notes and bonds; yield spreads on three-month Treasury bills customarily are 4 to 5 basis points (.04 to .05 per cent). Inside quotations, at which most large orders are executed, would reduce these spreads by perhaps one-half. The efficiency of the market organization is suggested by the fact that even if the "outside" quotations are used, the margin between bid and offered prices is no more than $\frac{1}{4}$ point on long-term bonds, $\frac{1}{16}$ on one-year certificates, and only $\frac{1}{100}$ point on three-month bills; per $100 transaction, these figures reduce to 25 cents, 6 cents, and 1 cent.

Size of transactions. The volume of securities which a dealer will buy or sell at the prices he quotes over the telephone depends upon a good many factors. Obviously, the most important conditioning factor is the dealer's judgment of the breadth of the market for the issue involved, and thus of his ability to reverse the transaction at a profit. If prices are declining and a supply of securities is overhanging the market, a dealer will be reluctant to buy more than a relatively small amount of the issue at his original quotation, although he might negotiate to take larger amounts on a declining price scale; alternatively, he might arrange to take the order on an agency basis rather than for his own account. Even in a declining market, however, a particular dealer might have a short position to cover or might know of a buyer for the securities (perhaps involving a succession of "swaps" in several issues) and be a willing buyer on a rather large scale. Moreover, individual judgments as to the likely course of prices frequently vary, and certain dealers might well be buying for position at the same time that other dealers are retrenching and reducing the size in which they will trade.

In short, the scale in which an investor may buy or sell a particular issue at a price close to prevailing market quotations depends upon the current supply-demand balance in the market, dealers' technical positions in the particular issue, and the general set of expectations as to the outlook for prices and interest rates currently shaping market attitudes. At most times, an investor may feel confident of being able to execute an order for $1 million or more long-term bonds, $3–5 million intermediate obligations, and $10 million or more short-term securities, without difficulty. In a strong and rising market, sell orders several times this size may be effected with ease but buy orders might take time to execute; in a falling market, even sell orders of this size might encounter some problems, but much larger purchase orders could be handled quickly.[7]

Dealer positions. An important characteristic of the Government securities market is the fact that the bulk of the vast volume of trading is executed on a dealer basis, with dealers buying and selling for their own accounts and at their own risk. Depending

7. The latter statement requires some qualification. At some times when prices are moving rapidly in one direction or another, the actual trading market becomes quite thin. Particularly when prices are falling sharply, dealer positions are likely to be quite limited, and problems might be encountered in filling a large purchase order—even though the market generally continues to fall.

upon their evaluation of the outlook, therefore, dealers are able to absorb temporary imbalances in the supply of and demand for particular issues, or in the total of all issues, in their own positions. For example, a net supply of short-term securities customarily comes into the market in the closing weeks of each year as corporate investors and others liquidate to pay taxes or dividends or to improve their cash positions in preparation for their year-end financial statements. Similar seasonal movements in aggregate demand or supply of Government securities occur at the other corporate tax and dividend dates, and for other reasons, throughout the year.

Dealers are able to minimize the impact upon interest rates of these purely seasonal movements by absorbing securities into position or by net sales from position. A similar stabilizing influence is exerted at times of Treasury financing, as noted in earlier chapters. Direct allotments of new issues to dealers do not ordinarily bulk large in the total of any Treasury financing operation, but dealers play an important role in the redistribution through the market of "rights" or "when-issued" securities. Whether the operation involves the refunding of an outstanding issue or the sale of new securities for cash, there is likely to be a temporary over-supply of the new securities until there has been time for investment demand to materialize in sufficient volume to absorb the issue. During this period, dealers' positions will be temporarily swollen. On balance, the fact that dealers buy for and sell from position means that price and yield movements are more orderly and less subject to seasonal or random influences than they would be in an auction market serviced by brokers.

At the same time, the controlling consideration in dealers' management of their positions is the intention to make a profit from the net spread between buying and selling price, and pursuit of this objective can add to the abruptness with which prices and yields adjust in response to cyclical influences. The total of dealer positions in Government securities is inversely correlated with the direction of interest rate movement, particularly when it is expected that rates will continue to move in a given direction for some time. That is to say, dealers should be expected to add to their positions as quickly as possible when interest rates turn cyclically lower and to reduce their positions as quickly as possible when interest rates turn cyclically upward. Statistics collected by the Treasury and the Federal Reserve System for 1958 show that in the six weeks following the sharp break in the market at the middle of June dealer positions were reduced by $2.1 billion. This liquidation undoubtedly accelerated the rate of price decline.

In part, this behavior would reflect intelligent speculation on the part of dealers, but it also is an unavoidable aspect of a freely moving market. Dealers consider their principal function to be that of traders, not speculators or investors in Government securities; but to be able to trade in size it is necessary to have an inventory of securities in position. Therefore, whenever the outlook suggests that dealers will not lose money by carrying securities in position—whether through declining prices or excessively heavy financing costs—they will choose to carry rather sizable positions, simply to facilitate their trading operations and, when financing rates are low, to add to their profits through the rate differential. But in the face of clear evidence that interest rates are turning higher, the potential loss on a long position outweighs the trading advantage it carries, and dealers are forced to lighten positions. A small net trading position does not mean that a dealer is unable to trade, although the job of matching bids and offers becomes much more complicated. Also, by selling certain issues short, a dealer may hedge a long position in other issues, thus maintaining a trading position that is protected against price movements. The difficulty with this procedure, however, is that it frequently is difficult to borrow securities to make delivery on a short sale, not to mention the fact that the ½ per cent charge on borrowed securities might make a short position expensive if maintained for any length of time. In any event, the net effect of the cyclical fluctuations in dealers' positions is to add to the rapidity with which interest rates adjust higher or lower at turning points in Federal Reserve policy by adding net dealer selling or buying to the similar adjustments being attempted by other investors at such times.

Published data on the size of dealer positions became available on a continuous basis only in 1961. These data plus the scattered evidence available for earlier periods suggest that, in total, the positions of the dealers typically amount to a billion dollars or more, and that fluctuations in these positions over the interest rate cycle may be as much as two or three billion dollars. Figure 1 depicts movements in total loans of New York City banks to brokers and dealers against United States Government security collateral and of Federal Reserve Repurchase agreements with these dealers for the period January, 1951, to December, 1957, plotted against the level of auction rates on new Treasury bills. The total of such loans fluctuated from almost $1.2 billion in June, 1952, to only $100 million in September of that year; loans subsequently rose to $800 million in July, 1954, fell to $100 million or less during much of 1956 and 1957, and then rose to about $900 million in December, 1957.

In general, two types of movements are evident in the data presented in Figure 1. First, there is a clear inverse relationship between interest rate movements and loan totals, suggestive of the cyclical changes in dealer positions described above. Second, there is a reasonably clear seasonal pattern, with loans increasing at mid-year and end-of-year, and declining in the opening weeks of most years; these movements suggest the seasonal changes in dealer positions discussed earlier. Many of the fluctuations not easily traceable to either seasonal or cyclical factors occurred at times of major Treasury financing operations.

It would be hazardous, however, to draw firm conclusions about either the size or the fluctuations in dealer positions 1951 to 1957 from the data on loans to dealers by New York banks and repurchase agreements written by the Federal Reserve Bank of New York. These institutions do not provide for all dealer financing needs, and their importance as sources of funds to finance dealers shifts seasonally and cyclically. Other commercial banks throughout the country provide part of the loan credit

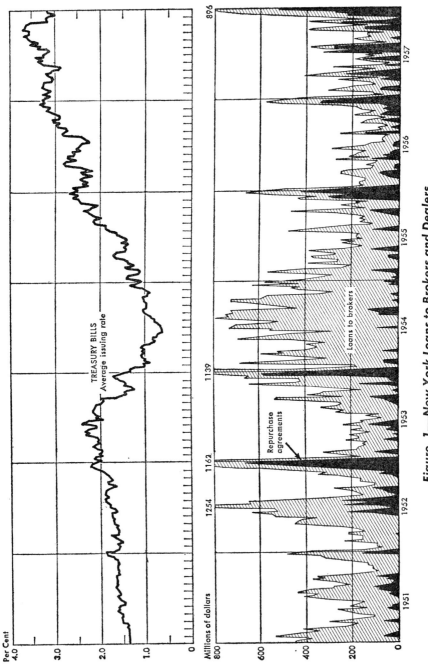

Figure 1—New York Loans to Brokers and Dealers
on Governments and Federal Reserve Repurchase
Agreements, 1951–1957

used by dealers, nonfinancial corporations have become an increasingly important source of funds (through repurchase agreements or "buy backs"), and a variety of other institutions participate from time to time in dealer financing.

The data on dealer positions which the Federal Reserve System began to publish in early 1961 give a more complete picture of the size of dealer inventories, but the series has not been available long enough to give a picture of changes in positions over the business cycle or to permit measurement of seasonal changes. In the four months March through June, 1961, a period of easy money and generally stable interest rates, total dealer positions averaged $2.4 billion and ranged from a low of $1.8 billion (late March) to a high of $3.2 billion (mid-May). The high in May coincided with the peak in bond prices and with a large Treasury financing. Holdings of issues within one-year of maturity accounted for more than 80 per cent of total positions, on average, and securities one to five years from maturity accounted for another 15 per cent. Positions in longer issues averaged less than 5 per cent and moved promptly from a plus to a minus (net short) when bond prices turned lower after the middle of May.

The new Federal Reserve data also provide interesting information on the sources of dealer financing. In the four months March through June, 1961, New York banks provided 23 per cent of the credit used by dealers, "out-of-town" banks supplied another 22 per cent, nonbank corporations accounted for no less than 47 per cent of the total, and all others 8 per cent. These data suggest the importance that repurchase agreements have achieved, since all of the funds supplied by nonbank corporations were in this form and a significant part of "out-of-town" bank financing also was through "r. p.'s."

The short period for which the data have been available does not permit firm generalizations about seasonal or cyclical shifts in the sources of financing. However, other evidence does suggest certain generalizations. Seasonal shifts in the sources of dealer financing are influenced by corporate cash requirements. Nonfinancial corporations may either invest temporarily surplus funds outright in financial assets maturing at or near the date the money will be needed, or they may purchase short-term Government securities, whatever their maturity, on a commitment by the dealer to repurchase these securities on the specific day that the corporation requires cash. Since corporate needs for cash tend to cluster around the quarterly tax dates, at dividend dates that are fairly uniform for many large corporations, and at statement dates, large blocks of securities ordinarily return to the dealers at these times to be financed elsewhere, frequently at the New York banks and sometimes on repurchase agreements with the Reserve Bank (if there is a concurrent credit policy need to supply bank reserves to the market).

A more important type of shifting in the source of funds for dealer financing probably occurs over the interest-rate cycle. It should be noted at the outset that, all else equal, dealers probably would prefer to finance their positions with the money-market banks in New York city, in spite of the fact that these banks customarily will lend only in clearinghouse funds and not in Federal funds. Financing in New York does not involve the cost of transferring securities that is attached to repurchase agreements, and the process of financing with one lender is considerably simpler and less expensive than scouring the country for funds from a variety of sources. However, all else is not equal. The lending rate to dealers at the New York banks customarily is higher than at other out-of-town institutions, banks, or corporations, and at times of money tightness it may be prohibitively higher.[8] This situation results from the fact that

8. For example, in the fall of 1957, the New York lending rate to dealers rose to 4½ per cent, approximately a full point above the yield on Treasury bills and even further above the coupon rate on other securities carried in dealers' positions. On the latter point, in computing the net cost of carrying positions, dealers measure the current return on their investment in position, rather than the effective yield to maturity, against the cost of financing. For instance, on January 31, 1958, the 2½'s of December 1967–72 were quoted at 93½ to yield 3.04 per cent to maturity, but a short-term dealer investment in these securities (assuming no price change) would accrue interest at 2½ per cent on a $93.50 investment, or a current rate of return of only 2.68 per cent.

214

in a tight money market the pressure on bank reserves and liquidity focuses with particular intensity on the central reserve New York City banks which, in a sense, bear the brunt of residual money market adjustments for the entire financial system. The New York banks at such times are forced to reduce liquidity reserves of all types, including dealer loans. The burden, then, is thrown upon the Government securities dealers to locate funds outside New York and, by so doing, channel reserves into the money center. It should be added that the large New York banks, two in particular, recognize a responsibility to finance the dealers if financing cannot be located elsewhere, but when money is tight they function only as "lenders of last resort" at more or less severe penalty rates. The net result probably is for a relatively larger proportion of dealer financing to be placed with New York banks when money is easy and these banks are in a position to lower their rates to compete for dealer loans, and for a relatively smaller proportion to be placed with New York banks when money is tight.

In summary, the development of the Government securities market as an over-the-counter dealer market rather than as an exchange auction market makes it necessary for the professional dealers in United States Government securities to carry inventories in order to facilitate the servicing of customer orders. Reliance upon corresponding investor sales and purchases in the market to balance out fortuitously from day to day, the only alternative to dealer inventories, probably would not allow for orderly execution of the volume of trades currently passing through the market. These inventories customarily are fairly large, but their size, per se, is not particularly important. The important elements in dealers' management of their positions are:

1. Seasonal imbalances in the supply of and demand for short-term Government securities are absorbed, in large part, in dealer positions, thus smoothing out short-term rate movements and providing continuity to the trading market.

2 1 5

2. Wide cyclical swings in dealer positions accelerate the rapidity of interest rate adjustments at times of fundamental shifts in expectations as to prospective rate movements and, presumably, increase the amplitude of rate movement over the business cycle.

3. Procedures developed by dealers to finance their positions have contributed to the development of a sensitive national money market.

Market mechanics. The volume of trading in the United States Government securities market since the Second World War and the development of that market as the key institution in the national money market have required highly refined market machinery, trading techniques, and market procedures. The important services performed by the market for the Treasury, for the Federal Reserve System, and for the national economy have been made possible, in a significant sense, by the intelligent origination of the proper mechanical procedures for the job that was to be done.

As noted earlier, virtually all transactions are executed over the telephone. The order may arise from an unsolicited inquiry from a customer or in response to a suggestion from the dealer and be completed in a single telephone conversation. It may involve several calls, as the customer "shops around" among the dealers for the best price or as the dealer defers making a firm bid or offer on the transaction the customer has in mind until he has an opportunity to check on potential sources of demand for or supply of the securities. In some very large buying or selling programs, particularly in intermediate or longer-term issues, the details may have been worked out in conversations between the dealer and the customer extending over several days, and execution of the order may take more than one day. Orders of this nature are sometimes taken by the dealer on an agency arrangement rather than as an outright purchase or sale.

Probably the greatest volume of transactions, both in number and in dollar value, result from more or less routine requests for bids or offers that are executed on the initial call or after a brief check of the market; dealers are reluctant to hold a firm bid or offer open for more than a few minutes for fear the market will move while the customer is hesitating. Execution of the order may call for "regular" delivery, *i.e.,* delivery of the securities and payment the following business day, or it may call for "cash" delivery, *i.e.,* delivery and settlement on the same day. Cash trades usually must be concluded well before the market closes (3.30 P.M., New York time) in order to allow time for the mechanical process of transferring ownership of the securities on that day. In addition, the contract may call for settlement in clearing house funds or Federal funds; all settlements made in funds located outside of New York are automatically in Federal funds, since settlement will be over Federal Reserve wires. There has been a tendency in recent years for more and more transactions in short-term securities to be for cash delivery and for settlement in Federal funds, and much the largest part of all transactions in such issues is now in this form.

Nearly all of the nonbank dealers use a single New York bank as clearing agent; the bank dealers use their own messengers and clearing facilities for transferring securities and making settlements. The clearing bank extends day-loans to the dealers to finance changes in their positions within a given day, and supplies Federal funds (in effect an overnight loan) where a dealer's payments in Federal funds have exceeded his receipts in this form during the day. The clearing agent bank does not ordinarily, however, extend regular financing to dealers. The clearing bank acts as custodian for the securities the dealers have in position, and upon receipt of instructions from a dealer, in reflection of a trade the dealer has executed, will deliver securities to their new owner or his agent and receive payment for the dealer's account or will receive securities the dealer has purchased and settle for them with its own check (either clearing-house or Federal funds). A small clearing charge is made by the bank each time it delivers securities, but not for receiving securities. In the event the transaction involves transfers of ownership to or

217

from a customer located outside the Second Federal Reserve District, the transfer is effected over the wires of the Commissioner of the Public Debt. For example, if a dealer instructs his clearing bank to transfer specified securities to Bank X in Chicago, the clearing bank will deliver these securities to the Federal Reserve Bank of New York subject to receipt of payment for account of the dealer. The New York Reserve Bank, as agent for the Treasury, cancels the securities and wires instructions to the Federal Reserve Bank of Chicago to issue and deliver identical securities to bank X upon receipt of payment to order of the dealer. No charge is made by the Treasury for wire transfers of any United States Government securities within one year of maturity, and a nominal charge is made for bonds or notes more than one year from maturity.

In addition to net purchase and sale transactions between a dealer and a customer, two other types of trades are important in the over-the-counter market for United States Government securities. These are professional transactions between dealers and swap transactions that involve two or more Treasury issues and, perhaps, more than one customer. The new Federal Reserve data suggest that typically about 30 per cent by value of all dealer trades are with other dealers. Dealers are in constant telephone communication with one another, checking market quotations and attempting to locate a supply of a particular issue (or issues) for which they have a potential buyer or a demand for an issue (or issues) which they have in position in unwanted size or which they have an opportunity to purchase but do not wish to add to position. All inter-dealer contacts of this sort are at arms-length, and every precaution is taken to avoid revealing information that might be advantageous to the other dealer. At the same time, the stream of inquiries from "the street" provide a trader with clues as to potential buyers or sellers of particular issues if he should have occasion to trade these issues.

Inter-dealer contacts and trading of this sort give the market an additional dimension and a fluidity that it would not have if all contacts were only between dealers and customers. Prior to 1956, dealers had informal arrangements known as "100 bond agreements" under which dealers agreed to purchase at least $100,000 of any issue at their quoted bid price or sell an equal amount at their quoted offer price. This arrangement was useful in maintaining reasonably uniform prices in the market, but some dealers felt the agreements were being abused, and most of them were abandoned in 1956. As a general rule, however, dealers will still support their quoted markets, even in the absence of the agreements, by buying or selling at least small amounts on inquiries from other dealers.

A large but indeterminate proportion of all trading in the over-the-counter market for Government securities involves swaps of one issue for another rather than net purchases or sales. In its simplest form, an investor acting on his own initiative or on a dealer's recommendation will sell one issue and simultaneously purchase another of similar maturity. His purpose may have been to readjust the maturity structure of his portfolio to fit his cash requirements (for example, by selling near-maturity bills and buying longer bills), to establish a capital loss or gain for tax purposes, or to take advantage of a yield differential that appears to promise an arbitrage profit.

Swap transactions are identical in all technical details to out-right trades, but their significance, as in the case of inter-dealer trading, is the greater fluidity and depth they impart to the market. Activity in swaps may be particularly pronounced immediately after the Treasury has placed a new issue with investors. The new securities ordinarily will carry a somewhat higher effective yield for a period after they are issued, and this higher yield provides the inducement for investors to sell other issues—usually shorter maturities—to buy the new securities. In the process of shifting about, the new Treasury security is gradually placed in firm hands with a minimum of disturbance to the market. From the point of view of a dealer, the swapping procedures that have been developed enable him to take into position larger amounts of a single issue than he might wish to

219

assume if it were then necessary for him to find outright purchasers of that single issue. By arranging the necessary swaps, the dealer can substitute in his position a variety of issues for the single issue he had purchased in size, and by so doing he is in a better position to find net buyers to reduce his over-all position to its size prior to the original large transaction. The ability to work off large blocks in this fashion is particularly important, as noted above, in maintaining continuity in the market following a large Treasury financing.

Trading arrangements and practices are substantially uniform for Government issues of all types, *i.e.,* bills, certificates, notes, and bonds. Perhaps the most important exception to this generalization is the tendency for the market to become thinner the longer the maturity of the obligation. Ordinarily, regular Treasury bills can be traded in large amounts with less difficulty than other types of Treasury issues, even though they are of similar maturity, because of the position that Treasury bills have come to occupy as the prime financial asset for liquidity investment and money-market adjustment. The constant flow of bills through the market in both directions gives to the Treasury bill market a depth and breadth not found, to the same degree, in the rest of the market. Although bills accounted for less than one-fourth of the publicly-held marketable debt at the end of 1960, it is likely that these instruments account for much the largest part of all trading in marketable United States Government securities.

The thinnest and least active portion of the Government securities market is in longer-term bonds, although this market can be characterized as thin and inactive only by comparison with the volume of trading in shorter-term Governments, certainly not by comparison with market depth or trading activity in any other capital market.[9] The reasons for the limited activity and relative lack of depth in longer-term bonds are self-evident and are implied in the discussion of motives for holding Govern-

9. In the second quarter of 1961, for example, trading in United States Government bonds more than ten years from maturity averaged almost $160 million per week.

ment securities in earlier chapters. In part, it is due to the relatively small and declining volume of longer-term securities outstanding. More importantly, it may be traced to the fact that funds ordinarily accumulate only slowly in the hands of institutions interested in investment in long-term Government securities. It is in the nature of longer-term securities, of course, that prices and trading activity should be more sensitive to interest rate movements and expectations of rate movements than prices and activity in shorter-term obligations. The potential price change, and thus potential profit or loss on an investment position, increases with the maturity of the instrument. Therefore, dealer positions in longer maturities vary relatively more than in other maturities. During prolonged periods of tight money and credit restraint dealers frequently comment that the limited "street" supply of long-term bonds is, in itself, a positive factor tending to limit trading volume. At the same time, when interest rates are rising or are expected to rise, dealers would be unwise to carry other than a minimum or carefully hedged position in long-term issues.

C. Role and Significance of the Government Securities Market

In terms of dollar volume of trading, the over-the-counter dealer market in United States Government securities is, by a wide margin, the largest financial market in this country and probably in the world. Participants in the market are the nation's largest banks, corporations, financial intermediaries, and the Federal Reserve System and Treasury. Individual trades are very large— running to the millions of dollars—and require immediate execution. Not only is the Government securities market the largest financial market in terms of trading volume, therefore, but the composition of its participants puts it in a class with the

London money market as the most sophisticated. The small group of professional dealers who stand at the center of this market, buying and selling at their own risk, must be constantly aware of all influences that might affect the market and must maintain a sure-footed agility in adapting to the stream of forces shaping price and interest rate movements. There is no regulation (official or otherwise) of prices or yields, and no protection for the dealer who allows himself to be caught long in a falling market or short in a rising market. The United States Government securities market is completely competitive and completely free to move in adjustment to changes in the demand for and supply of securities.

The true significance of the role currently filled by the Government securities market is only suggested, however, by citing the volume of trading and the sophistication of the investors participating in the market. Its fundamental importance lies in the fact that the debt instruments of the United States Government traded in this market constitute the principal supply of liquidity assets available to the national money market, and the shifts of asset ownership effected in the market reflect the liquidity adjustments of major firms in all industries and in all parts of the country. The availability of a large supply of uniform financial assets, bearing no credit risk, and the existence of a broad market in which these assets may be bought or sold in size, make possible a high degree of efficiency in the utilization of the money supply and give the national economy a financial viability that is its best insurance against the recurrence of financial panics of the sort the country has suffered in the past. It might be argued, and correctly, that if the Treasury debt were smaller or if it were so structured that it did not supply the liquidity instruments it now supplies, market processes would generate other liquid financial assets to fill the role now occupied by Government securities. The point is, however, that the debt does exist in its present form and through the intermediation of the Government securities market has provided the base for the most efficient and broadly pervasive money market the country has ever had.

The dealer market in Government securities also has direct links with the other major financial markets. Four dealers specializing in Government securities are also among the principal dealers in bankers' acceptances. Two dealers are members of the New York Stock Exchange, three are members of the American Stock Exchange, seven deal in "over-the-counter" stocks, and seven are dealers in tax-exempt bonds. Nearly all are members of the dealer selling groups that help to underwrite Government agency issues, and four are regular members of syndicates underwriting corporate securities and maintain markets in the bonds they help to underwrite. While this itemization is not complete, it suggests the direct links between the Government securities market and other financial markets that might be expected to serve as a channel through which the effect of important developments in one market would be quickly transmitted to all other markets. The more important linkage, however, grows out of the central position of Government securities themselves, at all maturities. For example, recent years have seen the growth of a high degree of correlation between movements of rates on bankers' acceptances and Treasury bills. Many investors move promptly from one instrument to the other when the rate spread widens or narrows. Simultaneously, many major borrowers in the acceptance market have the alternative of borrowing from a bank, and these borrowers shift back and forth promptly as the cost of acceptance borrowing moves in either direction in relation to the prime loan rate. The relation of market yields on longer-term Government securities to the corporate and tax-exempt bond markets has been spelled out in earlier chapters. At the rate differentials that have prevailed generally since the Second World War, capital funds most of the time have shifted out of Governments, with only official accounts and certain pension and trust funds as consistent net buyers. In one sense, the debt-management policies that have been followed have made the Treasury a major net supplier of capital funds.

It is not completely accurate to assign to the Government

securities market an autonomous and initiative position in the linkages with other markets, of course, since the Government securities market is but one segment in a highly complex financial apparatus through which investment funds are in constant motion both horizontally (among securities of different types) and vertically (among different maturities). At the same time, the volume of Government securities outstanding, their diffuse ownership distribution, the scale of market trading in these securities, and the highly organized market in which they trade give to Government securities—and the market through which they are traded—a central position in the total structure of financial assets and markets.

The Treasury places its new securities with investors on direct subscription, so that the broad and highly refined dealer market in Government securities has not been used directly to underwrite new issues in the way that corporate and tax-exempt bonds are underwritten. That is to say, the Government securities market is primarily a market in which investors transfer title to outstanding issues rather than a market centered about the placement of new securities with investors. At the same time, the earlier discussion of Treasury financing techniques has shown the assistance that the dealer market gives the Treasury in its financing operations through trading in "rights" and "when-issued" securities. A more important benefit accruing to the Treasury from the existence of the present facilities for trading United States Government issues is the liquidity characteristics imparted to these securities by the ease and rapidity with which they may be bought or sold, in almost any amount. The combination of no credit risk and easy marketability has resulted in the lodgment of a sizable part of the marketable debt in portfolios where it substitutes for money. The ability to lodge the war-created debt as a substitute for money probably has resulted in lower interest costs to the Treasury than would have been necessary to place less liquid securities. It should be remarked, however, that the liquidity imparted to short- and intermediate-term Governments as a consequence of their marketability—or shiftability—has not been entirely a blessing. The fact that it has been much easier and less costly to sell shorter-term securities, which do not require the diversion of investment funds in that amount from other uses, has perhaps been a hard-to-resist inducement to the Treasury to shorten its debt structure. Another way of looking at the same point is to conjecture that the broad market in shorter-term Government securities, and the aggressive selling techniques of dealers that have brought formerly idle cash balances into the market, have contributed to maintaining a positively sloped hypothetical new-issue rate curve throughout the years since the Second World War (although the market yield curve has sometimes been flat) despite the increasing concentration of debt in the short-maturity area.

The discussion thus far has appraised the importance of the over-the-counter market in Government securities from the point of view of its value to the Treasury and of the position it occupies in the money and securities markets as the mechanism through which residual liquidity and portfolio adjustments are made by buying or selling United States Government securities. The importance of the Government securities market in the national money market is not restricted, however, to its function as a clearing center for marginal liquidity adjustments through purchases and sales of short-term Government securities at the initiative of the investors. In their efforts to finance positions at minimum cost under the conditions of money and credit stringency that have obtained most of the time in recent years, dealers have been an initiating force in helping to extend the geographic and institutional perimeters of the money market. It was noted earlier that the rates charged on loans to dealers by New York City banks tend to rise during periods of pressure on the money market to levels that make carrying a trading position almost prohibitively costly. Dealers have responded to this situation by using their established customer contacts to search out pools of funds anywhere in the country that might be utilized, even for one or two days, to finance at rates lower than those quoted by the New York banks. Usually this financing takes the form of a repurchase agreement, under which an investor purchases short-term securities and the dealer simultaneously commits himself to repurchase these securities on a specified date and at the original sale price plus a fixed rate of interest. At times, the urgency of dealer financing requirements results in a rate of interest on re-purchase agreements higher than that available in the market on an outright purchase of securities of similar terms to that specified in the repurchase contract, in spite of the fact that the investor has complete protection against the risk of price fluctuation. Re-purchase agreements (other than those with the Reserve Bank) are written principally with out-of-town commercial banks and nonfinancial corporations, but state and local government funds, insurance companies, mutual savings banks, and others are sometimes drawn into the market.

No data have been collected on the average life of dealer re-purchase agreements, but comments by dealers suggest that it is typically fairly short. (Dealers are usually reluctant to tie up their positions on repurchase agreements for more than a few days because the securities often are not available for trading while they are out on repurchase agreements as they would be if they were financed on a loan.) Some part of the securities sold by dealers on repurchase agreement very probably take the place of outright sales that would have been made if the customer had not had the option of buying on repurchase agreement, but the typically short life of repurchase agreements suggests that a good part of the funds drawn into the money market on repurchase agreements would otherwise have been held for the few days they were available in idle balances. This is particularly true in the case of medium-size commercial banks that are too small to participate profitably in the Federal funds market but are able to employ their funds in repurchase agreements.

It is evident that the dealers in their efforts to finance positions have created a new type of financial asset that has neither credit nor money risk and that can be made as liquid (in terms of maturity) as the cash requirements of the investor dictate. By so doing, the professional dealers in United States Government securities have directly contributed to a more active and extensive money market and to economy in the use of money.

VII

Federal Reserve
Credit Policy
and Treasury
Debt Management

Federal Reserve policies aimed at regulating the availability of money and credit, together with the autonomous size and intensity of competing demands for funds at various maturities, are the most important influences upon the terms the Treasury must offer in its financing operations, upon the Treasury's ability to select the maturities at which it places its debt, and upon the ownership distribution of United States Government securities. At the same time, the Treasury's selection of securities to finance the public debt, the techniques employed to place these securities with investors, and the frequency and size of Treasury operations unavoidably affect the money and credit markets upon which the central bank is attempting to exert a regulatory influence. In point of fact, both central bank policy and Treasury debt policy have their ultimate effects upon the availability of funds and upon the structure of financial asset liquidity, so that they may properly be viewed as complementary aspects of a single area of public policy.[1] This chapter will attempt to outline the principles and techniques of modern Federal Reserve policy, particularly open market policy, and to trace the major relationships between Treasury debt management and Federal Reserve monetary and credit policy.

A. Purposes and Principles of Federal Reserve Open Market Operations[2]

When viewed over a period of time, Federal Reserve policies are seen to have achieved an expansive or limiting influence on the supply of money and on commercial bank credit in use, and to have been influential in determining the level of interest rates and the availability of credit of all types and at all maturities. Presumably these policies have also had an influence upon such economic magnitudes as aggregate demand for goods and services, general price levels, employment, etc. An influence upon these statistical measures and the magnitudes they represent is, of course, the ultimate objective of Federal Reserve

1. *Cf.* Earl R. Rolph, "Principles of Debt Management," *The American Economic Review*, 47, 3 (June, 1957), 302–320. Rolph defines debt management as follows: "National Debt management shall be taken to refer to any official action, by central banks as well as Treasuries, designed to alter the quantity and kinds of a national government's debt obligations outstanding in private domestic hands." Also, *cf.* G. L. Bach, "The Machinery and Politics of Monetary Policy-Making," *The Journal of Finance*, 8, 2 (May, 1953), 169–176. "Yet Treasury borrowing from the nonbank public piles up liquid assets in new securities in the same amount as borrowing from the banks piles up new money. Indeed, if we assume that excess reserves are fully utilized . . . whether the Treasury borrows from the commercial banks or the public has no effect on the quantity of money. Monetary and debt policy are not only hard to separate. Perhaps they shouldn't be separated but should be jointly used in a positive attack on economic instability."

2. See Robert V. Roosa, *Federal Reserve Operations in the Money and Government Securities Markets,* published by The Federal Reserve Bank of New York, 1956, for a more detailed explanation of open market operations.

policy. Such statistics do not, however, lend themselves to use as guides for the implementation of policy. In order to understand the relationships between debt management and Federal Reserve policies, it is necessary to look behind the ultimate objectives of these policies, in terms of money and credit availability, to the operational concepts that guide the implementation of central bank policy.

The immediate objective of Federal Reserve open market operations is to control the supply of bank reserves so as to achieve and maintain an availability of funds in the national money market which, all else equal, is expected to supply the economy with a volume of money and credit consistent with broad Federal Reserve policy objectives. The statistical and other information relied upon to guide day-to-day operations toward this end, taken together, measure the composite of "pressures" upon the money market. Operations are designed to regulate these pressures.

It should be recognized that there is no wholly adequate single guide which the Federal Open Market Committee may follow in scheduling its open-market operations to achieve desired changes in the money supply and in credit in use. The infinitely complex financial mechanism is subject to a host of influences, stemming from both the demand and supply sides, and the interplay of these influences continuously reshapes and redirects the flow of funds through the money and credit markets. Interest rates are responsive to the net impact of these influences, and changes in interest rate levels and rate relationships provide insights that are helpful in guiding Federal Reserve open-market operations. But day-to-day or week-to-week fluctuations in interest rates or in the market rate on a particular type of financial asset may result from a transient influence on market "psychology" or from a particular circumstance affecting one sector of the market and have little relevance to underlying conditions of money and credit availability. Similarly, the reserve position of the member commercial banks, as measured by current levels of excess reserves and of borrowing from the Reserve Banks, will ordinarily be closely correlated with the available supply of money and credit, but the true meaning of reserve statistics as measures of money and credit availability is strongly affected by the distribution of reserves as between the money centers and the "country" banks, by the expected duration of the current reserve situation, by the level of bank float, by the seasonal pressure or lack of pressure for new credit, and by a number of other factors. Reserve statistics alone are not a completely reliable guide to follow in scheduling open market operations.

Reserve data and interest rate data are, in fact, employed by the System Open Market Account, along with a great deal of additional information, in measuring the degree of pressure upon the money market and in guiding open market operations to control this pressure. The concept of "money market pressure" is, admittedly, difficult to define, but it has a quite tangible meaning to the money market specialist, and it cuts to the heart of the financial process as no other concept does. The myriad forms that credit extension may take, the diverse ways in which financial assets may be created all have one characteristic in common: they require an availability of money to the lender extending the credit. Institutions or individuals extending credit out of funds accruing from their regular flow of current receipts or out of idle cash balances are, individually, insulated from the effects of efforts by the central bank to regulate credit creation. But any lender that attempts to extend credit in greater amounts can do so only through the sale of financial assets from portfolio or in the form of its own liabilities. In so doing it will, in most cases, have recourse to the money market, and the degree of pressure being maintained in the money market by Federal Reserve policy determines the cost of this recourse and the absolute ease or difficulty of obtaining funds.

Before turning to a discussion of the implications of Federal Reserve policy upon Treasury debt management, a descriptive digression into the modern money market might be in order. The easiest way to visualize the money market is as an equilibrating mechanism through which short-term irregularities in the flow of funds are adjusted. Each cash transaction in the economy, whatever its purpose and whomever it involves, represents a transfer of funds from one holder to another. The great bulk of these transfers are offsetting as they affect any one bank, corporation, or other institution or agency. But on any given day, or in any week or month, some institutions lose funds on balance and others acquire temporarily excess cash. The function of the money market is to bring together the net demand for money and net supply of money growing out of this irregularity, through the medium of purchases and sales of highly liquid, virtually riskless short-term financial assets.

Commercial banks are the most important participants in the money market. Reserve shortages or excesses in small local banks, reflecting developments in the balance of payments in the region they serve, are reflected in the central money market for that section of the country. The bulk of these adjustments on any day or week will, in most cases, offset each other in the regional money market center. But the larger banks in that regional money center also are likely to find themselves with either a need for funds or an excess of funds from one day to the next. The cash adjustments made daily by the banks in the regional money market centers are made in a national setting. A bank in Dallas, for example, may buy or sell Federal funds with banks in San Francisco, St. Louis, Richmond, and so forth. But there is, in turn, a net residual from these adjustments, and the net supply of or demand for funds reflected by this residual comes into focus in the central money market in New York. All of the major banks throughout the country maintain correspondent relationships with one or more banks in New York, and some part of the day-by-day balance of money flows in the national money market may be reflected in transfers of funds into or out of New York correspondent balances. In addition, and indicative of the role played by these institutions, the New York City banks may, in a typical day, be involved either as buyers or sellers in one-half to two-thirds of the total dollar volume of Federal funds transactions for the entire country.

232

Detailed data on changes in the reserve positions of the central-reserve New York banks, and on the intensity and duration of the pressures upon their reserves, provide management of the System Open Market Account with one of its best measures of the availability of funds in the national money market.

It is obvious, of course, that the New York banks also must find methods of adjusting their reserves, in spite of the fact that they are, in a sense, the last link in the money market chain. One such method is by borrowing from the Reserve Bank; frequently, when the money market has been very tight, the borrowing of these institutions has accounted for more than one-half of total member bank borrowing. Also, they may buy or sell Federal funds or short-term Government securities. The latter procedure involves recourse to the dealer market in Government securities, transferring to the dealers the task of locating funds in the national money market to purchase securities sold by the New York banks.

The principal nonbank financial institutions—insurance companies, savings banks and savings and loan associations—are not important influences upon the money market. Typically, their daily money flow is small relative to their total assets and is reasonably predictable. Consequently, they operate on small cash balances and have little need to carry short-term money market assets in their portfolios for purposes of making quick cash adjustments. The larger nonbank corporations occupy an important position in the money market. Their operations have precisely the same motive as do those of commercial banks and all other participants in the market, *i.e.*, to adjust cash flows so that idle cash balances, earning no return, will be held at an operational minimum. Corporate treasurers have become very sophisticated in scheduling their money flows, very dexterous in keeping funds invested, and very enterprising in finding new short-term investment outlets. Some of the largest corporations operate on amazingly low average-deposit balances. The corporate treasurer must forecast his cash flow so that he can estimate when he will need any currently accruing excess funds or for how long any current shortfall in the cash flow will persist, and the maturities of the instruments he buys or sells will be determined by this estimate and by the relative cost or return of the various alternatives. Typically, the largest needs for cash will be at the quarterly income tax dates and at dividend dates. Every effort is made to arrange investment maturities, in the proper amounts, as close as possible to these dates and to other predictable dates when funds are needed.

In addition to these private institutions, state and local governments, foreign central banks, and the major international organizations are important factors in the money market. State and local governments, for example, receive tax revenues at periodic intervals through the year, and it is not possible to mesh payments exactly to this flow of receipts. Between the receipt of revenues and their scheduled disbursement, the funds will be invested in money-market instruments that mature as near as possible to the date when the funds will be needed. At other periods, these government bodies may sell short-term tax anticipation notes which, in turn, add to the supply of instruments to be purchased by commercial banks and other investors. As in the case of corporate operations in the money market, state and municipal governments attempt to minimize their risk exposure by buying obligations maturing as close as possible to the date on which the funds will be needed, so that it will not be necessary to sell in the market.

A foreign central bank or treasury has various alternative ways it may handle any dollar credits accruing to its account. It may leave them on deposit in this country. It may purchase gold, or it may transfer the funds to one of the other international financial centers, such as London or Paris. Finally, it may invest any funds in excess of a minimum working deposit balance in United States Government securities or bankers' acceptances. Most changes in foreign official balances take the latter alternative, investment of excess funds in money market instruments or, when dollars are needed, sale of such instruments. As in the case of the other participants in the money market, foreign and international institutions attempt to schedule the maturities of their investments to coincide with their estimated need for dollars to make settlements for which dollar exchange is required. The pattern of operations of these institutions is extremely varied, reflecting all of the influences that affect the balance of payments and international settlements of all the major trading nations. Frequently, the net impact on the money market is minimized by the fact that many of the purchases and sales are off-setting. But sometimes, as during the Suez crisis in the fall and winter of 1956, developments of far-reaching importance will bring the foreign and international institutions into the money market, on one side or the other, on a massive scale.

Chapter VI discussed the dealer market in Government securities at some length, and the function of dealers in the national money market need only be touched upon at this point. In discussing the role of commercial banks in the money market, it was pointed out that the net supply of or demand for funds in the banking system from day to day is reflected at the central money-market banks in New York City, but that these institutions, in turn, may have bought or sold United States Government securities in making their own reserve and portfolio adjustments. The dealers in Government securities who make a market for these New York banks and for all banks and participants in the money market throughout the country, therefore, are at the very heart of the money market. Part of the day to day changes in the availability of funds in the national money market is absorbed in the reserve positions of the New York banks, but an important part of it is reflected in the operations of the dealers in Government securities. Information on their activities is, therefore, an important part of the information available to the Open Market Committee and to the System Account Management in scheduling open-market operations aimed at regulating the money market.

One of the major problems frequently confronting dealers is to locate funds to finance the securities they are carrying in position. When the money market is seriously squeezed and dealers find themselves with large and perhaps growing positions, the financing problem becomes truly severe. The pressures bearing upon the New York banks and Government securities dealers at such times are the net residual of all the plusses and minuses of funds throughout the national money market. In other words, if there are sizable pockets of surplus funds in any money-market centers around the country these funds, presumably, have already been drawn into the money market and are not readily available to finance the dealers. The dealers' financing job, therefore, is to scour the country—commercial banks, nonbank corporations, state or local governments, savings banks, insurance companies—to find any remaining pockets of funds that can be borrowed, even for only one day, to finance the positions the dealers are carrying. Through this process, and through aggressive trading techniques, the dealers have been a primary influence in helping to develop a money market that extends into every corner of the country. A corollary of this development has been the sharp reduction in idle-money balances and increase in money velocity in recent years.

Out of the tens of thousands of transactions that occur in the money market each day, and out of the billions of dollars that change hands as participants convert liquid money-market instruments to cash or invest short-term funds in income-earning, near-maturity assets, a pattern emerges. This pattern of shifting restraint or ease is visible at the money-market banks and Government securities dealers in New York. There, the net supply of or demand for funds from one day to the next is reflected in changes in the liquidity of the central market institutions.

The funds employed to effect the unending stream of transfers of financial asset ownership through the money market come either from the existing money supply or from additions to the money supply. Liquid funds are made available in the money market and a simultaneous demand for these funds created through the normal seasonal shifts of liquid balances among industries, regions and firms. Other funds may flow into short-term

236

financial assets or be withdrawn from such assets as the result of changes in "idle" money balances in response to cyclical fluctuations in interest rates or to secular changes in financial practices. Still other funds may enter or be withdrawn from the money market through net changes in commercial bank asset portfolios, representing an increase or reduction in the money supply derived from changes in the total of reserves supplied by the Federal Reserve System. It is seldom possible in a particular money-market exchange of cash for financial assets to determine from which of these sources the cash has come, nor would it be particularly worthwhile to attempt to do so if it were possible. Through its adjustment of money-market pressures the central bank endeavors to exert a measure of control over the total availability of funds in the money market from all sources, and by so doing to regulate the increment to total expenditures for goods and services deriving from increases in the stock of primary financial assets.[3]

An important corollary of the foregoing description of Federal Reserve policy is that operations aimed at regulating the money market influence both the supply of money and the velocity of money, since the availability of funds in the money market is a function of MV and not of M alone.[4] Since the velocity of money ordinarily rises when the Federal Reserve System pursues a restrictive policy and declines when System policy is easy,

3. Defined as financial assets created by the ultimate users of the borrowed funds, as distinguished from financial assets created by financial intermediaries.

4. No attempt is made to define precisely the velocity concept referred to in this discussion, nor are precise measures of velocity or changes in velocity developed. Conceptually, velocity as used here refers to income velocity rather than transactions velocity. Changes in velocity are seen as supplying or withdrawing funds from the expenditure stream principally, although not exclusively, through the absorption or release of primary financial assets. That is to say, reference is to real changes in the level of "idle" or M_2 balances, however defined and however initiated, and to changes in financial or business practices (sometimes forced) that alter the M_1/Y ratio. The result of these changes is that, to a degree, financial assets other than money replace or are replaced by money in the asset structure of individuals, firms, and public bodies.

237

changes in velocity frequently are described as offsets to the effectiveness of central bank policy.[5] In one sense this is an accurate description since the achievement of a given policy objective in terms of effect upon the flow of expenditures resulting from changes in primary financial assets requires a greater change in M than would be necessary if V were constant. But Federal Reserve policy objectives are not defined exclusively with reference to changes in the money supply nor are the techniques of policy execution geared to achieve a specified change in the money supply. Rather, it is implicit in the manner in which operating Federal Reserve decisions are reached and in the analysis that guides these decisions that the proximate objective is to control the availability of funds in the money market and the ultimate objective is to regulate the rate at which new primary financial assets are created. This policy will allow for an increase in the total of primary financial assets over time in an amount somewhat greater than the supply of funds available from current real saving to purchase these assets, thus providing for a secular increase in MV (but not necessarily M alone) to service expansion in the dollar volume of economic activity, but the division of this increment as between M and V is largely irrelevant to the monetary authorities.

As a preface to discussion of the direct relationships between the management of the Treasury debt and Federal Reserve policy, it should be noted that there are rather well-defined, realistic limits upon the degree of money-market pressure or ease that the central bank may create consistent with its policy objectives. These limits may be indicated in terms of velocity changes. Keynes defined the "liquidity trap" as the minimum level of interest rates, the point beyond which further additions to the money supply would simply add to idle balances without significant effect on interest rates or the availability of credit. In a sense, this point defines the easy money limit of effective

5. For a discussion of velocity changes in recent years as they relate to Federal Reserve policy, see: W. L. Smith, "On the Effectiveness of Monetary Policy," *American Economic Review,* 46, No. 4 (September, 1956), 586–606.

credit policy; in Federal Reserve jargon, further ease would create a "sloppy" money market. At the other extreme, although Keynes does not refer to it, is what might be called the "illiquidity trap," the point beyond which further reductions in the money supply would cause interest rates to rise without check. In Federal Reserve jargon, this situation is known as a "disorderly market," and it defines the tight-money limit of effective policy. The easy-money limit is attained when open-market policy aimed at further ease simply adds to idle balances, reducing velocity without increasing the real availability of credit. The process of moving from this point toward greater and greater restraint involves moving up the velocity curve, reflected in the money market through an activation of idle balances for the purchase of liquid, short-term assets. It may be assumed that at some point, with a given liquidity preference, a velocity ceiling is approached, and an attempt by the System to impose still greater pressure on the market would create a condition in which the supply of assets was, for a time, absolutely greater than the supply of funds to take them off the market.[6]

B. Federal Reserve Policy and Treasury Debt Management

To repeat, Federal Reserve open-market operations, in combination with the other instruments of Federal Reserve policy, are intended to regulate the availability (which implies cost) of money and credit to potential users, and this regulation is effected through operations specifically designed to influence the availability of funds in the national money market. Effective quantitative control of money and credit through open market operations is achieved through the maintenance of more or less

6. It is unrealistic, of course, to think of liquidity preference as constant, but substitution of a set of liquidity preference functions does not affect the argument.

239

pressure upon the money market which, over a period of time, is intended to result in the desired change in money and credit in use, rather than through efforts to achieve as a proximate target a specific change in the money supply. "Changes in primary financial assets" may be substituted for "changes in money and credit in use" in the preceding sentence.

The concept of variable pressures upon the money market is important. These pressures may be applied to practical purpose between the limiting extremes of the "liquidity trap" and the "illiquidity trap." Efforts to push beyond these limits would, in the first case, be pointless since they could not increase the real availability of money and credit and would, in the second case, be self-defeating since they would be destructive of the orderly money-market processes upon which the viability of the financial economy rests. Operating within these limits, Federal Reserve open-market policy applies pressure that forces more or less economizing on money and credit. The free play of supply and demand for liquid funds, accompanied by free movement of interest rates, determines the allocation of available funds among competing uses for these funds.

Treasury operations in the management of the public debt are undertaken within the market environment established by Federal Reserve policy. The central bank does not underwrite the Treasury, nor does it specifically adjust its policies to the Treasury's financing requirements. In its efforts to place its obligations, in varying amounts and at various maturities, the Treasury is in open competition with all other users of borrowed funds; and to be successful in its financing objectives, the Treasury must adapt its offerings, as regards rate of interest, maturity, and offering techniques, to the availability of funds resulting from the combined influence of Federal Reserve policy and competing demands at various maturities.

At the same time, the techniques of Federal Reserve policy execution and the realistic limitations within which money and credit policy may be applied imply that the achievement of Federal Reserve policy objectives is also unavoidably influenced by Treasury debt policies. Pressure on the money market is the net product of the demand for money and credit and the available supply of money and credit. Therefore, since Federal Reserve open-market policy is adjusted to maintain a degree of pressure on the money market which, in turn, is expected to produce a general availability of money and credit consistent with the Open Market Committee's broad economic objectives, and since the Treasury may at times be the principal influence on the demand side in the credit markets, Federal Reserve operations may at such times find it necessary to adjust to the Treasury's financing requirements.

The actual policy followed by the Federal Reserve System is to attempt to maintain an "even keel" in the money market during periods of Treasury finance. Every effort is made to avoid overt System actions that might alter the supply-demand relationship or alter the set of market expectations existing in the period immediately before the financing. The concept of an "even keel" refers to the composite measure of market pressures, as discussed earlier, rather than to any specific statistical indicator.

During a Treasury exchange refinancing operation, the pressure on the market may increase at a given level of bank-reserve availability even though the operation simply replaces one security with another and does not, ultimately, add to the total of primary financial assets in existence. This increase in pressure results partly from the more rapid turnover of money incident to the transfer of ownership of "rights" and the frictions that are created in the money market by the enlarged activity. A development that sometimes is more important grows out of the dealers' practice of buying "rights" and selling "when-issued" securities. As a result of their operations, dealers sometimes have difficulty financing their positions in "rights." The added pressure upon the money market that ensues may lead the central bank to extend repurchase agreements to the dealers, which adds to bank reserves and, in terms of reserve measures alone, might suggest an easier Federal Reserve policy. However, such operations are necessary to maintain an "even keel" in the money market in terms of the net pressures upon the market. These reserve funds are recaptured upon maturity of the agreements, which usually is scheduled to coincide with the delivery date of the when-issued securities.

Maintenance of an "even keel" during a financing to raise new cash calls for a different type of operation. As noted earlier, commercial banks are the principal underwriters of new short- and intermediate-term Treasury issues sold for cash, and when there are no restrictions upon their subscriptions they also are important as underwriters of long-term cash issues. The effects of a Treasury cash financing upon the money market ordinarily occur at the time payment is made for the new securities rather than at the time subscriptions are received, although transfers of ownership of both the new securities and outstanding issues as preparations are made to pay for the new obligations may create money-market pressures during the "when-issued" period. At the time payment is made, commercial bank subscriptions are paid for through credits to Treasury tax and loan accounts, which add to total deposits and thus to total required reserves. Unless reserves are supplied to the market at this time to offset the sudden, sharp increase in required reserves, the money market will turn measurably tighter. That is to say, the Treasury in this case would have pre-empted a part of the available supply of credit, and other users of credit would find it necessary to adjust to the reduced availability.

In fact, the Federal Reserve System ordinarily supplies all or a large part of the new reserves required to prevent the payment for a new Treasury cash issue from adding to the pressure upon the money and credit markets. In other words, the central bank does not ordinarily allow the incidence of Treasury cash requirements to influence the conditions of money and credit availability sought by its policies. If the current policy of the central bank is aimed at an easy availability of funds, intended to promote expansion in the money supply, provision of the reserves needed by the commercial banks to pay for the new Treasury securities will mean that the banks will remain in an easy posi-

242

tion after the financing and the bulk of the new securities may remain lodged in commercial bank portfolios. The resulting increase in the money supply would be consistent with policy objectives. If, on the other hand, the Federal Reserve System is currently pursuing a restrictive policy, intended to restrain the creation of new money, restoration of the degree of pressure existing before the Treasury financing will still leave the commercial banks under sustained reserve pressure that will cause them to liquidate the new securities (or other investments) as rapidly as possible. In the latter case, the transfer of the newly-created money from Treasury deposits to private deposits as the proceeds of the financing are spent will make funds available to nonbanks which will find their way to the money market. The resulting easier atmosphere in the money market, in turn, will cause the central bank to withdraw reserves, increasing the pressure upon the banks to sell assets from their portfolios and thus reabsorbing the new money initially created by bank purchases of the new Treasury securities.

When the Treasury's cash financing represents intra-year tax anticipation borrowing within the framework of a balanced budget, the process can be a machine for money expansion when Federal Reserve credit policy is easy and a neutral influence when credit policy is restrictive. The neutral effect in the latter case results from the fact that the sale of the new securities initially to the commercial banks and their subsequent resale to nonbank investors as corporate income tax reserves accumulate may properly be considered as no more than a process through which the Treasury collects its taxes currently (albeit at an interest cost to the Government) to mesh with its current expenditure flow.

It follows from the foregoing analysis that Federal Reserve policies determine the incidence as between banks and nonbanks of debt retirement or placement, respectively, in the case of traditionally appropriate prosperity surpluses or recession deficits. The funds released to the financial markets by debt retirement from a Treasury surplus under conditions of restrictive credit policy would reduce bank-held debt to the extent the pressure of Federal Reserve policy upon commercial banks induced liquidation, and the new securities to finance a recession deficit would go into commercial bank portfolios to the extent that the Federal Reserve System supplied the reserves for their purchase.

In short, and abstracting for the moment from changes in the liquidity structure of total financial assets resulting from changes in the maturity structure of the Treasury debt, Federal Reserve policy and Treasury debt management may be smoothly meshed to achieve joint policy objectives when fiscal policy is appropriate or not grossly inappropriate to current economic conditions. The Treasury will have to pay widely varying rates of interest to finance or refinance its debt even under appropriate fiscal policy conditions, as it finances alternately in a market in which there are abundant funds for all uses and in a market in which it must place its securities in competition with other borrowers for a limited supply of funds. But it is unlikely, when fiscal policy is appropriate, that the necessitous character of Treasury financing requirements will threaten to force Federal Reserve policy beyond the limits of effective monetary and credit policy, outlined earlier.

Serious problems for both monetary and debt management may arise, however, when fiscal policy is inappropriate. In particular, a large Treasury deficit at a time when the central bank is attempting to restrain additions to the expenditures stream from new credit may pose almost impossible difficulties. The addition of net Treasury demand for credit to the demands from other private and public borrowers might force the central bank either to allow a greater increase in money and credit in use than its policy objectives call for or to impose a more restricted availability of funds upon other borrowers than could be justified by current economic conditions. Even if the central bank should attempt to force the funds to finance the Treasury deficit from other users of credit, thus holding total new credit creation to intended levels, it might be thwarted in this effort by the orderly market limits upon its effectiveness. That is to say, such an effort might create disorderly markets (an illiquidity trap) if other demands for credit are sufficiently interest-inelastic.

It should be stressed that the measure of the extent to which Federal Reserve policy has been subverted in this case is not to be found solely in the extent to which the additional Treasury securities have been placed with commercial banks. The net Treasury demand for credit is simply one part of total credit demand, and it would be irrelevant that all of the increase in Treasury debt was placed outside the banking system if the market pressure generated by the Treasury's financing requirements forced the Federal Reserve System to permit a larger increase in commercial bank portfolios of other assets than the central bank had intended. Moreover, a measure of change in the money supply may not be relied upon to indicate accurately whether or not the central bank has been successful in achieving its policies in the face of an inappropriate prosperity deficit. The growth in the money supply (currency and demand deposits adjusted) may have been no larger than intended, but this also could be irrelevant if there was a simultaneous increase in velocity. An inflationary employment of new credit may be reflected in either money supply or velocity, and, as noted earlier, Federal Reserve open market policy is designed (perhaps unconsciously) to regulate combined MV.

The latter point perhaps requires further elaboration. It is useful to define the net increment to the expenditure stream arising from credit in a given time interval as equal to the net increase in primary financial assets during the time interval. The funds employed to purchase the increase in primary financial assets may come, in variable proportions, from current liquid saving (either directly or channeled through an intermediary), through an increase in the money supply (representing net purchases of assets by the banking system, including the central bank), or from an increase in the velocity of money (representing a reduction in M_2, precautionary or speculative cash balances). It would be impossible, and pointless, to attempt to pair the multitude of new primary financial assets with the type-

245

source of the funds to purchase them. In the final analysis, the role of the central bank is to regulate the growth of total primary financial assets, without regard to the proportion of Government securities in the total or what type of investor purchases them, to an amount just enough in excess of the flow of liquid savings to provide for growth in the "effective money supply" at a rate that is neither inflationary nor deflationary. Exercise of this regulation requires that the central bank concern itself with both M and V to compensate for shifts between M_1 and M_2 (*i.e.,* changes in "k").

The foregoing discussion, which concludes that debt management is likely to have a significant influence upon the effectiveness of Federal Reserve policy only when fiscal policy is inappropriate, has abstracted from the influence the Treasury may have upon credit conditions and general liquidity through the maturity terms it sets on its securities. Although this influence is indirect and is not easily measured statistically, it is likely that the maturity terms the Treasury has used on its new securities since the Second World War, and the changes in the maturity structure of the Treasury debt that have resulted, have been an important influence, generally in a negative direction, upon the effectiveness of Federal Reserve policy.

It may be stated as a generalization without serious distortion of fact that the portfolio maturity distribution of investors of all types accurately reflect the expected term of the funds committed at various maturities. That is to say, commercial banks structure the maturities in their portfolios to reflect the demand nature of their liabilities and hold only relatively small amounts of truly long-term investments, insurance companies have little need in their portfolios for liquidity instruments and hold long-term investments almost exclusively, and so forth. A shortage of investments in a particular maturity area relative to the current supply of funds available for investment at that maturity may temporarily cause funds to be lodged in an inappropriate maturity (usually a maturity shorter than the appropriate one). Also, expectations as to future interest rate movements may cause temporary diversions of funds from their normal investment channel. Finally, there is at all times a marginal body of investment funds that may move easily either to somewhat longer or somewhat shorter term investment in response to interest rate differentials. By and large, however, within the broad maturity categories of short-term (out perhaps to two years), intermediate-term (to ten or twelve years), and long-term the maturity structures of investors' portfolios accurately reflect the nature of the funds invested and the purpose (investment portfolio or liquidity reserve) the investment is intended to serve.

It follows that any significant shift in the maturity structure of the Treasury debt probably is accompanied by a corresponding shift in the type of funds committed to United States Government securities. The transformation involves a realignment in the ownership distribution of the debt, but it may also involve some change in the function Treasury debt performs within particular portfolios. Thus, as outlined earlier, the massive movement of marketable Treasury debt toward a shorter maturity structure since the Second World War has been accompanied by shifts of ownership toward investors with shorter-term funds to invest and, within portfolios, by a growing tendency for United States Government securities to fill a liquidity rather than an investment role.

The movement of large elements of the public debt from the long-term range into the intermediate range and from intermediate into short debt since World War II, took place initially against the backdrop of an historically large money supply relative to national income and low income velocity of money, circumstances which suggest that "idle" cash balances were very large. The subsequent absorption of short-term Treasury debt has represented one aspect of the more efficient utilization of cash balances that has resulted in a significantly large increase in the income velocity of money. Treasury ownership data suggest that as the long-term bonds issued by the Treasury during World War II have moved into the intermediate-term area they have been liquidated by "long-term" investors and purchased

247

principally by commercial banks. Commercial banks, in turn, have sold Treasury bills and other short-term marketable Treasury securities to nonfinancial corporations, state and local governments, foreign official accounts, and other investors employing funds that formerly would have been held as cash balances. The concentration of new Treasury issues, both for cash and refunding, in the short-term area has worked in the same direction.

The release of funds into the expenditure stream through an increase in the velocity of money resulting from the investment of formerly idle cash balances is fully as inflationary as a direct increase in the money supply through net commercial bank purchases of financial assets. The process of velocity expansion outlined here has caused the funds released to expenditures through velocity change to flow through the financial markets and appear as a net addition to the supply of long-term funds available to support the capital boom of recent years. It is true that this process could not have operated to the extent it did if the economy had not had the pre-existing cushion of excess money that had been built up through the depression and war years. This cushion made it possible for the shifting to occur in size without creating a negatively sloped yield curve as a typical yield pattern. It is equally true, however, that the process could not have operated at all if the Treasury had maintained the maturity structure of its debt. It should be stressed again that "maturity structure" refers to the volume of securities outstanding in broad maturity areas; it does not refer to an artificial statistic such as the "average maturity of the debt." By allowing large segments of debt to move down the maturity scale without replacement, in a setting of large M_2 balances, the Treasury became directly responsible for "creating money" through increased velocity, money that was made available as long-term capital. This type of inflationary money expansion was most pronounced prior to 1958 and proved particularly difficult for the central bank to deal with. Because of the use to which these funds were put in supporting the capital and residential con-

248

struction booms through 1957, it probably was one of the most important elements in a tendency toward "over-employment" during those years.

C. Implications for Debt Management Policies

The most important implications of the foregoing analysis of the relationship between the central bank as the regulator of money and credit and the Treasury as a user of money and credit lie in the area of redefining the objectives of debt management. Since the Second World War, the objectives of debt policy mentioned most often by Treasury spokesmen, and by other "financial experts," have been to avoid (or reduce) debt monetization and to lengthen the maturity of the debt. The analysis in this chapter suggests that in the presence of an effective central bank and freely functioning securities markets neither of these is, as usually stated, a proper or meaningful objective of debt management.

Avoidance of "debt monetization" usually is discussed in terms of affecting, in some fashion, commercial bank ownership of United States Government securities. It should be apparent, if the analysis in this chapter is accepted, that the Treasury has very little control over the volume of Government securities owned by the commercial banking system or, for that matter, over any element of the ownership distribution of the public debt (except that portion of it owned by its own trust accounts).

Let us apply the most extreme test to this assertion. Assume that the Treasury were to adopt a rate of interest or other terms for its Series E and H Savings bonds which made these bonds substantially more attractive than competing outlets for personal savings. Also, assume that the mutual savings banks, savings and loan associations, and other savings institutions supinely accepted this Treasury move and did not apply for permission to increase their rates of interest to competitive levels (an unrealistic assumption). The funds derived from the increased net sales of Savings

249

bonds might then be employed by the Treasury to retire short-term securities held principally by commercial banks. At this, the first step in the process, it would appear that the Treasury has successfully "demonetized debt."

However, the money diverted from other savings institutions would result in a reduced availability of loanable funds at these institutions, causing them to liquidate secondary reserve assets to acquire funds to meet credit demands (this assumes, realistically, that there would be an income advantage in so doing). These short-term or intermediate-term securities (probably United States Government securities, since Governments account for much the greatest part of all secondary reserve assets) would be purchased by commercial banks, which would be employing the excess reserves released by the extinction of deposits incident to the Treasury's original retirement of bank-held Government debt. Ignoring for the moment the possible action of the central bank, only two circumstances could prevent the indicated outcome, in which the Treasury would simply succeed in diverting a body of funds away from financial intermediaries and directly into primary financial assets without in any way affecting either the money supply or the total of primary financial assets. First, the more attractive terms on the Savings bonds might induce an increase in personal savings, making possible a reduction in the money supply; however, what is known about saving habits would suggest that this is a most unlikely outcome. Second, demands for credit upon the financial intermediaries might be less than the current supply of savings, so that the diversion of funds would not necessitate sales of secondary reserve assets by the financial intermediaries. But in this case the "debt demonetization" would result from a deflationary tendency toward disequilibrium in the savings-investment relationship; it is not likely that the Treasury would be interested in promoting demonetization in a deflationary setting of this type.

Alternatively, the Treasury might sell an issue of long-term bonds directly to the nonbank financial intermediaries and employ the proceeds to retire bank-held debt. The results would

250

probably be the same. There is no reason to believe that the financial intermediaries would reduce their extension of credit to other borrowers because of their purchases of the new Treasury bonds so long as they held secondary reserve investments which it was marginally profitable to liquidate in order to transfer the funds to these other uses. Again, the commercial banks would, on balance, be the net purchasers of the securities liquidated by the nonbank intermediaries.

These simple illustrations have been detailed as a means of making two rather elementary points about the nature of Treasury debt and its ownership. First, there is nothing at all distinctive about United States Government securities that would make it realistic to analyze them as though they were, in some fashion, insulated from the normal interplay of supply and demand influences in the credit markets. Second, changes in total commercial bank assets, and particularly their holdings of Government securities, are regulated by central bank credit policy and not by Treasury debt policy. In the preceding illustrations, the retirement of bank-held Treasury debt in the first stage of the analysis would not have been replaced by subsequent bank purchases if the central bank had elected to withdraw the reserves released by the initial reduction in deposits. Such action would result from the action of the central bank, however, and not from the action of the Treasury debt managers. Banks' holdings of Government securities are one part of the assets in the banking system upon which the money supply is based. Changes in the total of these assets reflect the objectives of central bank policy and not the objectives of Treasury debt management. In fact, listing "debt demonetization" as an objective of public debt management policy, beyond being pointless, tends to obscure the proper allocation of function and responsibility as between the Treasury and the Federal Reserve System.

The second inappropriate objective frequently cited for debt management is to "lengthen the maturity of the debt." As the analysis in this chapter has shown, changes in the maturity structure of the debt can have profound influence upon the availability of funds at different maturities, upon the structure (and perhaps the level) of interest rates, and, in a setting of excess liquidity such as has characterized the postwar years, upon the income velocity of money. That is to say, changes in the maturity of the public debt affect the liquidity structure of financial assets. Thus, given the anti-inflationary or anti-deflationary direction of economic policy at any particular time, the Treasury might wish, respectively, to lengthen or shorten its debt. But such lengthening or shortening is the *means* employed to pre-empt or supply capital funds, to reduce or increase income velocity, to lessen or add to the liquidity of financial assets; it is the means to achieve an objective, not the objective itself. One exception to this statement might be noted. To the extent that the shortening of the debt structure has piled up a floating debt so large that the physical task of constant refunding by itself exerts a disturbing effect upon the functioning of the credit markets, the Treasury might properly adopt an objective of some debt extension as an independent objective of debt management. The "housekeeping problem" in this situation, however, could ordinarily be resolved by improved financing techniques and would not, by itself, justify an aggressive program of debt lengthening that could not be supported in terms of its influence upon the interest rate structure and the availability of capital funds in the current economic setting.

It should be stressed that the changes in debt maturity structure with which this discussion is principally concerned are those that involve shifts *between* broad maturity areas and not merely shifts *within* maturity areas. For example, a debt-management program that did not change the total amount of debt outstanding in the area beyond ten or twelve years or the debt in the intermediate two- to twelve-year range, although it extended the maturities of the securities in these areas, would not be defined as debt lengthening or shortening for purposes of this discussion. While such changes within maturity areas would have an influence upon the liquidity of investors' Government portfolios, particularly in the case of commercial bank holdings of intermediate-term issues, they need not require a redistribution of debt among owners nor a reclassification of the purpose of the portfolio, as between secondary reserve and investment purposes, within individual portfolios. Of course, it is not possible to establish sharp dividing lines between short-, intermediate-, and long-term debt, but it is conceptually accurate to distinguish between these categories in a loosely defined framework and to conclude that significantly large changes in the distribution of the debt among these categories are accompanied by similar changes in the type of funds committed to Government securities.

It has been pointed out that the almost steady shortening of the debt structure in the postwar period through 1957 provided incentive for an increase in the velocity of money, and that the inflationary support given by this development to the capital boom as this "new" money was made available to the capital markets was particularly difficult for the Federal Reserve System to deal with within the realistic limits upon the pressure the central bank is able to maintain on the money and credit markets. The strenuous effort to lengthen the debt during the first half of calendar 1958 has been mentioned earlier as providing impressive evidence of the dangers in *this* type of policy. Between the end of October, 1957, and the end of June, 1958, the Treasury issued some $4.0 billion of new securities carrying maturities of twelve years or longer and $17.8 billion of new securities carrying initial maturities of two to twelve years, while reducing the under-one-year debt by $4.2 billion. The result of these operations was a pronounced shift in the maturity structure of the debt that required a corresponding shift in the types of funds committed to Government securities.

In fact, however, these operations were carried out against a background of other demands for long-term funds that were at record levels. The addition of a $4 billion United States Government demand for long-term funds to the record takings by other borrowers meant, barring a sharp increase in the flow of liquid savings or the creation of new money by the banking system to flow into the capital markets, that not all of the new long-term

253

obligations could be sold. The commercial banks did add $7.5 billion to their portfolios of Government securities, entirely in the intermediate-term category. These purchases did not even equal new Treasury issues in this maturity area, however, so that the usual process through which commercial banks purchase intermediate issues sold by long-term investors shifting into new long-term obligations was short-circuited by the Treasury's debt policy. The net effect was the placement of a volume of *both* intermediate and long-term obligations in the market that was far in excess of any realistic estimate of the supply of funds actually available for investment at these maturities.

The sale of these securities was made possible in the first instance by the fact that the economy was in recession and Federal Reserve policy was directed at an easy availability of money and credit. Interest rates were in a declining trend, and investors' expectations generally projected this trend for an indefinite period into the future. Consequently, a large part of the new securities issued in this eight-month period—United States Government and other—were taken into speculative "underwriting" positions of dealers, brokers, individuals, and other investors. The common characteristic of these investors was that they were employing short-term funds (loans from banks, nonbank corporations, and other lenders) to carry intermediate and long-term securities on the expectation that declining interest rates would give them a speculative profit. As a consequence of this speculation, the Treasury's debt policy of pre-empting long-term funds, which was singularly inappropriate for a period of recession, probably had minimum influence upon the availability and cost of funds to other borrowers in the capital market so long as the expectation of declining interest rates continued. At mid-year 1958, however, when clear evidence of economic recovery began to emerge, these expectations had to be revised, and the ensuing liquidation of speculative positions forced interest rates sharply higher and for a period created disorderly trading conditions in the bond markets. By the end of 1958, these securities were largely placed with investors employing funds of a type appro-

254

priate to the maturity of the securities, but this result was achieved only against a reduction in the flow of new corporate and tax-exempt bonds at a period of early recovery when such a reduction in the availability of capital funds might be questionable economic policy.

In short, massive realignment of the maturity structure of the Treasury debt in either direction requires a proportionately massive absorption and release of funds in the affected maturity sectors. The investment practices of various investor groups have sufficient marginal flexibility to absorb relatively small changes in debt structure without significant ownership redistribution or effect upon the allocation of types of funds to United States Government securities, but changes in debt structure that exceed this amount must influence the supply of funds to other borrowers, particularly in the long-term markets. Consequently, decisions to shorten the debt structure by not replacing issues as they move from longer to shorter maturities, thus using the debt as a source of long-term funds, or to lengthen the debt structure by pre-empting long-term funds should, ordinarily, be taken in full awareness of their role in economic policy. If it is assumed that the Federal Reserve System functions effectively, then the availability of funds in the money market at any given time accurately reflects Federal Reserve policy intentions, and the distribution of these funds among various investment types and maturities will reflect the source of the funds, the strength of competing demands, and the (after-tax) interest rate structure. A debt management decision to lengthen or shorten debt will disturb the pre-existing equilibrium and make the Treasury a positive rather than a neutral influence in the market. Ideally, this influence will supplement the current policy of the Federal Reserve System. Unless it is consciously designed to have this effect, or unless debt policy is designed to be neutral, it probably will have effects upon money market pressures and upon the availability of funds that will tend to be contradictory to central bank policy. Until the last two years (1959 and 1960) contra-

255

dictory policies have characterized the years since the Second World War.

This rather lengthy attempt to show that efforts to prevent or reduce "debt monetization" (in the sense of commercial bank ownership) and to lengthen the debt (as distinguished from debt-maturity policies linked to broad economic policy) are not, as such, meaningful debt-management objectives, has as its purpose the clarification of what the realistic objectives of debt management might or should be. It is perhaps not very important that recent Treasury administrations have enunciated irrelevant objectives; high-sounding slogans are acceptable political devices so long as they do not get in the way of policy execution. In fact, however, it sometimes appears that the slogans have been accepted as valid objectives, causing attention and energies to be focused upon irrelevancies at the expense of a pragmatic, first-things-first approach to the management of the public debt. The following chapter attempts to bring debt management into proper focus and to outline realistic objectives and the techniques that would simplify achievement of those objectives.

D. Rates of Interest on United States Government Securities

Little has been said in this discussion about the determinants of the rates of interest the Treasury will find it necessary to pay in financing its debt. Actually, there is very little that can be said. At any point in time, the existing structure of interest rates on primary financial assets of all types will reflect the current demands for funds at various maturities and the current supply of funds available at these maturities (the latter being a function, in part, of Federal Reserve policy), the tax status of the different securities and of the different groups of lenders, relative degrees of credit risk, traditional investing practices of some groups of lenders, expectations as to future levels of interest rates, and a complex of more or less irrational prejudices, notions as to "normal rate relationships," etc., that fall under the umbrella of "market psychology." The market rates on outstanding United States Government obligations adjust themselves to the proper levels, at their respective maturities, which will reflect the fact that they are free of credit risk, fully taxable, non-callable, easily traded in large size, and any other special features they might possess. New Treasury issues must, accordingly, bear interest rates that will enable them to sell, given their features, in competition with all other demands for funds at the specified maturity.

All that the foregoing says is that the rate of interest on United States Government securities, as for any market price, is a function of supply and demand, the latter encompassing the prices of acceptable substitutes relative to their degree of substitutability, the structure of tastes, and the state of expectations. There might, however, be some justification for restating the obvious. As discussed in earlier chapters, the service cost of the public debt has been a consideration in debt policies for the past century, and this concern—along with misapplication of the economic theories growing out of the depression of the 1930's— resulted in subordination of all other debt-management and credit-policy objectives to the maintenance of low interest rates until the inflationary results of such a policy in a full-employment economy were at last recognized. The notion that rates of interest on United States Government securities can somehow be insulated from the influences that affect interest rates generally is by no means dead in spite of the lip service paid in recent years to "market determination" of rates.

In developing a rational approach to debt management it must be recognized that there are only two ways in which the level of interest rates on United States Government securities can be determined. Either the level of rates may be determined by fiat and maintained by subordination of the central bank to this purpose, in which case the public debt becomes an extension of the

257

money supply and all market rates of interest adjust to the Government rates, or the level of rates is determined through competition of Government securities on a nonpreferential basis with all other demands for funds.

Within the meaning of competitive determination, an influence may be exerted upon the level of rates on United States Government securities by changing their characteristics or by affecting the determinants of demand. For example, all or part of the public debt might be made wholly or partially tax-exempt. Or a larger "captive market" might be established by imposing a requirement that some or all financial institutions must carry minimum "secondary reserve" portfolios of Government securities. These and similar innovations have one characteristic in common; they alter the position of interest rates on United States Government securities in the structure of rates by methods that effect a redistribution of income as their only economic influence. Judgment as to whether the income redistribution resulting from any particular action of this sort is justified would rest upon a combination of economic and socio-political factors. Such judgments and the analyses upon which they would rest lie outside the scope of this study. Whatever changes in the parameters of market rate determination might be made, the market would promptly adjust interest rates to their proper relationship, and the technical debt-management decisions required of the Treasury would be substantially the same at the new pattern of rates as they were at the old.

In short, interest rates, and thus the service cost on the public debt, should not be a primary influence in debt-management decisions. Unlike private borrowers, the Treasury has no freedom of choice as to whether or not it shall borrow or repay debt in response to interest rate changes; this decision is implicit in fiscal policy. It has a choice at any time as to the maturity at which it will borrow, but the economic-policy role of debt management overrides interest cost considerations in these decisions. Changes in the tax status of Government securities and similar actions that might influence interest rates have an income effect that makes the decision one of broad economic policy rather than a technical debt-management decision. The Treasury has no choice but to pay the "going rate" for its borrowing while pursuing debt-management policies calculated to achieve specific effects on the availability of funds to other borrowers, and so on.

VIII

Conclusions:
Objectives and Techniques
of Treasury
Debt Management

A. Review of the Debt

On December 31, 1960, the total gross debt of the United States Government was $290.4 billion. Of this total, $82.5 billion represented securities held by United States Government agencies and trust funds and by the Federal Reserve Banks and, for purposes of this study of public debt management techniques, may be ignored. An additional $3.4 billion consisted of matured debt and special issues bearing no interest and also may be ignored. The portion of the public debt with which this study is concerned, therefore, amounted to $204.5 billion of publicly-held marketable and nonmarketable securities. Approximately 32 per cent of this total was owned by individual investors at the end of 1960, 30 per cent by commercial banks, 10 per cent by non-bank corporations, and the remaining 28 per cent by insurance companies, savings banks, state and local government bodies, and a miscellaneous group of investors.

The largest part of the investment of individuals in United States Government securities (approximately two-thirds) was in nonmarketable Series E and H Savings bonds; some $43.1 billion of these Savings bonds were outstanding at the end of 1960, almost all held by individual investors. In view of the relatively steady performance of this component of the debt in recent years, there also is justification for excluding it in the discussion of possible improvements in techniques of debt management. It is conceivable that a sufficiently large proportion of the millions of individuals who currently buy and own Series E and H Savings bonds might become so sensitive to relatively small interest-rate differentials as either to force the Treasury to change interest rates on these bonds more frequently as market rates of interest change or to otherwise alter or abandon the program. There has been no evidence to this point, however, that such a development is a likelihood in the years immediately ahead. It seems more likely that a continuation of the present selling program, particularly the Payroll Savings arrangement, at or about the present 3¾ per cent rate of interest paid on these bonds, with only infrequent rate adjustments, will result in sales that approximately offset redemptions of outstanding bonds. Therefore, the management of this stable and well-placed portion of the debt should be continued in its present form.

Subtraction of the Series E and H Savings bonds from the $204.5 billion of publicly-held, interest-bearing debt outstanding at the end of 1960 leaves approximately $161.5 billion of public holdings to be managed through the Treasury's debt-management program. Commercial banks were the largest single group of investors in these securities, accounting for nearly 40 per cent of the total. Individuals owned 15 per cent of the total, and nonfinancial corporations, state and local governments, insurance companies and mutual savings banks (combined), and miscellaneous investors each accounted for roughly equal proportions of the remainder.

It would not be realistic to exclude the other public nonmarketable securities—Series F, G, J, and K Savings bonds and

Investment Series A and B bonds—from the debt for which the Treasury will have to devise improved management techniques. Sales of Savings bonds of the J and K series were suspended during 1957 (sales of F and G bonds ended five years earlier) and it is unlikely that the Treasury would wish to attempt a new series of redeemable bonds directed toward the more sophisticated investor group in the face of market interest-rate movements of the amplitude that has developed in the past few years. Therefore, it is reasonable to conclude that Series F, G, J, and K Savings bonds—outstanding in an amount of $4.4 billion at the end of 1960—will continue to be refunded, in effect, with marketable securities as they mature or are redeemed. The same conclusion applies to the Investment Series A and B bonds as they mature, are redeemed (Series A), or are converted into marketable notes (Series B). Some $400 million of publicly owned 2½ per cent Investment Series A bonds will mature in 1965 and $3.2 billion of publicly owned 2¾ per cent Investment Series B bonds will mature in 1980. In all probability it will not prove feasible, even if it should be considered desirable, to sell nonmarketable securities to replace these bonds, and as they are redeemed, converted, or mature they will be replaced by marketable obligations. Consequently, the maturities and redemptions of Series F, G, J, and K Savings bonds and of Investment Series A and B bonds should properly be treated as part of the Treasury's task in managing its marketable debt over the years ahead.

Table 18 indicates the maturity distribution, as of December 31, 1960, of the publicly-held debt with which this chapter is concerned. More than 35 per cent of the total $161 billion— some $59 billion—fell in the less-than-one-year maturity area. Another 38 per cent—$61 billion—was scheduled to mature within one to five years. Only 15 per cent of the debt was more than ten years from maturity, and less than 10 per cent was more than fifteen years from maturity. Of the latter figure, nearly 35 per cent was owned by insurance companies and mutual

Table 18—Publicly-Held Marketable Treasury Debt by
Type and Maturity, December 31, 1960
(Billions of dollars)

Maturity	Bills	Certificates	Notes	Bonds*	Investment Series Bonds	F, G, J, and K Savings Bonds†	Total
1961	35.6	8.9	3.6	10.4	—	0.7	59.2
1962	—	—	13.2	7.1	—	1.0	21.3
1963	—	—	7.5	6.7	—	0.4	14.6
1964	—	—	11.2	3.8	—	0.3	15.3
1965	—	—	2.6	6.3	0.4	0.3	9.6
Subtotal	35.6	8.9	38.0	34.3	0.4	2.7	120.0
1966	—	—	—	2.5	—	—	—
1967	—	—	—	1.3	—	—	—
1968	—	—	—	2.8	—	—	—
1969	—	—	—	5.7	—	—	—
1970	—	—	—	3.4	—	—	—
Subtotal	—	—	—	15.7	—	1.5	17.2
1971	—	—	—	2.2	—	—	—
1972	—	—	—	7.4	—	—	—
1973	—	—	—	—	—	—	—
1974	—	—	—	0.5	—	—	—
1975	—	—	—	—	—	—	—
Subtotal	—	—	—	10.1	—	—	10.1
After 1975	—	—	—	11.0	3.3	—	14.3
Total	35.6	8.9	38.0	71.0	3.7	4.2	161.6

* Partially tax exempt bonds included at first call date.
† Investment Series Bonds and Series F, G, J, and K Savings bonds included since they will, presumably, be refunded with marketable securities at maturity.

savings banks, and virtually all of the remainder was held by the "all other" category of investors (individuals, personal trusts, pension funds, etc.).

B. Review of Financing Operations

Exclusive of operations in Treasury bills, the Treasury came to market with a cash or refunding offering on seventy-six separate occasions, or between seven and eight times per year, on average, in the ten years from 1951 to 1960, inclusive. In twenty-eight cash offerings (the earliest of which was in 1952), a total of $69.7 billion was raised; the average cash offering amounted to approximately $2.5 billion. In forty-eight exchange offerings, new securities were issued in a total amount of $374.7 billion, or an average of nearly $8 billion per exchange.

These operations, because of their frequency, their size, and often the way they have been handled, have been something more than a nuisance to everyone involved. Each financing operation has involved a separate set of decisions with respect to the securities to be offered, the terms to place on these securities, and the range of detailed conditions to attach to the offering. Consequently, the debt-management officials at the Treasury have scarcely completed one financing before it has been necessary to begin thinking of the next one; there has been little opportunity to concentrate upon long-range planning that might ultimately get them off the treadmill. Moreover, the very fact that it is necessary to return to market so frequently places limits upon what is possible in a given financing, particularly at times when the money market is tight and the competition for funds severe. The Government securities market is almost always still digesting the last big placement at the time the Treasury returns to finance its next issue, and there is a tendency for the market to look ahead for a month or two to still the next offering. Boxed in in this fashion, the Treasury has found that in a period of rising interest rates almost no rate is satisfactory to sell longer-term obligations, since investors expect a still higher rate the next time around.

The Federal Reserve authorities, as well, are restricted in their freedom of policy action by the frequency and size of Treasury financing operations. As noted earlier, the Federal Reserve System pursues an "even keel" policy for a few weeks before and after each major Treasury financing in order not to alter either basic supply-demand relationships or investor expectations during the financing period. This approach frequently has meant that the central bank must squeeze its own policy decisions into the interstices between the Treasury's debt operations. Moreover, the size in which the Treasury finances has sometimes made it necessary, both on cash and refunding operations, for the Federal Reserve System to supply more reserves to the banking system than it would have supplied if problems had not arisen in the absorption of new Treasury issues. While these reserves ultimately are recaptured, an element of control over money and credit is sacrificed.

Perhaps most important is the influence that Treasury debt operations have had not only upon the Government securities market but upon the markets for all other types of fixed-income obligations as well. As a major Treasury financing operation approaches, trading in all types of bonds is affected. The terms set by the Treasury can sharply influence all other rates of interest, and at times they serve as benchmarks to which other rates must adjust. This potential influence necessarily makes for a cautious approach to commitments by both investors and underwriters as a Treasury financing approaches. If the Treasury offering involves the replacement of short-term debt with intermediate or longer obligations, the sheer amount of funds which may be drawn from other uses in a brief period of time sometimes involves radical shifts in investment portfolios of a broad range of investors and equally sharp realigments of interest rates to stimulate these portfolio adjustments.

Frequent Treasury financing operations and the size of these operations thus tend to keep the capital markets off balance a good share of the time. Perhaps fully as important as the frequency and size of these operations, however, has been the uncertainly created by the fact that, with the exception of Treasury bills, the Treasury has not established a routine or predictable pattern for refunding maturing obligations. In any given operation, the market knows that the new securities offered by the Treasury may range from very short term to very long term, without regard to whether the securities being refunded are certificates, notes, or bonds. Treasury officials have frequently stated that they will issue intermediate or long debt whenever market conditions suggest that such issues could be sold successfully. Typically, therefore, each financing operation as it approaches has the anticipatory impact upon all bond markets of a long-term offering. Uncertainty as to what the Treasury will offer, in combination with the frequency and tremendous size of these offerings, has been a massive source of instability in the capital markets. In addition to the influence this uncertainty has had upon the orderly functioning of security markets, it is more than likely that it has involved the added cost of higher interest rates for all borrowers, the Treasury included. Such higher rates (higher than would have obtained in the absence of this source of uncertainty) would logically be necessary to compensate investors for the added uncertainty, particularly in the setting of heavy capital demand and rising interest rates that has generally characterized the past decade.

C. Shifting Maturity and Ownership of the Debt

The maturity distribution of the Federal debt has shortened almost steadily since the end of the Second World War. In February, 1946, immediately following the Victory Loan campaign which completed World War II financing, about 27 per cent of the public marketable debt was more than fifteen years from maturity, nearly one-third was more than ten years from maturity, and no less than 56 per cent was five years or more from maturity. By December, 1960, the maturity structure showed only 6 per cent of the public marketable debt more than fifteen years from maturity, only 7 per cent more than ten years from maturity, and only 18 per cent more than five years from maturity.

A drastic shift in ownership and portfolio function of public marketable United States Government debt accompanied its movement to a shorter maturity structure. As would be expected, the movement took the form of larger and larger use of Government securities for liquidity and secondary reserve purposes and their replacement in investment portfolios by other types of financial assets. In the ownership distribution of the public marketable debt, this movement was marked by a decline in the holdings of insurance companies and mutual savings banks from 17 per cent of the total in 1946 to 8 per cent in 1960 (the decline in the ratio of Government securities to total assets of these institutions was much more pronounced). Commercial bank ownership actually was reduced, from 42 to 28 per cent, as the liquidity requirements of investors of all other types provided a market for the much enlarged short-term Treasury debt.

The enlarged supply of short-term, liquid, risk-free Government securities over the past several years led to an upward adjustment in short-term rates of interest which, in combination with aggressive selling and education campaigns by Government securities dealers and other market specialists, has resulted in the replacement of income-earning assets for idle cash balances in liquidity positions of institutions of all types. Rising income velocity of money fed by this development has constituted an inflationary addition to money expenditures that has been particularly difficult for the Federal Reserve System to deal with.

Concerned not only by the inflationary consequences of the shortening maturity structure of its debt but by the added burden of more frequent refinancing imposed upon debt management by a huge floating debt, the Treasury, at least since 1952, has made strenuous efforts to place new debt outside the short-term area. These efforts have taken the form of optional offerings of intermediate or longer-term securities in combination with a short-term offering in most refundings, of advance refunding offers to holders of issues still some distance from maturity, and of an announced policy of offering longer-term securities for cash or refunding whenever market conditions suggest that such securities could be successfully placed. By and large, these efforts have not been successful, although the development of the advance refunding technique during 1960 holds promise for greater success in the future. The lack of success is particularly apparent if the criterion applied is not solely in terms of preventing further shortening of the debt but also encompasses the integration of debt management with credit policy toward common objectives. The Treasury generally has not been able to sell longer-term obligations during periods of strong competing demands for capital funds and rising interest rates, *i.e.*, during periods of economic boom. Consequently, nearly all financing at such times has been at short term. On the other hand, the Treasury has successfully sold intermediate and long-term obligations in substantial size in periods when competing demands for funds have been depressed and interest rates have been in a declining phase, *i.e.*, during periods of economic recession. The net effect upon the cost and availability of capital of the Treasury's efforts to maintain the maturity structure of its debt, therefore, has been to offset at least part of the effect of Federal Reserve policy. The two policies have been in rather direct conflict.

The cyclically aggravating character of the Treasury's debt policies has been recognized by the debt-management officials, and during the recession year of 1954 (but not during 1958) opportunities to sell long-term bonds were not taken precisely because of a wish to avoid competing with other borrowers. Caught between the Scylla of inability to sell bonds when other investments were available to investors and the Charybdis of an economic theory which dictated that bonds should not be sold when other investments were not available to investors, it sometimes appeared to the Treasury officials that "there is no good time for the Treasury to sell long-term bonds." The burden of the argument in this study is that the Treasury has been unable to sell long-term bonds whenever it chose only within the context of the techniques it has employed. There is in logic no reason why the United States Treasury should not be able to compete on equal terms with all other borrowers. Recognition of this principle and revision of the financing techniques which have made its application impractical at times of heavy capital demands are fundamental to the development of debt-management policies which will make the public debt an instrument for economic stability rather than a source of economic disturbance.

What are these techniques in the management of the longer-term debt that have contributed to the difficulty of selling Treasury bonds? First is the practice of selling long-term securities in large blocks. The placement of long-term bonds requires either that true long-term funds be available to take them down or that long-term investors sell other, shorter maturities to intermediate investors, and so forth down the maturity structure. (An advance refunding, of course, bypasses this problem by substituting a longer maturity for one that still represents longer-term funds.) If long-term funds are not immediately available to purchase all of a long-term Treasury issue, the unplaced securities must be underwritten by commercial banks, dealers, or other investors employing shorter-term funds until either the steady flow of liquid savings has provided the long-term funds to purchase the new securities or long-term investors and others have had an opportunity to make the necessary portfolio adjustments to absorb the new bonds. Seldom can it be expected that there will be a large volume (as much as one billion dollars) of long-term funds immediately available in the market for investment in Treasury securities. Therefore, on large offerings some amount of underwriting is required, and at most times a substantial amount. The larger the supply of unplaced securities in under-writing (or speculative) portfolios, the more vulnerable the market is to developments suggesting higher interest rates and the longer is it likely that the market will remain in this vulnerable position. The end result, particularly at times of a tendency toward higher interest rates, is likely to be distress selling that creates higher rates than would otherwise have resulted, a more or less demoralized Government securities market for a protracted period that makes it almost impossible for the Treasury to sell another longer-term issue, and a record of underwriting losses that makes it more difficult for the Treasury to get under-writing the next time it finances. To avoid these results the Treasury must gear the sale of its long-term bonds to the rate of accrual of long-term funds, thus holding the amount of underwriting to a minimum both in amount and in the length of time the new securities are in underwriting positions.

The second shortcoming in the Treasury's program for selling long-term debt is the irregularity of new offerings. Institutional savings in insurance companies, savings organizations, trust funds, etc., and the flow of funds from amortization of outstanding debt accumulate at a fairly steady and predictable rate over time. As these funds accumulate they are invested immediately. In fact, larger institutional lenders customarily commit their projected cash accruals well in advance of receipt so as to remain as nearly fully invested as possible at all times. When there is almost complete uncertainty as to when the Treasury will next offer a new long-term issue, it is not feasible for investors interested in Government bonds to accumulate funds in liquid form as an advance commitment for investment in new Treasury securities. Consequently, such funds either go into other investments or, in the case of "captive investors" who are required to purchase Governments, are used to purchase Government securities in the market from other investors who are liquidating and shifting to other investments. The latter development tends to depress market rates of interest on Government bonds relative to other investments, so that when the Treasury surveys the market to determine potential demand for new Treasury bonds at a new issue rate consistent with current market rates it discovers that there is very little interest. A program of regular offerings of Treasury bonds at predictable intervals could encourage investors to commit funds for investment in the next issue, with these funds invested temporarily in short-term Government issues, and would tend to hold market rates of interest on Government securities at levels competitive with other investment so that the potential pool of funds available to the Treasury would be enlarged. Such a program of bond offerings would make Treasury debt management more nearly consistent with current investment practices in the financial markets.

Third, the procedure followed in determining rates of interest

270

on new issues of Treasury bonds has complicated the problem of selling such securities. As noted above, the failure to maintain a steady flow of new bonds has frequently allowed the market rate of interest on Treasury bonds to develop a spread below rates on competitive investments so broad that the demand for a new issue priced in relation to market rates has been very limited. In addition to the fact that the market rate base to which a new issue rate would be related has frequently been un-realistically low, the Treasury has tended to think in terms of a spread between market rate and new-issue rate that was too narrow. During periods of heavy capital demand, new-issue rates on corporate bonds sometimes are as much as one-half point above yields on comparable outstanding issues, part of the spread reflecting tax advantages and other considerations (such as call provisions) which might tend to hold yields on outstanding issues down and part constituting the premium necessary to place a sizable block of new bonds. Similar willingness to offer a new-issue rate substantially above market yields on outstanding issues will be necessary if the Treasury is to be successful in selling bonds at periods of strong competing demands. To some extent the barrier to such a policy has probably been administrative unwillingness to pay the necessary rate of interest. In larger part it probably has been due to the combination of a statutory interest rate ceiling and political pressures opposed to high interest rates. Whatever the sources of the resistance to competitive new issue rates, they must be overcome if the Treasury is to develop a rational program for handling the maturity structure of its debt.

The fourth important shortcoming of debt-management techniques in selling longer-term debt during most of the postwar period was the practice of permitting longer-term debt to reach maturity before replacing it in the maturity structure. The use of advance refunding in 1960 and 1961 should correct this deficiency. As discussed in the preceding chapter, the character of the funds invested in any given Government security may for analytical purposes be assumed to be determined by the term to

271

maturity of the security. That is to say, the funds invested in a security with one or two years—or less—to run to maturity will ordinarily be short-term funds, and the purpose of the investment will be for liquidity or secondary reserve. This conclusion follows without regard to the original maturity of the obligation. A long-term bond becomes a steadily more liquid investment as it moves toward maturity, and changes in ownership or in function within a portfolio adjust the character of the funds committed to the obligation to conform with its liquidity characteristics. Therefore, by the time a Treasury bond approaches maturity the long-term funds originally committed to it have been lost to the Treasury, and it is pointless to offer the current holders of the issue—who have short-term funds invested—an opportunity to exchange for a new long-term bond. A rational debt management program would attempt to *prevent* the loss of long-term funds in order that the Treasury would not at one period be a large supplier of capital funds and at another a large user of capital funds, particularly since the pattern over recent years has been to supply capital in a boom and withdraw capital in recession. There are two ways in which this might be done, either through optional exchange offerings before bonds move into shorter maturity ranges, the advance refunding procedure developed by the Treasury in 1960, or through a technique of offerings of new bonds that regularly replaced the securities moving out of the long-term area, with the funds raised in this way used to retire bonds at call date or maturity.

D. A Neutral Objective for Treasury Debt Management

Much of the discussion and writing on objectives of Treasury debt management since the Second World War has analyzed ways in which debt management might be used as a positive instrument of economic policy in combination with Federal Reserve policy. In particular, it has been suggested that shifts in the maturity structure of the debt might be employed to affect economic liquidity and the availability of funds at different maturities in a manner intended to promote orderly economic growth. These suggestions imply that the Treasury has already developed the ability to regulate the maturity structure of its debt and, to this extent, have ignored the fundamental problems that have plagued Treasury officials. The first job is at the technical level, to develop those techniques that will reduce the unintended disturbing influence that Treasury debt operations have exerted on the capital markets and that will enable the Treasury at all times to maintain administrative control of the debt. The "neutral objectives" for debt management suggested in this study do not deny that Treasury debt management might eventually be developed as an important economic policy instrument; they are intended only to give recognition to a first-things-first approach that would solve the technical problems of managing the debt before tackling the theoretical problem of what policy ends might be achieved through debt management.

Some maturity structure objective is necessary as a proximate goal during the period of technical innovation. It is suggested that the Treasury direct its operations toward preventing further changes in the maturity structure of the debt, in the sense that the arrangement of maturities of publicly-held marketable debt by broad maturity areas existing at the end of 1960—or at whatever point in time the objective is adopted—be maintained. Very roughly, this would mean that approximately one-third of the publicly-owned marketable debt (which is defined to include F, G, J, and K Savings bonds and the Investment Series bonds) would be in the under-one-year range, approximately one-half in the one- to ten-year range, and about one-sixth in the over-ten-year range. Maintenance of this debt structure would be neutral in the sense of the discussion in Chapter VII.

The current debt structure represents what has already happened. Whatever inflationary consequences flowed from the

273

shortening of the debt since the end of the Second World War are now part of history. To attempt to lengthen the debt so as to move back to some previous maturity structure would simply create an entirely new set of economically disturbing repercussions, this time deflationary. The capital funds drawn out of Treasury bonds in earlier years are now embedded in financial assets representing industrial plants, residential homes, etc.; they can not be recaptured. Lengthening the public debt could be achieved only by diverting capital funds from the current flow, pre-empting them from current investment expenditures. There could be no logical justification for such a policy, except in marginal amounts and for the explicit purpose of creating just such a diversion for economic stabilization purposes. At the same time, to allow the maturity structure to shorten further would, as in previous years, tend to supply capital funds, perhaps again through upward pressure on the income velocity of money. The "neutral" objective recommended here would be intended as a technically achievable goal that would have a generally neutral effect and that would, therefore, allow central bank policy, working through responsive money and credit markets, to exert a more precise influence upon money and credit availability.

It might appear that adoption of a "neutral" maturity objective for Treasury debt management, in the sense of a stabilized maturity distribution, would constitute abandonment of debt management as an instrument of public economic policy. In fact, it would constitute nothing more than recognition of the fact that in the present state of technical knowledge of Treasury finance a more ambitious objective is not feasible. And, after all, achievement of this "neutral" objective would represent a significantly more desirable performance of debt management than has been realized thus far.

Leaving aside for the moment questions as to the type of securities to be sold, methods of selling them, and the other technical questions, the "neutral" maturity objective would maintain approximately 30–35 per cent of the public marketable debt (excludes Treasury and Federal Reserve holdings) in securities within one year of maturity, 45–50 per cent in securities within one to ten years of maturity, and 15–20 per cent in securities more than ten years from maturity. Assuming $160 billion public marketable debt (as defined earlier) outstanding at the end of 1960, some $50–55 billion would be within one year of maturity, about $75–80 billion one to ten years from maturity, and $25–30 billion more than ten years from maturity. Changes in the total of public marketable debt outstanding, as a result either of fiscal surpluses or deficits, could then be distributed among maturity areas in a manner designed to synchronize with the counter-cyclical objectives of monetary and fiscal policy. Ideally, these changes might be expected to concentrate in the short-term area. Thus, if we assume a "cyclically balanced" budget for purposes of analytical simplicity, the budget deficits in periods of recession would be financed through the sale of liquid short-term securities and budget surpluses in periods of economic boom would be used to retire liquid securities. In fact, the record suggests that the budget—and thus the public debt—does not behave in this cyclically balanced fashion, so that decisions as to the maturity area from which debt should be retired or into which new debt should be placed will not always be this simple. Economic policy objectives at the time, market conditions, and limitations on what it is realistically possible to do will determine the maturity effect of these changes in the total public marketable debt; it would not be too fruitful to attempt to outline all the possible circumstances and courses of action in this study. Therefore, the "neutral" maturity objective applies principally to the outstanding debt that is to be refunded. Net cash borrowing or repayment, except as they are intra-cyclical, can not by definition be neutral, and their effects upon the maturity structure will reflect immediate policy objectives at the time the borrowing or repayment occurs.

If Treasury debt management is to be a truly neutral economic influence, it must seek as a second objective—in addition to a stable maturity pattern—to minimize its impact effect upon the financial markets. Pursuit of this objective would require that it make at least four changes in financing practices:

1. Routinize financing in order to eliminate, so far as possible, all uncertainty as to the maturity of the securities the Treasury will offer in any given financing.

2. Arrange the size of all offerings so that the amount of securities offered at any maturity at one time will be consistent with the market's absorptive capacity for securities of that type.

3. Finance in a way that recognizes a clear distinction between debt of different maturities. In particular, recognize the short-term debt as a distinct body of debt that is routinely and regularly rolled over at maturity and that is not, in refunding, in any way intermingled with intermediate or longer-term debt.

4. Refund intermediate and longer-term debt in a manner that does not rely upon voluntary exchange refunding at maturity to maintain the debt structure.

Techniques that would minimize impact effect of Treasury debt management are discussed in the following section.

E. Techniques of Debt Management

1. THE SHORT-TERM DEBT

While it is not possible to derive an exact estimate of the amounts of funds that might be available at any one time for investment at various maturities in the under-one-year area (in any event these amounts shift from one period to the next), perhaps it could be assumed that the distribution of short-term Treasury securities outstanding at the end of 1960 is consistent with the "normal" distribution of these liquidity reserves. That is to say, approximately 50 per cent of the funds invested in under-one-year Government securities might ordinarily be available for three months or less, an additional 25 per cent for three to six months, and the balance for periods ranging from six months to one year. Such a distribution in late 1960 was consistent with a short-term-yield curve that had a moderately pronounced positive slope.

Using this rough guide to distribute the total $50 to $55 billion of short-term debt indicated by the discussion in the preceding section would yield approximately $27 billion within three months of maturity, $14 billion three to six months from maturity, and $6 billion in each of the third and fourth quarters from maturity.

What types of securities might the Treasury include in its short-term debt to achieve this distribution? First, it is clear that the regular weekly issues of three-month and six-month bills should be maintained approximately as now constituted. These securities are sold at auction each week on a routine schedule, and their sale has virtually no effect upon the market or upon investor expectations. Some $17.5 billion of three-month bills were owned outside of official accounts at the end of 1960, and about $5.4 billion of four- to six-month bills were so owned. In addition to the three-month and six-month bills, the publicly-owned short-term debt at the end of 1960 included approximately $5.8 billion of securities sold initially with a one-year maturity, with $1.4 billion scheduled to mature in January, July, and October and $1.8 billion in April, 1961. The one-year bills have a somewhat greater impact on the market at the time they are auctioned than the shorter bills, but by the end of 1960 they had been well absorbed into the permanent debt.

The adoption of the six-month and one-year bill cycles in 1958 and 1959, respectively, went a good distance toward bringing order out of the chaotic short-term debt situation that had existed prior to 1958. Through these instruments, the bulk of the under-one-year debt was placed on a routine rollover basis, with substantial benefits for the functioning of the market. Beginning in early 1961, the Treasury added slightly to the six-month bill issues and moved to increase each of the one-year issues to $2.0 billion. These actions were wholly consistent with further

277

improvement in the short-debt structure. In addition, it may be assumed that the short-term debt at the end of each calendar year will include $3 billion or so of tax-anticipation bills scheduled to mature at both the following March and June tax dates. Even in a fiscal year in which the budget is balanced, the uneven pattern of corporate tax collections would call for this type of intra-year short-term financing.

Finally, the longer-term-debt schedule worked out later in this chapter would provide for approximately $12 billion of such debt moving into the under-one-year range each year. For purposes of simplicity, it may be assumed that the latter debt component would be equally distributed by quarters. The resulting under-one-year debt would take the form as indicated in Table 19.

Table 19—Suggested Short-Term-Debt Structure*
(Billions of dollars)

Maturing in	3-month Bills	6-month Bills	One-year Bills	Tax-anticipation Securities	Short Bonds and Notes	Total
1st quarter	19.0	—	2.5	3.0	3.0	27.5
2nd quarter	—	6.0	2.5	3.0	3.0	14.5
3rd quarter	—	—	2.5	—	3.0	5.5
4th quarter	—	—	2.5	—	3.0	5.5
Total	19.0	6.0	10.0	6.0	12.0	53.0

* Excludes Federal Reserve and Treasury holdings.

This distribution roughly approximates the distribution recommended earlier.

The short-term-debt structure suggested in Table 19 is very similar to that prevailing at the end of 1960. The principal changes are the substitution of larger amounts of bills, particularly one-year bills, and of longer securities that have shortened to within one year of maturity for the certificates of indebtedness now outstanding. Coupon-bearing certificates create refinancing problems, if for no other reason than the fact that the Treasury has customarily employed two or more issues of different maturity in their refunding, and these financings often have been serious causes of market uncertainty. There is no reason, of course, why one-year certificates of indebtedness could not be used as readily as one-year Treasury bills, but their unfortunate record suggests that there might be virtue in removing temptation from the Treasury's way if a truly routine short-term-debt program is to be developed. Also, their elimination would reduce the number of times the Treasury must come to market each year.

It should be stressed at this point that the precise dollar amounts used in the preceding discussion, while correctly adjusted to current investor practices and to the structure of the Treasury debt as of December, 1960, are illustrative only. Within the broad framework of the short-term debt outlined here there is considerable latitude for adding to or reducing one or more of the short-debt components relative to the total. Also, the total of short debt may change with the passage of time, as a consequence either of changes in the *total* of publicly-held debt resulting from budget deficits or surpluses or of changes in the debt structure resulting from efforts to link debt management to counter-cyclical monetary and fiscal policy. What is of lasting importance in the preceding discussion is the emphasis upon careful scheduling to provide an availability of short-term securities consistent with the availability of investment funds and an orderly flow of short-term debt to maturity at a pace and in forms that can be refunded with minimum disruption of the financial markets and of central bank policy.

2. INTERMEDIATE DEBT

Table 20 summarizes the structure of the publicly-owned intermediate and longer-term marketable Treasury debt outstanding as of December 31, 1960 (including Series F, G, J, and K Savings bonds and Investment Series bonds in marketable debt, as explained earlier).

In the following discussion, suggestions on restructuring intermediate and long-term debt rest upon two conclusions with

279

**Table 20—Publicly-Held Treasury Marketable Debt More Than
One Year from Maturity December 31, 1960
(Billions of dollars)**

Period to Maturity	Marketable Notes	Marketable Bonds	Other*	Total
1–5 years	33.5	24.2	2.4	60.1
5–10 years	—	15.9	1.5	17.4
10–15 years	—	10.2	—	10.2
15–20 years	—	1.3	3.3	4.6
20–25 years	—	2.8	—	2.8
25–30 years	—	2.3	—	2.3
30–35 years	—	2.5	—	2.5
35–40 years	—	2.1	—	2.1
Total	33.5	61.3	7.2	102.0

* Series F, G, J, and K Savings Bonds and Investment Series A and B bonds.

respect to the distribution shown in Table 20. First, the concentration of securities in the one- to five-year area represents
principally the secondary liquidity reserves of commercial banks
and other investing institutions, and while some reorganization
within this area is possible, the bulk of the funds invested here
would not readily move out to longer maturity if the Treasury
were to attempt to lengthen its debt structure by moving significantly large blocks of these securities to longer-term areas.
Second, the clustering of the debt more than five years from
maturity in the five-to-ten and ten-to-fifteen-year ranges reflects
the movement toward maturity of issues originally of longer
term, particularly the large wartime 2½ per cent "tap" issues,
and it is assumed that the largest part—or at least a substantial
part—of these bonds are still held in long-term investment portfolios. Consequently, it should be possible to achieve a more
even distribution of this debt in maturity areas beyond five years
without draining new long-term funds into Treasury securities
from other uses.

Consistent with the "neutral" objective for Treasury debt
management outlined earlier in this chapter, Table 21 summarizes a proposed maturity structure for the intermediate
and longer-term debt that would regularize this portion of the
debt and provide for an even flow of securities toward maturity

**Table 21—Suggested Structure of Intermediate and
Long-Term Debt
(Billions of dollars)**

Years from Date to Maturity	Notes	Bonds	Total
2 years	8	4	12
3 years	8	4	12
4 years	8	4	12
5 years	8	4	12
Subtotal	32	16	48
5 to 10 years	—	25	25
Cumulative subtotal	32	41	73
10 to 15 years	—	10	10
15 to 20 years	—	10	10
20 to 25 years	—	10	10
Subtotal	—	30	30
Grand total	32	71	103

without radically altering the amounts of "investment funds" and "liquidity reserves" invested in United States Government securities. Comparison with Table 20 shows that the most important shifts would be the movement of several billion dollars from the one-to-five-year into the five-to-ten-year range and of a few billion dollars into later maturity categories. Movement of this volume of debt even this much further out in the maturity structure might encounter serious obstacles.

The discussion in Chapter IV suggests the nature of the obstacles the Treasury might encounter in even this modest effort at debt lengthening to achieve a more orderly flow of securities toward maturity. Many of the principal types of investing institutions that regularly purchase longer-term obligations—*i.e.,* life insurance companies, mutual savings banks, savings and loan associations, *etc.*—probably would not be interested in substantial amounts of longer-term Government securities even at rates of interest equal to high-grade corporate bonds. There are, however, three sources of funds which might be available to the Treasury for the suggested debt reconstruction. First are the holdings of one-to-five-year or five-to-ten-year obligations that originally were of longer term by institutions that would be willing to lengthen in an advance refunding. Second is

the prospect that some rather sizable amount of bank investments in the one-to-five-year range might rather readily move
longer if there were sufficient interest-rate incentive. And third
is the prospect of tapping somewhat larger amounts of funds
from such investors in high-grade obligations as personal trusts
and pension trusts through rates of interest more directly competitive with rates on other top-quality bonds. With respect to
the latter source, it might be mentioned that the analysis in
Chapter IV shows that an increasingly large proportion of the
longer-term public debt is likely to move into the hands of these
investors. They have become increasingly sophisticated, however, and it is to be expected that in order to attract and hold
funds from the personal and pension trusts the Treasury will
find it necessary to pay rates of interest that are competitive with
rates available on other investments. In time, the differential
between high-grade, noncallable corporate bonds and Treasury
bonds might virtually disappear, a circumstance that would
require rather fundamental revisions in the thought patterns of
public officials and of market specialists.

Turning first to the financing of intermediate debt in the one-
to-five-year maturity sector, it should be noted that the most
important characteristic of this body of securities is its ownership distribution. Of the $60 billion of publicly-owned Treasury
bonds and notes from one to five years to maturity outstanding
at the end of 1960, some $33 billion, or 55 per cent, were owned
by commercial banks.[1] The remainder were held in the liquidity
reserves or investment portfolios of a wide range of institutions,
including nearly $4.2 billion, or 7 per cent of the total, owned
by insurance companies and mutual savings banks. Nonfinancial
corporations and savings and loan associations held small
amounts (4 per cent and one per cent, respectively), but the
largest part not owned by commercial banks fell in the "all other"
category (33 per cent), for which a detailed breakdown is not
available. Reports from Government securities dealers on the

1. Data from the Treasury's Survey of Ownership have been increased by
10 per cent to adjust for commercial banks not included in the Survey.

types of institutions trading these securities suggest that state and local government agencies hold large amounts as employment for construction and other funds not scheduled for expenditure in the near future; and that foreign official accounts also hold sizable amounts.

As a general rule, these short-intermediate securities are not purchased for long-term investment purposes, in which case liquidity or marketability would not be a consideration, but for a secondary reserve purpose which emphasizes some degree of liquidity and marketability. The funds employed represent money for which there is no immediate or predictable need for other purposes but which might be needed if the rate of money inflow should decline or if other demands for credit should expand. Because of the purpose which these investments are intended to serve, most major banking and other institutions attempt to schedule their portfolios so as to have a distribution that will provide a steady flow into the short-term sector. From the point of view of Treasury debt management, therefore, the most desirable distribution of short-intermediate debt is one that provides a fairly even amount in each annual maturity and thus conforms with investor demands.

The fact that commercial banks also held 55 per cent of the five-to-ten-year maturities at the end of 1960 suggests that these maturities also constitute a second line of liquidity. Bonds in this range are considerably less liquid, however, and commercial banks and most other institutions holding intermediate obligations generally attempt to arrange their portfolios so as to have a much larger total of funds invested in the one-to-five-year maturity sector than in the five-to-ten-year area. Table 20 (see p. 280) shows that total publicly-held Treasury securities outstanding at the end of 1960 in the one-to-five-year intermediate area was nearly four times as large as the total in the five-to-ten-year maturity area. While the recommended debt structure reflects investor preferences for shorter-term intermediates, it does not accept the actual distribution as of December, 1960, as one that necessarily reflected investor requirements or the

283

most desirable structure from the Treasury's point of view. Intermediate debt was rather unusually concentrated in the one-to-five-year area at that time, reflecting the heavy reliance upon notes during 1959 and part of 1960, when the 4¼ per cent limitation upon interest rates on Treasury bonds forced the Treasury to rely upon notes in its efforts to move debt beyond one year. As mentioned earlier, commercial banks in particular might be encouraged to lengthen slightly by more attractive rates.

It is possible, therefore, that the Treasury's publicly-owned intermediate debt might be restructured so as to shift about $12 billion of securities in the one-to-five-year range out to slightly longer maturities, as suggested in Table 21, without encountering serious conflict with investor's preferences. If this were to be done, the shorter-intermediate debt might include in each annual maturity roughly $8 billion of Treasury notes originally issued with a five-year maturity and $4 billion of Treasury bonds originally issued with a longer maturity. On this schedule, $12 billion of debt would reach maturity each year and $12 billion would enter the five-year area through the sale of $8 billion new five-year notes and the movement toward maturity of $4 billion of the longer bonds.

The longer-intermediate debt might, then, include $4 billion of Treasury bonds in each annual maturity, each issue sold initially with a ten-year maturity, and, in addition, the residue of a $10 billion block of bonds originally sold with a twenty-five-year maturity. As discussed in more detail later, the latter bonds would be fully callable in the last ten years of their life, and the debt schedule outlined in this chapter contemplates that they would be called in even amounts during the sixth to tenth years. Therefore, the amount of bonds in the five- to ten-year range actually would total $25 billion, as shown in the table, only on average. During the year that the $10 billion block of long-term bonds reached a point ten years from maturity, the five-to ten-year total would be $30 billion. It would then be reduced each year as these long-term bonds were redeemed until, as the last of this block was retired, a new $10 billion block would reach the ten-year mark.

The detailed techniques for issuing the intermediate-term (one-to-ten-year) notes and bonds called for in these recommendations would require few innovations upon present techniques with the exception of the all-important adoption of a regular program that would be pursued, without substantial interruption, year after year. A total of $12 billion new intermediate-term securities would be issued each year, including $8 billion five-year notes and $4 billion ten-year bonds. The program probably would require that the Treasury be in the market four times each year, although after an orderly debt schedule has been established it might prove possible to do the job in two operations each year. Since the maturing securities would have been sold initially to commercial banks and other investors interested in maintaining an orderly spacing in their secondary reserve portfolios, it is likely that there would be relatively less shifting among groups of investors over the life of the securities than is now the case. With the ownership distribution of the maturing securities presumably including large numbers of investors interested, for portfolio purposes, in replacing this issue with securities of a maturity equivalent to its original maturity, an exchange option rather than cash refunding is indicated. By offering a par-for-par exchange for the maturing securities, the Treasury would make it easy for these investors to maintain their portfolio structure. At the same time, an additional amount of the new securities would have to be sold for cash if the total outstanding were not to be reduced through the attrition from investors that submit the maturing securities for cash. The cash portion might be offered at the same fixed price (par or a price either side of par) employed in the exchange offering, or it might be offered at auction. Probably the latter alternative is preferable in order to assure the necessary underwriting in a period when interest rates are rising and in order to limit speculative "free riding" and padding of subscriptions. Underwriting probably would come principally from the professional Government securities dealers and from the larger commercial banks, as it does in rolling over the regular three-month, six-month, and one-year bills that constitute the bulk of the short-term debt.

Assuming that these intermediate financing operations were scheduled four times a year, the total offering in each operation would be roughly $3 billion, consisting of $2 billion five-year notes and $1 billion ten-year bonds. On the basis of past experience, attrition on the exchange to be covered through the cash offering would typically run in the neighborhood of 5 to 10 per cent, or something between $150 and $300 million. In periods of restraint on money and credit, and rising interest rates, the cash portion probably would be larger than this, perhaps rising to as much as $500 million. Given the opportunity for dealers and other "underwriters" to protect themselves at such times by allowing for the necessary risk cushion in the prices they bid for the new securities, however, it is unlikely that the recommended size of this financing and the amount of underwriting it implies would at any time be too large for the market to absorb. It should be recalled, also, that the reduction of uncertainty through the institution of a regular and orderly refunding program would do a great deal to create a new and more favorable setting for Treasury finance.

Assuming that the Treasury should adopt an orderly program for its intermediate debt, as recommended here, in which the maturity and amount of the new securities would be known in advance, there still would remain the problem of setting interest rates on the new obligations. Since the implementation of such a program would tend to hold market rates on securities in the five- and ten-year areas in line with the rate of interest necessary to place the next new issues at these maturities, it follows that the Treasury would have a reasonably good market base upon which to price. The amount of spread above market rates necessary to place the new issues would vary with market conditions but might be expected to range between ⅛ and ¼ per cent in yield. Experience with a regularized debt management program would be necessary to determine just how much new-issue premium was required to assure a successful operation while at the same time holding the Treasury's interest cost to a minimum. One practice begun by the Treasury in 1958 that should be continued as a means of pricing more precisely is the offering of securities at fractional discounts or premiums. It is not practical to vary coupon rates by fractions smaller than eighths, but by varying the price on either side of par it is possible to obtain decimal pricing. If an auction procedure is employed to sell the cash portion of each issue, cash subscriptions might be scaled in decimals or in the standard ¹⁄₃₂ of a price point above or below the price on the Treasury's exchange offering, preferably the former.

The process of converting to an orderly intermediate-debt schedule will be complicated somewhat by the fact of the rather disorganized structure presently existing. Table 18 (see p. 263) shows that as of December, 1960, the securities outstanding in public hands in the one- to ten-year maturity range were distributed as follows:

Year	Amount in billions
1962	$21.3
1963	14.6
1964	15.3
1965	9.6
1966	2.5
1967	1.3
1968	2.8
1969	5.7
1970	3.4

There are various methods that might be employed to redistribute this debt into the schedule outlined earlier, or whatever similar schedule the Treasury might adopt, but the important first step is to adopt a definite schedule as a target and to direct each refunding operation in notes and bonds toward filling in the schedule. If, as recommended, the short-term debt is clearly segregated and separate financing methods applied to it, it will be fairly simple to sort out the maturing issues of notes and bonds for which exchange offerings into new five-year notes and ten-year bonds are to be made. In handling large maturities it might be useful to offer a strip of notes or bonds containing equal or specified amounts of two or more issues; exchange subscriptions would receive specified proportions of each issue offered by the Treasury.[2] Special treatment might be required to refund maturing F, G, J, and K bonds and Series A Investment bonds which will mature in an amount of nearly $4 billion over this ten-year span. These bonds might be offered exchange into ten-year bonds, or they might be paid off in cash. In any event, attrition from the nonmarketable bonds, in particular, and from marketable bonds and notes as well, is likely to be quite large during the early years of debt reformation. Therefore, occasional issues will probably have to be sold for cash, with maturities and amounts carefully scheduled to fill in the gaps in the debt structure. In addition to these techniques, it would be most desirable that some of the very large bond issues, such as the 2½'s of August, 1963, the 2¼'s of June and December, 1962, and the 2⅝'s of February, 1963, and February, 1965, be offered one or more options to convert into a strip of six- to ten-year bonds well before they reach maturity. The Treasury would, of course, if it offered a pre-maturity conversion of this sort, reserve the right to limit total allotments to an amount in accord with its overall debt-structure objectives.

The recommended restructuring of the intermediate debt cannot be accomplished in a few months. It will require carefully directed effort over a period of years. During this transition period the important consideration will be that every effort in the intermediate area be part of the total plan. Occasions will

2. Small subscriptions, *e.g.,* less than $50,000, might be allowed exchange into a single issue selected by the subscriber.

arise when it will be possible to accomplish more "debt lengthen-ing" than called for by the program. At other times it will appear impossible to sell even the limited amounts of intermediate bonds and notes called for by the program. Under these varying condi-tions the Treasury must, if it is ever to achieve an orderly process for refunding its debt and market understanding that it is seek-ing orderly processes, adhere doggedly and single-mindedly to its program. The only alternative is the kind of "catch-as-catch-can" debt-management program that has been followed since the end of the Second World War, with its concomitant creation of uncertainties that disrupt the financial market and its generation of inflationary forces that thwart the central bank.

3.   LONG-TERM DEBT

In some respects, the program recommended for the management of the long-term Treasury debt is the simplest. It calls for the sale of only $2 billion twenty-five year bonds each year. Yet, in only three years since the Second World War—1955, 1958, and 1960—has the Treasury been successful in selling long-term bonds in this amount. The historical record and the analysis in this study have repeatedly stressed the shortcomings in the Treasury's program for selling long-term bonds. These short-comings are summarized earlier in this chapter, and it is toward correcting them that the long-term financing program presented here is directed.

The first and most important step is for the Treasury to come to market at regular and predictable intervals with offerings of long-term bonds to replace those that are moving down in the maturity structure. If it is known that the Treasury will be in the market two times or four times each year with an offering of long-term bonds, investors interested in such bonds will have an opportunity to accumulate funds in advance for their pur-chase. In a sense, the Treasury will be in a position to share in the funds that major investing institutions commit in advance. Morcover, the procedure of regular offerings will have the

289

effect of preventing the market rate of interest on Treasury bonds from drifting out of touch with competitive investments. The fact of a steady supply of new Treasury bonds will tend to establish and maintain a rate relationship between these bonds and other instruments at which the Treasury will be able to compete effectively for investors' funds.

It is recommended, therefore, that the Treasury adopt a program of selling approximately $2 billion of twenty-five year bonds each year, and that the rate of interest and price of these securities be adjusted to whatever effective rate of return is required from period to period to sell bonds. One of the competitive advantages Treasury bonds have had is their long no-call period. It is suggested that the twenty-five year Treasury bonds be made noncallable over the first fifteen years of their life but callable thereafter. Another advantage most Treasury bonds have possessed is their acceptability at par in payment of estate taxes; it is recommended that this feature be retained. These bonds should be attractive to personal trusts and public and private pension trusts, which probably now are the largest investors in long-term Government securities, and for balanced portfolio purposes they should have some attraction, at competitive rates of interest, to mutual savings banks, insurance companies, and other institutional investors.

Two other shortcomings of Treasury management of its long-term debt have been the practice of waiting until long-term securities have reached maturity before refunding them and the failure to recognize the realistic limits on the market's ability to absorb new long-term securities in a brief period. The suggestion that a relatively fixed amount of new long-term bonds be issued each year, rather than waiting for a bond issue to reach maturity before refunding, implicitly corrects the first shortcoming. With respect to the second—the size of new Treasury bond issues—it appears likely that if the techniques outlined below are employed the Treasury should be able to issue $1 billion bonds in each operation. That is to say, the Treasury might offer $1 billion twenty-five year bonds in connection with two of its four operations in intermediate issues each year.[3]

It seems entirely feasible for the Treasury to conduct its long-term financing in two operations each year, with an offering of $1 billion bonds in each operation. These bonds would be twenty-five year obligations on initial issue, except that for purposes of minimizing the number of bond issues outstanding and thus facilitating trading in the issues it would be advantageous to reopen each new bond issue until it had been built up to a $10 billion total. By the time this had been achieved, the last bonds sold to round out the issue would be only twenty-one years from maturity on issue. The Treasury would employ the proceeds of the long-term bonds as they were sold to call and retire the issue of bonds that had moved within its ten-year call period. If $2 billion of old bonds were called for retirement each year, the total of the issue would be redeemed in the sixth year before maturity. Calls of $1 billion, based either upon random selection of a prefix letter or upon a first-issued, first-called basis, preferably the former, would be made at least four months before the bonds were to bcome payable.

In spite of the difficulties encountered by the Treasury in selling long-term bonds during the past decade, the technical details in selling bonds under the program suggested here probably would be quite uncomplicated. The market would know that as a regular practice the Treasury would offer approximately $1 billion new long-term bonds in connection with, for example, its February and August financing operations. There would be virtually no uncertainty as to this program, and the market could therefore adjust in advance to the known size and maturity of the Treasury offering. Given this advance knowledge, and the additional knowledge that the new bonds would be priced

3. Nothing was said earlier about the timing of these operations within the year. For various detailed reasons, including avoidance of conflict with tax dates and periods of seasonal pressure on markets and scheduling in line with seasonal flows of investment funds, the preferable months probably would be February, May, August, and November for the intermediate-term financing, with long-term financing included in February and August.

competitively, investors would have an opportunity to adjust their portfolios in preparation for absorbing the new Treasury bonds. The latter process would be encouraged if the Treasury made provision for preferential exchange of the bonds that had been called for payment into the new bonds. Thus, for example, bonds with from six to ten years still to run to maturity might be called, on the basis of prefix letter selected at lottery, in April for payment in August. These bonds would be given the option of exchange into new long-term bonds in August, and would begin immediately, in April, to trade as "rights." In a regular program of this sort, there is every reason to believe that a large proportion of the called bonds would still be held in long-term portfolios and would be exchanged for the new bonds, and also that there would be good demand in the market for the "rights" out of current accruals of investment funds.

While the largest part of each semi-annual issue of long-term bonds would probably be issued on exchange for called bonds, there would in each operation be some bonds turned in for cash, and it would therefore be necessary to accept cash subscriptions to cover the full $1 billion offering. As in the case of the cash components in issues of five-year and ten-year obligations, it is suggested that the cash subscriptions be on the basis of competitive auction. Dealers in Government securities would be encouraged to seek out prospective cash purchasers of the new bonds and to bid aggressively to get enough bonds to provide for these customers. Other bids from the dealers, for their own portfolios, would be scaled down in price. In addition to this encouragement to dealers to underwrite the new issues of bonds, the Treasury might give serious thought to paying a commission to dealers, *e.g.,* one-fourth point, for all bonds awarded through them, both cash and exchange. This procedure would provide direct incentive to the dealers to encourage customers to exchange called bonds for the new issues and to seek out potential cash purchasers of the new bonds. In this way the Treasury would create for its new bonds a broad underwriting group of professional firms with a direct stake in the success of each new issue.

The plan for long-term financing proposed here would contemplate no discrimination among investor groups and, thus, no preferential allotments. One of the problems that has often plagued the Treasury in its intermediate and long-term financing in the past has been the incidence of speculative free-riding which has resulted in poor initial placement of new bonds and subsequent pressure on the market as the speculators attempted to unload their holdings. Would the proposed plan, particularly the abandonment of preferential allotments to "real" investors, lead to even greater speculation? This outcome is unlikely; in fact, it is more likely that the techniques recommended here would reduce or eliminate such speculation. Speculation in new United States Government bonds has been made possible principally by two Treasury practices. First, in exchange offerings, the offering of long-term bonds in exchange for maturing securities the greatest part of which were held as short-term investments, has created a large supply of "rights" to be purchased by free-riders. Second, in cash offerings, the practice of awarding minimum subscriptions of a specified amount in full, frequently with small cash payments, has encouraged speculation; a good share of the free-riding has been by small investors who receive their bonds under the "minimum allotment in full" provision. The program recommended here would offer a limited amount of bonds in exchange for bonds which, in most cases, would still be held by long-term investors, so that the potential supply of "rights" available to speculative free-riders probably would be small. On the portion sold for cash, subscriptions for bonds would be allotted in full, without regard to the size of the subscription, based wholly on competitive pricing, and because of the market sophistication required to compete in an auction it is unlikely that the usual speculators would become involved. In short, the program suggested here would be calculated to place as many of the new bonds as possible directly with long-term investors and the balance with experienced bond dealers, serving

293

in an underwriting capacity, who would not disrupt the market in placing their awards with ultimate investors.

Once the long-term debt program was fully established, the Treasury, through the sale of $2 billion twenty-five year bonds each year, would have a permanent debt outstanding in the maturity area beyond ten years of $30 billion. There would be only three issues, each totaling $10 billion, spaced at five year intervals. Such a long-term debt structure would provide a group of issues large enough to assure maximum tradability.

The process of transition from the present debt structure to this arrangement of the long-term debt will, however, call for very careful planning and, clearly, further use of the advance refunding procedure to place long bonds. The total publicly-owned Treasury debt still more than five years from maturity at the end of 1960 amounted to $42 billion (including Investment Series B bonds and a small amount of J and K Savings bonds). Of this total, $26.7 billion will mature within twelve years. Three-fourths of the latter figure consists of $20.4 billion of optionally dated 2½ per cent bonds issued during the Second World War.

The ownership data at the end of 1960 suggested that the bulk of the funds invested in the 2½ per cent "tap" bonds still represented longer-term investment money. With the passage of time, however, it must be expected that these bonds will move into shorter-term portfolios and the long-term funds will be lost to the Treasury unless action is taken to prevent this occurrence. In October, 1960, in its first advance refunding into long-term obligations, the Treasury exchanged nearly $4 billion of 1980, 1990, and 1995 bonds for an equivalent amount of four of the shorter issues of 2½ per cent "tap" bonds.

It is unlikely that new long-term bonds could be sold in normal course in sufficient volume to offset the loss of long-term funds as the remaining "tap" bonds move into the intermediate and short-term areas. Thus, if the Treasury were to sell $2 billion of long-term bonds per year beginning in calendar 1961, it would have sold only $10 billion through 1965, by which time the longest of the World War II bond issues—the Victory 2½'s of December, 1967–72—would have moved within seven years of maturity. The massive increase in the supply of bonds in the "bank maturity range" might lead to a tendency for commercial banks and investors with similar liquidity requirements to reach out for these securities while simultaneously pressing shorter-term issues upon short-term nonbank investors (always assuming that interest rates and rate expectations indicated this policy). Long-term funds would be lost to the Treasury. The subsequent efforts to rebuild the total of long-term Treasury bonds outstanding would then involve net *withdrawal* of investment funds over the following ten years, which would make the execution of the Treasury's debt-management program significantly more difficult and might accentuate rather than mitigate cyclical tendencies in the private economy. Finally, allowing this block of bonds to move into the intermediate and short- and intermediate-term area would, for several years, make it almost impossible for the Treasury to develop a rationalized program for managing its intermediate-term debt along the lines described earlier.

The indicated solution to the problem of the present longer-term debt structure is further pre-maturity conversion offerings to holders of the "tap" bonds, similar to the successful operation in October, 1960, to *prevent* the loss of the largest part of the long-term funds presently committed to investment in these securities. Such offerings, if they are to be made, should be made as early as possible in order to "lock in" as many of the long-term funds as can be saved. An offering that would be consistent with the long-term-debt program recommended earlier would extend to owners of the remaining "tap" bonds, or some part of them, an option to convert their holdings for a strip of 1975, 1980, and 1985 bonds. The subscriber might be required to take equal amounts of each issue of the new bonds, with the exception that small subscriptions might be allowed to go entirely into one issue.

While further conversion offerings to the holders of the "tap" bonds is clearly suggested by considerations of debt structure and the related considerations of sound economic policy, the costliness of advance refunding operations raises questions that can be answered only with reference to explicit valuation of the importance of preventing the type of inflationary impulse to be expected from further shortening of the Treasury debt structure. Since this study is of debt management, and since a principal conclusion is that inadequate debt management has been a primary force for inflation in recent years, the conversion is considered to be justified. The conversion offering would constitute an option to investors to change, to their own advantage, the terms of a contract to which they are still bound for a period of years; the option is costly to the Treasury to the extent of the difference between the 2½ per cent rate on the outstanding bonds and the rate the Treasury has to attach to the conversion bonds to make the operation a success. In the October, 1960, advance refunding, for example, the additional interest cost to the Treasury over the remaining life of the old bonds tendered for exchange was nearly $350 million. This was, in a sense, the cost to obtain a somewhat better maturity distribution. While undesirable in this respect, such advance refundings appear to be absolutely necessary in terms of the neutral objectives for debt management adopted in this study. At the same time, they should be recognized as deviations from sound debt-management techniques—"crash" programs dictated by circumstances—rather than in any sense a part of a soundly conceived debt-management program.[4]

4. The very intricate tax questions, pricing problems, etc., involved in a large conversion offering of this sort are not dealt with in this study. One point might be noted, however, with respect to the matter of pricing. In order to make the conversion attractive it is necessary only that the Treasury offer a rate of interest that provides an alternative that is so attractive to the holder of the bonds that he cannot refuse it; it is not necessary that this rate match current market rates of interest. Ignoring tax considerations, an investor selling his "Vics" at 86, for example, and buying a thirty-year corporate bond (or mortgage, or other type of investment) would have to get a coupon yield of 4½ per cent on his new investment in order to realize an effective yield of 3⅜ per cent on the par value of his original investment. Therefore, if issue rates on high-grade corporate bonds are in the neighborhood of 4½ per cent, an alternative return of 3⅜ per cent on a Treasury conversion offering would be quite attractive and, in fact, 3¼ per cent might do the job.

F. Concluding Comments on the Techniques of Treasury Finance

The implicit theme throughout this study of Treasury financing techniques has been that in each period of America's history the debt managers have had a set of problems, circumstances, and broad public policies to deal with which have defined the objectives of debt management and which, in turn, have necessitated the development of financing techniques best adjusted to achievement of these objectives. In the post-Civil War period the problems were an unfunded debt and a dual currency system based, in part, upon this debt. Later, in the late nineteenth and early twentieth centuries, the problems revolved about the need to assure a debt of adequate size and proper type to sustain an inadequate monetary system organically tied to the public debt. The 1920's called for debt management aimed at structuring a debt that would provide a steady flow of maturing securities to be retired out of the proceeds of budget surpluses and sinking fund appropriations. And in the 1930's the debt managers were called upon to finance steadily large deficits in a fashion that moved the payment date for the new securities well into the future since the prospect of surpluses to repay debt was, at best, a distant one.

The key problem of the post-World War II years has been— and is—to provide for the maintenance through refunding of a huge public debt which, realistically, is not going to be reduced by significant amounts in the foreseeable future. This debt has replaced most other types of marketable obligations in the short-term area, and it represents the largest part of all liquidity reserves of all types of institutions. Other components of the debt are the core of secondary portfolio reserves of commercial banks and other institutions, and longer-term Treasury bonds are important in the portfolios of many pension funds and institutional lenders. The gross size of the public debt and the massive size of the financing required to service the debt have been disruptive

297

influences, respectively, as the Treasury has been a principal influence in the availability of funds at different maturities and as its financing operations have had a jolting impact which even highly developed financial markets are not equipped to withstand. This study concludes that the key objective of post-World War II debt management—imposed by the need to refund rather than repay, by the very size of the debt relative to other economic magnitudes, by its role in the financial economy, and by the unavoidable nature of Treasury-central bank relationships—is orderliness. Orderlinesss is required in maintaining the debt structure in order that Treasury finance may not unwittingly be a disequilibrating force in the economy, and it is necessary in arranging financing techniques so that the Treasury can avoid a dominating and disruptive effect upon the functioning of the money and credit markets.

If orderliness in these two areas is to be achieved a well-thought-out and doggedly adhered to program of debt management is required. It is upon this premise that the foregoing detailed set of suggestions for a rational debt-management program was developed. The numbers employed, by themselves, are of little significance except that they are one set of numbers that meet the requirement of orderliness. And there is, of course, considerable latitude in the development of techniques; the techniques recommended in this chapter are, however, consistent with contemporary market practices. While individual analysts and technicians will dispute various elements in the proposed program, the need for orderliness within some fully articulated program remains and it is recognition of this principle that this study argues for.

The study has carefully avoided recommendation—or even consideration—of financing practices that are not compatible with accepted practices in the financial markets. Such practices include the use of lottery bonds, purchasing-power bonds, the sale of preferred stock in Government corporations, and other well-meant but uninformed suggestions. There is absolutely nothing to recommend these practices in an orderly debt-management program in the mid-twentieth century. And, in fact, they are not needed. The author concludes that the Treasury is, beyond question, able to regain and retain control of its debt, to manage the debt toward a neutral economic objective, and, ultimately, to employ the debt as an integrated element of broad economic policy. While attainment of these ends will require a willingness to pay whatever rate of interest is necessary to sell Treasury obligations at various maturities, there is no reason to believe that the neutral orderly program outlined in this study would threaten to drive interest rates to politically or socially unacceptable levels. Should this circumstance ever arise, however, the policy authorities might be well advised to look first at tax policy and fiscal policy before fixing the blame on debt management.

Bibliography

Books

Abbott, Charles C., *Management of the Federal Debt,* New York, McGraw-Hill Book Company, Inc., 1946.

——, *The Federal Debt, Structure and Impact,* New York, Twentieth Century Fund, Inc., 1953.

Bogart, Ernest L., *War Costs and Their Financing,* New York, D. Appleton and Company, 1921.

Bolles, Albert S., *The Financial History of the United States, from 1789 to 1860,* New York, D. Appleton and Company, 1883.

Buchanan, James M., *Public Principles of Public Debt,* Homewood, Illinois, Richard D. Irwin, Inc., 1958.

Childs, C. F., *Concerning U. S. Government Securities,* Chicago, R. K. Donnelley and Sons Company, 1947.

Dalton, Hugh, *Principles of Public Finance,* London, George Routledge and Sons, Ltd., 1936.

Dewey, Davis K., *Financial History of the United States,* New York, Longmans, Green and Co., 1928.

Eccles, Marriner, *Beckoning Frontiers, Public and Personal Recollections,* edited by Sidney Hyman, New York, Alfred A. Knopf, 1951.

Fisk, Harvey E., *Our Public Debt,* New York, Bankers Trust Co., 1919.

Friend, Irwin, Hoffman, G. Wright, Winn, Willis, *The Over-the-Counter Securities Markets,* New York, McGraw-Hill Book Company, Inc., 1958.

Goldsmith, Raymond W., *Financial Intermediaries in the Saving and Investment Process in the American Economy, 1900–1952,* New York, National Bureau of Economic Research, Inc., 1957.

Harris, Seymour E., *The National Debt and the New Economics,* New York, McGraw-Hill Book Company, Inc., 1947.

Hepburn, A. Barton, *History of Coinage and Currency in the United States,* New York, The Macmillan Company, 1903.

Loeser, John C., *The Over-the-Counter Market,* New York, National Quotation Bureau, Inc., 1940.

Love, Robert A., *Federal Financing,* New York, Columbia University Press, 1931.

Lutz, Harley L., *Public Finance,* New York, D. Appleton and Company, 1932.

Mellon, Andrew W., *Taxation: The People's Business,* New York, The Macmillan Company, 1924.

Mitchell, Wesley C., *A History of the Greenbacks,* Chicago, University of Chicago Press, 1903.

Moulton, Harold G., *The New Philosophy of Public Debt,* Washington, D.C., The Brookings Institution, 1943.

Murphy, Henry C., *National Debt in War and Transition,* New York, McGraw-Hill Book Company, Inc., 1950.

Myers, Margaret, *The New York Money Market,* Vol. I, edited by B. H. Beckhart, New York, Columbia University Press, 1931.

Noyes, Alexander D., *Forty Years of American Finance,* New York, G. P. Putnam's Sons, 1898.

———, *The War Period of American Finance,* New York, G. P. Putnam's Sons, 1926.

Oberholtzer, D. T., *Jay Cooke, Financier of the Civil War,* Philadelphia, George W. Jacobs & Co., 1907.

Paish, F. W., *The Post-War Financial Problem,* London, Macmillan and Co., Ltd., 1950.

Patterson, Robert T., *Federal Debt Management Policies, 1865–1879,* Durham, North Carolina, Duke University Press, 1954.

Pigou, A. C., *A Study in Public Finance,* London, Macmillan and Co., Ltd., 1951.

Porter, Sylvia, *How to Make Money in Government Bonds,* New York, Harper and Brothers, 1939.

Sherman, John, *Recollections of Forty Years in the House, Senate and Cabinet, An Autobiography,* New York, The Werner Co., 1895.

Shoup, Carl, Friedman, Milton, and Mack, K. P., *Taxing to Prevent Inflation,* New York, Columbia University Press, 1943.

Stewart, Paul W. and Tucker, Rufus S., *The National Debt and Government Credit,* New York, Twentieth Century Fund, Inc., 1937.

Studenski, Paul, and Krooss, Herman E., *Financial History of the United States,* New York, McGraw-Hill Book Company, Inc., 1952.

Winn, Willis J., "Government Securities," from *Investment of Life Insurance*

Funds, edited by D. McCahan, Philadelphia, University of Pennsylvania Press, 1953.

Withers, William, *The Public Debt,* New York, The John Day Company.

Pamphlets

Bankers Trust Company, *The Investment Outlook for 1958,* and for prior years. New York.

First Boston Corporation, *Securities of the United States Government.* New York, 1958.

Grunewald, Adolph C., *Investment Policies of Public Pension Funds: Present and Prospective.* Municipal Finance Officers Association of the United States and Canada, Special Bulletin 1957 C, June 1, 1957.

Institute of International Finance of New York University, *Management of the Public Debt.* New York, February 18, 1946.

Lanston, Aubrey G., *The Funding Program of the 1920's and the New Funding Program.* New York, Aubrey G. Lanston and Co., Inc., March, 1953.

————, *Problems Posed by Our Public Debt.* New York, First Boston Corporation, November 1945.

McGill, Dan M., *Fundamentals of Private Pensions.* Homewood, Illinois, Richard D. Irwin, Inc. Published for the Pension Research Council, Wharton School of Finance and Commerce, University of Pennsylvania, 1955.

National Industrial Conference Board, Inc., *Financial Management of Pension Trusts.* Studies in Business Policy, No. 66, New York, 1954.

New York Clearing House Association, *The Federal Reserve Re-examined.* New York, 1953.

Robinson, Marshall A., *Federal Credit and Creditors.* Hanover, New Hampshire, The Amos Tuck School of Business Administration, May, 1954.

Roosa, Robert V., *Federal Reserve Operations in the Money and Government Securities Markets.* New York, Federal Reserve Bank of New York, July, 1956.

Savings Banks Trust Company, *Savings Banking in a Competitive Economy.* New York, August, 1957.

Articles

Alhadeff, D. A., "Monetary Policy and the Treasury Bill Market," *American Economic Review,* Vol. 42, No. 3, pp. 326–346 (June, 1952).

Anderson, Benjamin M., "A Manageable Public Debt," *The Tax Review,* Vol. 9, No. 5 (May, 1948).

Bach, G. L., "The Machinery and Politics of Monetary Policy-Making," *The Journal of Finance,* Vol. 8, No. 2, pp. 169–176 (May, 1953).

Neckhart, B. H., "A Debt Policy for a Prosperous America," *The Annals,* Vol. 266, pp. 186–195 (November, 1949).

Blyth, Robert B., "Factors Affecting Treasury Financing," *The Commercial and Financial Chronicle,* Vol. 181, No. 5430 (May 19, 1955).

Brockie, Melvin D., "Debt Management and Economic Stabilization," *The Quarterly Journal of Economics,* Vol. 68, No. 4, pp. 613–628 (November, 1954).

Burgess, W. Randolph, "Progress on Public Debt," *The Commercial and Financial Chronicle,* Vol. 185, No. 5632 (April 25, 1957).

Carr, H. C., "The Problem of Bank-held Government Debt," *American Economic Review,* Vol. 36, No. 5, pp. 833–842 (December, 1946).

Cohen, Jacob, "A Theoretical Framework for Treasury Debt Management," *American Economic Review,* Vol. 45, No. 3, pp. 320–344 (June, 1955).

Conklin, George T., "Treasury Financial Policy from the Institutional Point of View," *The Journal of Finance,* Vol. 8, No. 2, pp. 226–234 (May, 1953).

Cooke, H. J., and Katzen, M., "The Public Debt Limit," *The Journal of Finance,* Vol. 9, No. 3, pp. 298–303 (September, 1954).

Culbertson, John M., "The Term Structure of Interest Rates," *The Quarterly Journal of Economics,* Vol. 71, No. 4, pp. 485–517 (November, 1957).

"Dealers in Government Securities Sign Pact," *Finance* (May 25, 1944).

Donovan, C. H., "Debt Management and Federal Reserve Credit Policy Since 1945," *The Southern Economic Journal,* Vol. 20, No. 3, pp. 231–242 (January, 1954).

Garvy, George, "Rivals and Interlopers in the History of the New York Security Market," *The Journal of Political Economy,* Vol. 52, No. 2, p. 133 (June, 1944).

Kareken, John H., "Monetary Policy and the Public Debt: An Appraisal of Post-War Developments in the U.S.A.," *Kyklos,* Vol. 10, Fasc. 4, pp. 401–431 (1957).

Kemmeru, Donald L., "Is the Cycle of War Bond Selling Completed?" *The Commercial and Financial Chronicle,* Vol. 174, No. 5058 (October 25, 1951).

Lanston, Aubrey G., "The Government Bond Picture," *The Commercial and Financial Chronicle,* Vol. 179, No. 5326 (May 20, 1954).

Matthews, D. Walton, "The Federal Debt—How it Might be Lengthened," *Bankers Monthly,* Vol. 74, No. 5, pp. 19–22 (May 15, 1957).

McCracken, Paul W., "The Public Debt: Hindrance or Advantage to Credit Controls?" *The Journal of Finance,* Vol. 8, No. 2, pp. 159–168 (May, 1953).

Miller, Donald C., "Reconciling Monetary Management and Debt Management Policies," *The Journal of Finance,* Vol. 1, No. 4, pp. 368–386 (December, 1950).

Murphy, H. C., "Essentials of a Sound Debt Program," *The Annals,* Vol. 266, pp. 180–185 (November, 1949).

Murray, Roger F., "Federal Debt Management and the Institutional Investor," from the Symposium on Institutional Investments, *Law and Contemporary Problems,* Durham, North Carolina, Duke University School of Law, 1952.

Patterson, Robert T., "A Major Error in Refunding," *The Journal of Finance,* Vol. 7, No. 3, pp. 421–433 (September, 1952).

Porter, S. F., "Gambling in Governments," *Scribner's Magazine* (December, 1938).

Ratchford, B. U., "The Economics of Public Debts," *Public Finance,* Vol. 3, No. 4, pp. 299–310 (1948).
———, "Some Aspects of Debt Management in the United States," *Public Finance,* No. 2, pp. 133–152 (1955).
Reinhardt, Hedwig, "On the Incidence of Public Debt," *Social Research,* Vol. 12, No. 2 (May, 1945).
Robinson, Marshall A., "Federal Debt Management: Civil War, World War I, and World War II," *American Economic Review,* Papers and Proceedings of the 67th annual meeting of the American Economic Association, Vol. 45, No. 2 (May, 1955).
Robinson, Roland I., "Monetary Aspects of Public Debt Policy," *Postwar Economic Studies,* No. 3, Washington, Board of Governors of the Federal Reserve System.
Rolph, Earl R., "Principles of Debt Management," *American Economic Review,* Vol. 47, No. 3, pp. 302–320 (June, 1957).
Roosa, Robert V., "Integrating Debt Management and Open Market Operations," *American Economic Review,* Papers and Proceedings of the 64th annual meeting of the American Economic Association, Vol. 42, No. 2, pp. 214–235 (May, 1952).
Seltzer, Lawrence H., "A Uniform Treasury Certificate as Bank Reserve," *Commercial and Financial Chronicle,* p. 1087 (February 28, 1946).
Slichter, Sumner H., "Curb Inflation With a Purchasing Power Bond," *The Commercial and Financial Chronicle,* Vol. 173, No. 4994 (March 15, 1951).
Smith, W. L., "On the Effectiveness of Monetary Policy," *American Economic Review,* Vol. 46, No. 4, pp. 588–606 (September, 1956).
Smutny, Rudolph, "Advantages of Treasury's Long-Term Bond Sales," *The Commercial and Financial Chronicle,* Vol. 181, No. 5410 (March 10, 1955).
———, "Effects Upon the Bond Market of a Restrictive Credit Policy," *The Commercial and Financial Chronicle,* Vol. 183, No. 5544 (June 21, 1956).
Snavely, William P., "The Asset Reserve Plan: an Appraisal," *The Southern Economic Journal,* Vol. 21, No. 4, pp. 425–434 (April, 1955).
Spencer, Girard L., "The Government and Municipal Bond Market," *The Commercial and Financial Chronicle,* Vol. 180, No. 5360 (September 16, 1954).
Stein, Herbert, "Monetary Policy and the Management of the Public Debt," *American Economic Review,* Vol. 42, No. 5, pp. 866–875 (December, 1952).
Thomas, Woodlief, "Lessons of War Finance," *American Economic Review,* Vol. 41, No. 4, pp. 618–631 (September, 1951).
Walker, Charles E., "Federal Reserve Policy and the Structure of Interest Rates on Government Securities," *The Quarterly Journal of Economics,* Vol. 48, No. 1, pp. 19–42 (February, 1954).
Wallich, Henry C., "The Philosophy of Public Debt Management: Some Implications of the Patman Inquiry," *The Journal of Finance,* Vol. 8, No. 2, pp. 196–205 (May, 1953).
Winterhalter, Le Roy F., "The Banks and Government Bonds," *The Commercial and Financial Chronicle,* Vol. 182, No. 5488 (December 8, 1955).

Woodward, Donald B., "Public Debt and Institutions," *American Economic Review*, Papers and Proceedings, Vol. 37, part 2, p. 157 (May, 1947).

Public Addresses

Bell, Daniel W., Address to the Investment Bankers Association, October 19, 1942, reprinted in United States Treasury *Annual Report for 1943,* p. 390.

Blyth, Robert B., *Appropriate Size of Short-Term Debt,* address before the American Finance Association, New York, April 13, 1955.

Cassaza, Alfred J., *Bank Investment Policy in a Cyclical Economy,* an address before the Savings and Mortgage Conference, the American Bankers Association, New York City, March 11, 1958.

Humphrey, George M., Address before Investment Bankers Association of America, December 1, 1953; contained in the *Annual Report* of the Secretary of the Treasury for 1953, pp. 250–255.

Lanston, Aubrey G., *Federal Financing and the Debt Limit,* address before the National Industrial Conference Board's meeting on the financial outlook, Dallas, Texas, March 20, 1958.

———, *Treasury and Federal Reserve Policies,* an address before the National Industrial Conference Board's discussion on the financial outlook, St. Louis, Missouri, November 15, 1956.

Leland, Simeon E., *The Government, the Banks, and the National Debt,* address before the Institute on Business Problems, University of Pittsburgh, January 16, 1946.

———, *The Impact of the National Debt Upon Banks and the Capital Markets,* address to Mortgage Bankers' Farm Services, Purdue University, Lafayette, Indiana, June 27, 1945.

Murray, Roger F., *Pension Funds and the Capital Market,* remarks at a meeting of the National Industrial Conference Board, New York, September 17, 1952.

Van Cleave, Robert, *Government Securities in Your Liquidity Position,* paper delivered to the Twelfth Annual Convention of the National Savings and Loan League, Cleveland, Ohio, May 23, 1955.

Government Documents

Federal Reserve Bank of New York, *Annual Reports.*

Federal Reserve System, Board of Governors, *Annual Reports.*

———, Board of Governors, *Survey of Common Trust Funds.*

United States Congress, *Conflicting Official Views on Monetary Policy: April 1956.* Hearings before the Subcommittee on Economic Stabilization of the Joint Committee on the Economic Report, June 12, 1956. 84th Congress, 2nd Session.

———, *Monetary, Credit and Fiscal Policies.* Statements submitted to the Subcommittee on Monetary Credit and Fiscal Policies of the Joint Committee on the Economic Report, 81st Congress, 1st Session, 1949.

————, *Monetary, Credit and Fiscal Policies.* Hearings before the Subcommittee on Monetary Credit and Fiscal Policies of the Joint Committee on the Economic Report, 81st Congress, 1st Session, 1949.

————, *Monetary, Credit and Fiscal Policies.* Report of the Subcommittee on Monetary Credit and Fiscal Policies of the Joint Committee on the Economic Report, 81st Congress, 2nd Session, 1950.

————, *Monetary Policy: 1955–1956.* Hearings before the Subcommittee on Economic Stabilization of the Joint Economic Committee, December 10 and 11, 1956, 84th Congress, 2nd Session, 1956.

————, *Monetary Policy and Management of the Public Debt.* Replies to Questions (Parts I and II) of the Subcommittee on General Credit Control and Debt Management of the Joint Committee on the Economic Report, 82nd Congress, 2nd Session, 1952.

————, *Monetary Policy and Management of the Public Debt.* Hearings before the Subcommittee on General Credit Control and Debt Management of the Joint Committee on the Economic Report, 82nd Congress, 2nd Session, 1952.

————, *Monetary Policy and Management of the Public Debt.* Report of the Subcommittee on General Credit Control and Dbet Management of the Joint Committee on the Economic Report, 82nd Congress, 2nd Session, 1952.

————, *United States Monetary Policy: Recent Thinking and Experience.* Hearings before the Subcommittee on Economic Stabilization of the Joint Committee on the Economic Report, December 6 and 7, 1954, 83rd Congress, 2nd Session, 1954.

United States Senate, *Welfare and Pension Plans Investigation.* Report of the Committee on Labor and Public Welfare. April, 1956.

United States Treasury Department, *Annual Reports* of the Comptroller of the Currency. Various years.

————, *Annual Report of the Secretary of the Treasury on the State of the Finances,* 1865 to 1957, inclusive.

Periodical and Statistical Sources

Best and Company, *Aggregates and Averages,* various dates.

Federal Reserve System, Board of Governors, *Federal Reserve Bulletin.*

————, Board of Governors, *Federal Reserve Chart Book.*

Institute of Life Insurance, *Life Insurance Fact Book,* various years, New York.

New York Stock Exchange, *Fact Book.*

Securities and Exchange Commission, *Report on Current Assets and Liabilities of U.S. Corporations.*

United States Savings and Loan League, *Savings and Loan Fact Book.*

Unpublished Material

Brimmer, Andrew F., *Some Studies in Monetary Policy, Interest Rates, and the Investment Behavior of Life Insurance Companies,* unpublished dissertation, Harvard University, October, 1956.

Harris, Marcus A., *The Over-the-Counter Market for United States Government Securities,* unpublished thesis submitted to the Graduate School of Banking, Rutgers University, 1948.

Smith, Arthur J. R., *The Growth of Public and Private Debt in the United States, 1914 to 1948,* unpublished dissertation, Harvard University, March, 1955.

Index

Aaa corporate bonds, 97–8, 150–2
"accord" between Federal Reserve
 System and Treasury Department,
 1, 55, 62–4, 65–72, 90, 94, 115–16,
 117n, 143
Act of 1900, 200
Act of April, 1917, 24
agency basis trading by dealers, 208,
 216
agency (Federal) debt/issues, 77–8,
 112, 135, 150, 223
allotment of new securities, 25, 38,
 169–71, 176–7, 182, 187–8, 189
 table, 190–6, 228, 255, 288, 293
American Bankers Association 156,
 157, 159, 165
*Annual Report of the Board of Gover-
 nors of the Federal Reserve System
 for 1939*, 41n
Annual Reports, U.S. Treasury Department: 1881, 16n; 1882, 16n;
 1883, 16n; 1892, 19; 1895, 18n;
 1925, 29n; 1929, 33n; 1943, 47n;

1951, 62n, 67n; 1952, 67n, 68n;
 1953, 195n; 1956, 170n
Assistant to the Secretary for debt-
 management matters, 156n, 165
Astor, John Jacob, 8n
Attorney General of United States,
 155n
attractiveness of U.S. Government securities offerings, 96, 106, 109, 111,
 184, 228, 290, 296n
attrition, *see* cash turn-in
auction bills, 180
auction technique, 19, 21, 37, 39, 176–
 80, 182, 203, 285, 292, 293
"average debt maturity" concept, 3,
 29, 56, 159, 165, 248

Bach, G. L., 229n
Baird, Julian, 81, 85, 156n
bank float level, 231
"bank holiday" of March, 1933, 36
*Bank Investment Policy in a Cyclical
 Economy*, Cassaza, 110n